THE GURDJIEFF MOVEMENTS

THE GURDJIEFF MOVEMENTS

A Communication of Ancient Wisdom

Wim van Dullemen

HOHM PRESS
Chino Valley, Arizona

Cover Design: Becky Fulker, Kubera Book Design, Prescott, Arizona

Cover Image: Cover photograph made by Fatih Azman during the presentation, 24 September 2013, of Gurdjieff's Music and Movements, directed by Wim van Dullemen and Christiane Macketanz, at the 10th Konya International Mystic Music Festival. © the Directors of the Konya International Mystic Music Festival; *www.mysticmusicfest.com* Used with permission.

Interior Design and Layout: Becky Fulker, Kubera Book Design, Prescott, Arizona

Library of Congress Cataloging in Publication Data:

ISBN: 978-1-942493-34-1

Hohm Press
P.O. Box 4410
Chino Valley, AZ 86323
800-381-2700
http://www.hohmpress.com

This book was printed in the U.S.A. on recycled, acid-free paper using soy ink.

Original translation of Dutch text by: Gerard Scanlan and Pascalle Videler.

Contact with the author of this book is possible at:
www.gurdjieff-movements.net

CONTENTS

PREFACE

I prefer people talking nonsense about important matters rather than keeping silent, because from the ensuing argument and fighting the truth will out.

– Diderot

On two occasions, my life has been touched by something extraordinary. These differed from all other intense experiences, good or bad, which I have known like any other person, in that both times it seemed as if a power manifested itself. A power, the existence of which I could not have imagined, the source of which seemed to reside outside of me. From its independent core, far from me, shrouded in invisibility, this power briefly illuminated me, the result of a mere coincidence, the way a searchlight dances its beam across all manner of objects as it glides swiftly forward through the dark.

The first time this occurred I was thirteen years old and confined to bed by a protracted illness. As all I could see was the ceiling above my bed, my sensory perceptions increasingly focused on my hearing. The sounds of the street that reached my room unfolded before me into fixed patterns, in which I managed to distinguish the individual steps of the nightly passers-by. Because I had a contagious disease, only my mother looked after me. She was seriously ill herself at the time, and to bring me food or to change the bed linen she had to climb two long flights of stairs. At each step she paused, took a deep breath and sighed. That sound still torments my soul today.

Some time later, I was given a small radio and perchance I heard half an hour of recordings by a blues pianist from Chicago: Jimmy Yancey. That half hour not only determined my fate as a musician, but I am still convinced it also cured my illness. Never again did I experience music with such intensity. I have heard famous pianists, such as Horowitz, play live, and studied countless others through their recordings, but none of them managed to touch me so deeply. The desperation of my adolescent existence, like a fly at the bottom of a bottle, was gone. Deep within the keys, behind the vital rhythms, a life resounded whose simplicity, resignation, humanity, hope and love had taken on a vibration my nervous system absorbed like a dry sponge soaks up water.

A decade went by before it happened for a second time. The doors of a dilapidated dance hall in the then Jewish Quarter of Amsterdam swung open and a small group of hippies interested in Gurdjieff's ideas, myself among them, walked in for their first lesson in Gurdjieff's dances. We were welcomed by a handsome woman, of small stature, and Oriental appearance. Her relaxed countenance immediately put us at ease. Without wasting time, we were lined up in rows as if we had joined the army, and she demonstrated a powerful physical exercise, in which she moved her arms, legs and head separately.

An old lady, seated at a piano more elderly than she, hammered out a strange, almost hypnotic melody, as she desperately searched for the right keys. The movements my body performed while hearing this music had a sudden effect on me. It was as if a blinding light filled everything in the dance hall, including me, and I was convinced that I had stumbled across something of incredible meaning and power. That was my first encounter with Gurdjieff's Movements.

The difference between these two experiences is that the first one was never repeated, not even after I could play Jimmy Yancey's pieces note by note, and listened to his music again and again as attentively as I could. I often tried to understand this, without success. The second experience, on the other hand, has recurred many times, albeit in a different form each time. The study of this phenomenon, Gurdjieff's Movements, has occupied my life since I discovered it. This book forms the embodiment, the results of years of research.

Both these experiences shared an intensity that held an inescapable commitment.

The initial impetus for this book came from Dries Langeveld, chief editor of *Bres Magazine*, a philosophical and esoteric Dutch monthly to which I contributed articles on a regular basis throughout the nineties.[1] On one occasion, while visiting Dries in his office to discuss a new article, he remarked that there were more than enough books written on Gurdjieff to fill an entire library, but not a single word was to be found anywhere about his most significant creation, his Movements. He raised his hands in a gesture of despair and incomprehension, adding: "On the Gurdjieff Map, they are nothing more than a large blank spot. They are the great 'Terra Incognita' of his work. There is absolutely nothing about the most elementary details such as: how many Movements are there, when were they created, how did they come about, where can you study them, what developments will they undergo and what did his pupils ultimately do with them?"

"Pupils," Dries repeated softly, lost in his thoughts while attempting to pour coffee in a near impossible situation—standing between the towers of books that littered his study—and concluded his musings with: "Write about them Wim, try to explain as accurately as possible what is going on here. If something has gone wrong, analyse it. Don't attribute blame needlessly, but don't humor anyone either. We're not into pretending that everything is fine when it isn't here."

For the most part I agreed with Dries. I believe the creation of the Movements to be one of the most important manifestations of human genius from the twentieth century and I was concerned about their legacy. Major questions arose regarding how Gurdjieff's pupils had treated his legacy and what their motivation had been. This is what this book is about; it is not about Gurdjieff.

---

1 *Bres*, a bi-monthly "Magazine for religion, science and gnosis" (www.bresmagazine.nl)

Dries Langeveld, a great expert on every aspect and school of thought within spirituality and blessed with encyclopaedic knowledge, died shortly after this conversation. He is often in my thoughts and it is with fond memories that I reflect on him. I am so glad that I did what he asked me to do.

His criticisms are understandable. It looks suspiciously as though a small, elitist circle has appropriated Gurdjieff's Movements. I have attempted to describe the complexity of the causes that led to this situation from all sides. Gurdjieff's pupils went their separate ways after his death, founding new schools, which sometimes worked together, but not without great tension between them at times. This resulted in an opaque network that I intend to illuminate in detail in this book. However, more importantly than all the facts about Movements is that in this book an example is given of what could happen, and in this case what did happen, to the knowledge and rituals of an esoteric teacher after he passed them onto his pupils.

A MOMENT OF REFLECTION . . .

Or better still, a large step backwards, like the worshippers in the Echternach procession have to do before they can take two steps forward. Who am I to venture into this hornets' nest, and am I capable of providing a faithful report? This is a question I asked myself many times after Dries Langeveld had requested that I write this book.

I encountered Gurdjieff's teaching fifty years ago and it has been the compass that has determined my life's direction. I was originally involved as a member of the largest organization in this field for fifteen years. I accompanied dance classes on the piano for one of Gurdjieff's personal pupils. After this, as a travelling troubadour playing Gurdjieff's music, I met many of his surviving pupils, some of his children, and I came across a wide variety of communities practising his "Work" – the code name for the whole of Gurdjieff's ideas and directions. I played his music in concert halls, I teach his dances in various countries and publish articles on his teachings, which, like warp and weft, are closely knit with my personal hopes and despairs. Can I still be objective? Of course not. Would a report by an impartial outsider not be preferable? Probably not.

Gurdjieff's teaching is being studied by an ever-growing number of people. They can be classified on a sliding scale marked with various stages. The first stage includes all those who study this material individually. Next come the open study groups, followed by the closed hierarchical structures. Eventually, the line comes to a halt at the last stage: in the murky world of sects. The third category is the most important for the study of Gurdjieff's Movements. The closed circles of the "Gurdjieff Work" have large memberships and above all hold most of the knowledge. In these structures, opinions are being prescribed peremptorily from above, as is common in hierarchies, with the result that everyone is cautious when an outsider is present. The outsider, in general, will not hear more than his own voice, like a hollow echo from a well, so that it is just as unfeasible for an outsider to observe objectively.

Every observer perceives the complex mosaic of reality through a screen onto which gradually more and more personal associations are projected. The transparency of this screen determines the quality of the observation and the opinion that is formed based on this. The reader should be wary of all opinions, of mine, but especially his or her own. Since the observer's vision says as much about the observer as the object under observation, I believe it only fair that the reader knows which associative patterns have colored and shaped my observations. This is the reason why, from time to time, I relate my own experiences, in the form of anecdotes, in this book.

As a warning, it is clearly stated here that the facts are incomplete and the anecdotes subjective. The justification for their publication is that this is the first attempt at a historiography and quantification of Gurdjieff's Movements. I hope most sincerely that this book will initiate a process in which others supplement the inadequacies in this presentation.

I am sure that my vision of the historical development of Gurdjieff's Movements will meet with some resistance. Many will disagree with me, but I think that the length of time and intensity I devoted to this matter form a good basis for expressing my opinion. Above all, if we live in a free country, such expressions of opinion are permitted all the time. This becomes something we take for granted, but I know a number of people who think very differently about this matter. While writing these sentences, I saw their faces, one after another, appearing in my mind's eye. Slowly they emerged, but with an uncanny sharpness, while it is generally rather difficult to remember faces. They were people who staked their lives during the Second World War on the right to form, express your own opinions and live by them. They were broken or beaten to deafness in concentration camps. Sometimes, their hands shook so much that they could not even light a cigarette. Their complexions ash grey. They combated the rise of fascism in Spain, as members of the International Brigade, and printed free speech pamphlets on old printing presses in their cellars throughout the war. It was my job to compile their medical files so that they could apply for a state pension. They made an indelible impression on me. I love them very much, all these years later, and with the example they have given me, I would be deeply ashamed if I kept a well-founded opinion to myself.

> Truth exists.
> The maximum a single individual can comprehend of the truth is called consciousness.
> The courage to face this is honesty.
> To live accordingly, this is power.

These principles have guided me in writing the following pages.

I am grateful to all who have assisted me, in one way or another, in writing this book. The definitive version of my text that follows owes a lot to the competence, dedication and understanding of Regina Sara Ryan, Editorial Director, Hohm Press.

– Wim van Dullemen

PART I

BACKGROUND

1

GEORG IVANOVITCH GURDJIEFF

The world comprises a whole mass of people and a few individuals

– D.H. Lawrence

Who was Gurdjieff? When once asked "Who are you?" he answered: "Who are you?"

Gurdjieff left a deep impression on the people who met him. Usually positive, though not always. Most people regarded him as an exceptional man who brought about a turning point in their lives. They spoke about him in glowing terms, described him in their intimate diaries and in the books they published, so many in fact that they would fill a good-sized bookcase. Sometimes, even someone who just saw him for an instant could not help but write a book about him. It is striking, however, that a woman who had known him her entire life gave him the shortest description of all. "Mr. X," and nothing more. For her, Gurdjieff was an unfathomable phenomenon.[1]

There is almost no one still alive who knew him personally. The only way to get to know Gurdjieff is through his works. "Man is the sum of his deeds," wrote the author Albert Camus, and Gurdjieff left his tracks in very different worlds: in music, in dance, but above all in the world of mysticism. He was someone we refer to as a "teacher," someone who preached a "spiritual teaching." I would like to clarify briefly what I mean by this. The words "spiritual teaching" may evoke associations with vague ideas, of little value in real life which is

---

1 The wife of author P.D. Ouspensky: Sophie Grigorievna Maximenko.

governed by hard facts. Anyway, such is the case for me. I see no sense in a spiritual teaching as an end in itself. The teaching only acquires meaning when it answers a question and, as such, the possibilities or impossibilities of that teaching can only be verified in the inner world—in *myself*. That question cannot be theoretical, nor hatched from a logical mental process. The question arises from the daily experience of the inescapable fact: that I/you do not know. This last word, "know," should be in capitals. The question can only be kept alive by a deep desire for understanding.

Gurdjieff contemplated the meaning of life on earth and especially the meaning of human life. The words in which this question is expressed have become a cliché, and are at odds with its content. So I will repeat the question here in the words of the French surrealist André Breton, in a statement that is the opening line of an oracle: "Was man given a place under the sun, only to suffocate in an animal skin?"[2]

Gurdjieff was born in 1877, according to all official records (although he indicated 1866 as the year of his birth), in what is now the border region between Russia and Turkey, in a melting pot of races, cultures and religions. It has been generally assumed that his mother was of Armenian descent, but recent research has revealed that she was Greek, as was his father. Gurdjieff spent his youth in archaic, almost biblical conditions. His father became a cabinetmaker out of sheer necessity after an epidemic decimated his flock of sheep, but he was also well known locally as an *Ashik*.[3] His father's songs and ancient stories left a lasting impression on Gurdjieff, whose

2 From the article about his deceased friend Jacques Vaché in "Les pas perdus" 1924.

3 The word *Ashik* refers to an itinerant singer of traditional songs, who accompanies himself on a simple, portable stringed instrument. In the eastern part of Turkey, where this tradition is still alive, the instrument in question is usually a long-necked lute, the Saz, with three double strings. The *Ashik* is held in high esteem and is considered as an important purveyor of culture. The Turkish word *Ashik* is derived from the Persian word *Ask*, meaning love. More literally, *Ashik* means: "He whose music evokes feelings of love." It is interesting to note that the old Dutch word *Minstreel* conveys this meaning very precisely.

education was entrusted to the Patriarch of the Armenian-Orthodox Church in Kars.

Gurdjieff's life had two clearly distinguishable phases. In the first phase: his longing for a hidden knowledge that would close the gap between religion and science, and explain to him the miraculous events he witnessed as a child, drove him to a long period of travelling and expeditions in the East and the Near East. Or so it would appear, because not much is known about this period. The historical picture first became clear in 1912, when Gurdjieff turned up as if from nowhere in Saint Petersburg. This is where the second phase of his life began: the bestowal of his insights on others, acquired during his travels and forged together by his inner discipline. He succeeded in securing the commitment of a number of striking pupils, such as the author Ouspensky and the composer de Hartmann.[4]

The Russian Revolution forced him to flee Russia, together with some of his pupils. First to Georgia, then to Turkey, finally settling in a country estate at Fontainebleau in Paris in 1922, the seat of his "Institute for the Harmonious Development of Man." At Fontainebleau, Gurdjieff accommodated pupils and those relatives who had managed to escape the Turkish crusade against Armenia (his father and one of his sisters fell victim to this genocide), as well as a number of other Russian exiles. The community at Fontainebleau—a commune "*avant la letter*" —was set up along patriarchal lines. Gurdjieff's pupils, comprising just part of the community, plied a multitude of disciplines, such as heavy physical work, memory and concentration boosting exercises, and the dances and physical exercises called "Movements." These Movements were Gurdjieff's creative choreographic interpretations of the dances and rituals he had seen and studied during his travels. The accompanying music was his own, but the scores were arranged for piano solo and

4 Chapters 3 and 11 will provide the necessary background information about these two people.

orchestra by the composer Thomas de Hartmann. These dances were presented to the general public in theatre performances in Paris in 1923, and in various American cities—such as in New York's Carnegie Hall—in 1924, and were intended to promote his Institute, making it more widely known. In spite of a controversial reputation in the press, Gurdjieff drew in pupils from England and America. Although the Institute for the Harmonious Development of Man only existed for a few years, this period can still be considered as a heroic episode in Gurdjieff's life as a teacher.

A serious car accident in 1924 forced Gurdjieff to reconsider his possibilities and the future. He disbanded the Institute and devoted his time exclusively to writing in order to preserve his teaching for posterity. His main work was a trilogy, titled *All and Everything.*[5] The first and most voluminous part of this triptych is the most important, and also Gurdjieff's magnum opus. It is an allegory in which the principal character, Beelzebub, sets out his critical view on humanity to his grandson. The two remaining parts can be considered autobiographical.

During his first years as a writer, Gurdjieff composed a lot of music too, again in cooperation with de Hartmann. This time, the motivation was to compose pieces of music to accompany the reading aloud of his books, in the manner of a *Gesamtkunstwerk*,[6] but once the flow of music was set in motion, it could no longer be stemmed. Between 1925 and 1927, more than two hundred solo pieces for piano were created: musical childhood memories, sketches of the music he heard during his travels, and arrangements of liturgical choral music and hymns from exceptional monasteries. In all these pieces, usually of

[5] G.I. Gurdjieff, *All and Everything,* First series. *Beelzebub's Tales to His Grandson,* Lowe and Brydone, London, 1950.

[6] It is important to note that the composer Alexander Scriabin and painter Wassily Kandinsky, who both developed the concept of *Gesamtkunstwerk* in the direction of "Synaesthesia," were close friends of Thomas de Hartmann.

short duration like a musical miniature, it often remains unclear where the "memory" ends and where "Gurdjieff" begins.

By the time he had completed his books in 1935, not only was his country estate sold in the aftermath of the 1929 Depression, but also the number of people interested in his teachings had decreased dramatically. Shortly before the Second World War, a new circle of young, this time French, pupils was formed and, after a fifteen-year gap, he resumed teaching Movements classes. Post 1945, in the last years before his death, Gurdjieff received a steadily increasing stream of visitors in his Paris apartment: former and new pupils, both those interested and the merely curious. During the dinners for his guests, which Gurdjieff presided over like an old school patriarch, he summarized his teaching for the last time, in symbolic or cryptic statements, such as in this "toast" proposed to his table companions: "A worthy goal for a person is to die an honorable death . . . this is only possible if you work on yourself . . . if you do not do so, you will perish like a dog." The melancholic sounds of Gurdjieff's harmonium concluded these evenings.

One of the four biographies dedicated to Gurdjieff is from the pen of James Webb, an author of a number of works of key importance about the historic development of esoteric systems.[7] The fact that even this eminent historian believes that an intrigant in the political power struggle for Tibet around 1900, of Tibetan or Mongol descent, is one and the same person as Gurdjieff—a highly unlikely thesis—shows how little is actually known about Gurdjieff's background. His life before 1912 will therefore remain a fertile ground for speculations, sometimes most absurd. This is unlikely to change.

---

7 James Webb, *The Harmonious Circle, An Exploration of the Lives and Work of G.I. Gurdjieff, P.D. Ouspensky and Others*. Thames and Hudson Ltd., London, 1980. The other three biographies are: J.G. Bennett, *Gurdjieff: Making a New World*, Harper & Row, New York, 1973; James Moore, *Gurdjieff: The Anatomy of a Myth, Element Books, Dorset, 1991; Paul Beekman Taylor,* Gurdjieff: A New Life, Utrecht, 2008.

THE MAN, THE MYSTERY, THE SPIRITUAL TEACHER

A precondition for "spiritual teaching" is that it must be practiced by the person who teaches it. A human being, as he or she is, not what he claims or writes to be, is the living proof of the authenticity of his teaching. Unfortunately, this criterion is not so easily applicable to Gurdjieff. He remains unfathomable, even during the historically traceable part of his life, post 1912. He remains hidden behind the masks of the roles he played, as virtuoso as a travelling actor of times past, who could stage a compelling drama in an overcrowded market with the simplest of props. He remains shrouded in a haze that blurs the border between science and charlatanism, and between his compassion for humanity and his provocative role patterns. Those who study Gurdjieff in more depth discover that contradictions are the rule rather than the exception. Gurdjieff claimed that he was forced to lead an unnatural life in order to pass on his ideas to humanity, who were enslaved by a concerted effort of hypnotic forces as well-organized as multiplication tables. Humanity was in the grip of these cosmic "laws," which are not at all concerned with the human's well being. And furthermore, the existence of these laws are not even surmised.

Gurdjieff's decision to remain hidden in his role-playing, which he employed consciously to separate his teaching and his person, can also be taken as a piece of good advice. An open question is better than a closed one and takes us back to ourselves. It is better to doubt than to lose ourselves in illusory certainties.

Gurdjieff is no longer the anonymous mystic he was during his life, known only to a small circle. His books have been translated into many languages, public appreciation of his music is growing, and all kinds of groups and organizations, of which just a few are based on historic ties with Gurdjieff, attempt to put into practice his views and methodologies—summarized in the code words "The Gurdjieff Work." His ideas have spread like concentric circles on the surface of a pond after a stone has been tossed in. This dissemination takes the ideas out of their context, simplifies, commercializes and gradually intermingles them with other psychological and religious disciplines, often omitting to mention Gurdjieff as the source. However, the opposite is also true. Recent additions and interpretations of his ideas are sometimes wrongly attributed to him. A striking example of this is the proliferation of theories about the "enneagram," a mathematical symbol that was indeed introduced by Gurdjieff, but was never intended as a blueprint for character typology into which it has now degenerated.

The question of who Gurdjieff was remains unanswered and this lays it open to myth distortion. It is as if we are dealing with a ghost, roaming around in the stately, though somewhat dilapidated country estate of his teaching. The mirrors in the rooms and corridors do not reflect anything more of him than a passing shadow. Inhabitants of neighboring villages have mixed feelings about this haunted house, some speak in hushed voices about the mysterious phenomena that take place, others laugh about them. In the meantime, the local merchants do great business as busloads of tourists arrive to see this country estate for themselves. Those organizing guided tours and excursions, laying it on thick as they relate these tales, are really cashing in! After the tourist season ends, they happily count their profits, with the same gleam in their eyes that you see in rats when you spot them in the dark.

This realm of shadows is anything but satisfying if you wish to study Gurdjieff's teaching or, as is the case in this book, his dances in more depth. It is normal to want a face you can put to this, a human aspect to hold on to. Which is why I present an image here that appeals to me more than all the other "shadows in the mirrors of the stately home." It is a brief, concise excerpt from a novel, which as such has nothing to do with Gurdjieff or his ideas, written by Fritz Peters.[8] This author spent his childhood years with Gurdjieff, who was almost a second

[8] Arthur A. Peters, *The Descent*, Signet Books, New York, 1953.

father to him. In this passage, Peters describes an old man staring at the rising sun. Firstly, it strikes the man that people deem themselves so important that they even believe that the sun rises especially for them. "As though the sun would tune its service to suit them. As though the sun, so high and far away, could become aware of the image that people had of it." Then the man imagines that he himself has become the sun. Unconcerned, he watches how the earth brought people into his light through its slow rotation, and simultaneously returns other people to the cold grip of darkness. What has been given must be taken back. He saw people left to the mercy of cosmic powers that are unconcerned with what people call their "lives" or their "existence." A beginning and end exist for mortals, not so for the sun. "The old man began to feel his own insignificance, his true place in the world."

It could very well be that Peters is conveying an impression of Gurdjieff that he had as a child. This assumption is reinforced by the fact that the man described here is the father of the protagonist of the story. In this excerpt from Peters' book, the earth is viewed from a great distance, no doubt the same position Gurdjieff adopted in his most important book. The old man is possibly a memory of Gurdjieff, spontaneously returning from the author's subconscious. In any case, I cherish this description as, for me, the most real of all personal impressions I have ever heard or read.

MEETING JOHN BENNETT

Another measure of a "spiritual teacher" is the level of his pupils. They too are an indication, albeit indirect, of the quality of the teaching. This is how it appeared to me when, at the end of the summer of 1965, I decided to approach one or more of Gurdjieff's pupils. I had just finished reading Gurdjieff's first book—a guest at the bar where I worked had suggested I might find it an interesting read. I remember in particular that it was a very beautiful summer, because I had chosen the roof of our house, right in the middle of the ring of canals in the old center of Amsterdam, as my regular spot for a quiet read. I did not have a clue what the book was about. I just remember how captivated I was by the appearance of the city from above in the softly vibrating light of a summer day, the sea of roofs interspersed with treetops, the cry of seagulls and the glistening of the water in the canals. The feeling of freedom that this gave me somehow dovetailed wonderfully with the atmosphere in the book. After I had, by my measure, made a sincere effort to understand what this book was all about, I arrived at the conclusion that I was not going to make any more progress on my own. I was determined to establish contact with one of the author's pupils, if any of them were still alive.

Within a very short time, and after a series of the most unlikely coincidences, as if the one occurrence evoked the next like a magic formula, I found myself sitting opposite John Bennett, one of Gurdjieff's most important pupils, who gave me a piercing look from behind his desk.[9] Our eyes met and it was as if two chemicals had mixed indissolubly. His eyes emitted a kind of black light that shone right through me, so powerfully that I could no longer perceive his face very clearly, and it slowly transformed into the black granite masks of the Buddha statues I had once seen in a museum. Suddenly, I seemed to be standing in a large dark hall, my own inner self, with my past on the one side, and my future on the other, and an inaudible voice saying that

---

[9] John Godolphin Bennett (1897-1974) was an autodidactic mathematician and also studied Eastern languages and various religions. His career began with the British Secret Service in Constantinople. He later became the coordinator for the British coal research laboratory and contributed to the successful turnaround in this industry which utilized coal as a raw material for new synthetic materials in addition to its traditional use as fuel. He met Gurdjieff for the first time in 1920 in Constantinople. Several years later, he stayed briefly in Gurdjieff's Institute in the Prieuré, a stately home in Avon, municipality of Fontainebleau, near Paris. After this, he maintained regular contact with Ouspensky and only after Ouspensky's death did he renew his contact with Gurdjieff. He described his experiences with Gurdjieff in a number of books.

my future could only become reality if I could realize my potential myself. This inaudible voice further said that all of God's creation is a drama in which the one possibility is realized, while the other is not.

I recovered my composure and asked him what kind of person Gurdjieff actually was. After all, an inquiry is what I had come to do in the first place. He answered: "I can assure you that Gurdjieff was a good man." Mustering all my courage, I asked him, with all the naivety of youth: "This force that you have shown me, which I think is very unusual, did you get that from Gurdjieff?" His expression became quiet and thoughtful, as if he was looking at himself rather than at me, and he said softly and resigned, "Yes," and a few seconds later, "but not *only* from him." After that, we spoke at length, and our meeting was occasionally interrupted by what would become a fixed ritual, in which Bennett would apologize that the conversation had gone on long enough and would leave the room. Then his secretary would enter to show me out. Each time, I refused to leave, after which I could hear her saying despairingly in the other room: "Sir, the young Dutchman still refuses to go." Bennett then would re-enter the room as if nothing had happened and resume the conversation at the point we had left off.

Without question, John Bennett was an exceptional individual, tall and lean, and even now, over fifty years later, I can recall every detail of his ascetic head. Perhaps because his is the only face that I cannot imagine could ever possibly show the slightest trace of fear. Another emotional expression, however, did not escape my notice. When we talked about how, after his death, Gurdjieff's work disintegrated into various organizations which chose to adopt a hostile rather than a cooperative attitude towards one another, I saw in a flash, in less time than a match head needs to flare up, how his face turned ashen, flush with great grief. I remember to this day how surprised I was that a person with powers like his could not mask his grief, but I did not respond to this. Instinctively, I felt that whatever had happened at the time was none of my business. Immediately after this, he recovered his unusual vitality. Everything he focused his attention on that afternoon was balanced on a fine line, which seemed to emphasize his own calmness even more.

As our conversation came to a conclusion, Bennett advised me to contact the "Institut Gurdjieff" in Paris because of my interest in Gurdjieff's music, which I heard then for the very first time on crackling old gramophone records, and in the Movements which I really wanted to learn. On parting, Bennett escorted me outside through the small garden in front of his unpretentious redbrick house. I asked him if we would see each other again. He answered: "We have met once, and we will meet again." In the lost and lonely feeling that came over me, these words sounded like a sick joke.

Doubt is normal, even healthy in many cases, but I never doubted that a teacher and a teaching that can evoke the qualities that John Bennett possessed must be very special. It was the first, but for me also the most important talk I ever would have with one of Gurdjieff's pupils. And I have made the acquaintance of many of them since. This conversation answered my question about who Gurdjieff was. Indirectly, yes, but sufficiently for me.

~

We often forget the extent to which the physical shape of a man determines our ultimate impression of him. That is why I would like to conclude with a final impression of Gurdjieff, from a very different quarter. The indifference with which a German official looked at Gurdjieff, for him no more than a number in an endless queue of Russian refugees seeking shelter after the revolution in their country. The official had to describe Gurdjieff's physique on the visa application form. He penned: "Very strong!"[10]

---

10 I have a copy of this document in my archive. It is an application for a residence permit, in Germany, completed in the German Embassy in New York and signed by Gurdjieff. The document is not dated with any particular year, but it must be from 1921.

2

INVENTORY AND CLASSIFICATION OF GURDJIEFF'S LEGACY

Art without a magical component does not exist. Great magic cannot exist without great art.

– Valentin Bresle

When Gurdjieff died, on the 29th of October 1949 at Neuilly, near Paris, he left an oeuvre comprising a script for a ballet, three books, three hundred musical compositions and just as many dances, which are referred to as his "Movements" in this book. In addition, there are sound recordings of him playing the harmonium, and on occasion recordings of his voice, made in the twilight years of his life. This is the most direct and tangible part of his legacy, exceptional in its diversity. Of course, there have been religious figures who have written philosophical treatises, such as Teilhard de Chardin, and also philosophers who composed music, such as Nietzsche, but Gurdjieff's legacy is beyond comparison, given the three fields that it covers. And then, there is the sheer volume of the works! The first book alone has 1300 pages of India paper in small print. His Movements are set out in the smallest detail: one single Movement comprising a complexity of combined multiple roles. His musical compositions appear to have been composed in passing, in the midst of his creative eruptions, in just a matter of years. How should this legacy, created with such passionate energy, be regarded?

A preliminary inventory presents us with three main elements, each representing a different discipline, three independent worlds as it were: Gurdjieff's books, music and Movements. These elements originate directly from Gurdjieff. He wrote his books himself in his own words. His music, though not scored by him, is still clearly his. His Movements have been passed on by several of his pupils independently and we can assume that around 250 of them have been preserved in a historically reliable form.

In the first place, Gurdjieff was an esoteric teacher and not an author, composer or choreographer. When I mention Gurdjieff's teaching, I mean his own words of explanation that he gave in a form that was comprehensible for each and every one of his small circle of pupils in the first stage of his teaching, from 1912 to 1924. Why then are his teachings missing from the elements of his legacy? The reason is that the logically structured component of his teaching reached us exclusively through his pupils and, as such, cannot be mentioned in the same breath as the aforementioned elements of his legacy. It should also be considered that the content of the pupils' words is colored by the reader's or listener's subjective associations, and on top of this altered in the course of time by the "spirit of the times." Words lack the precision of the mathematical physical positions, movements and rhythms of Gurdjieff's Movements that leave no room for doubt or vagueness. Words are more vulnerable to false interpretation, manipulation and even sheer fabrication.

An attempt to classify the elements of this legacy immediately raises questions of how this should be tackled. Are they interconnected, and if so in what way? How do his books, music and Movements relate to his teaching? Are all parts equally important? Or does one of them form the center of gravity, around which the other parts revolve as mere illustrations, or clarifications, of the core? This last question is essential, because after Gurdjieff's death his legacy has been studied by groups, institutes or organizations that focus on one of the components at the expense of the others, depending on the preferences and tastes of those leading these groups. Therefore, each group or organization has already answered this question. Their answers are far from unanimous.

For an analysis and historiography of the Movements, it is necessary to examine the aforementioned questions, although I do not labor under the illusion that I can completely answer them. All I can do is present and classify the facts as I understand them, defining keywords, providing them with a historical framework. No matter how rudimentary and clumsy the definitions of these keywords may be, they will hopefully prevent us from losing our way and serve to keep us on a negotiable path.

ART, SCIENCE OR OTHERWISE?

Under which banner can the components of Gurdjieff's legacy be accommodated? Gurdjieff's music and his Movements can clearly be categorized as "art," but does this apply to his books too? The blend of mythical, fantastic and autobiographical elements they comprise argue in favor of this, were it not that many believe that the books proclaim a new kind of science about the human and the cosmos. Should they be classified as esoteric?

In the above paragraph, words like "art," "science" and the "esoteric" are bandied about. The meanings of these words float around us like leaves falling from a tree, carried along on every gust of wind. Let us set up these three keywords in relation to each other as if they were the corners of a triangle. Entering the silent realm of geometric abstractions, we will label the points of the triangle and look at what they have in common and where they differ from each other.

Art is an irrational domain in which the question of truth or falsehood is irrelevant. The fact that a work of art exists is its truth. Science is a rational endeavor, in which the veracity of statements or propositions can be tested through logic or experiment. The result of such investigation is either a confirmation or negation of their correctness. The esoteric, a banner that accommodates all religions and a wide variety of occult and mystical ideas, may meet with a response from the inner being, borne out by the fact that since time immemorial, every religion and culture has been in search of an answer to "the ultimate question," as described by Gurdjieff and Breton in the previous chapter. Unfortunately, the truth or falsehood of all these ideas can never be proven. Were this the case, humanity would have been spared insufferable misery, religious wars and genocides. The irrational system of the esoteric is on good terms with the other irrational system, the arts. Gurdjieff's legacy is proof of this.

Let us consider this from a broader perspective and continue our geometrical exercise with the triangle we have imagined. Let us suppose that the triangle's origin was a single point, from which, over time, three lines grew longer and further apart, to such an extent that they have now become wholly alienated from each other. This geometrical picture is close to the historical truth. In ancient times, art, science and esotericism formed a unity, and each in its own way testified to a harmonious universe, created and governed by a higher intelligence than that of the human. Over the course of time, scientists did their job so well that this view of the world, in which they had a deep-rooted faith, was played out. Sir Isaac Newton was one of these scientists. He was not just deeply religious, but also spent more time on treatises about alchemy than on physics. Even so, he is *the* father of contemporary physics. Only in the nineteenth century, a period so aptly called "Flight from Reason" by historian James Webb, did the paths of science and esotericism part for good. It is no coincidence that the devotees of esoteric systems are often nostalgic for the past—for those distant days when science, art and religion formed a whole—that they display a weakness for ancient monuments, such as pyramids, Aztec temples, shrines overgrown by forests, medieval cathedrals, Tibetan monasteries and such. Beliefs and ideas that have drifted miles apart, historically speaking, such devotees of the esoteric attempt to reunite within themselves. This is not exclusive to them. All of us are the products of history and doomed to personify random hybrids of the rational and the irrational.

For some, Gurdjieff's books are the harbingers of a new science, but can they actually be classified as such? This is an important question, even more so because bridging the gap between Western sciences and Eastern mysticism was one of Gurdjieff's goals. His first and most important work, *Beelzebub's Tales to His Grandson*, is about as accessible for an approach employing a logical conceptual basis as a raw piece of marble. The reader feels something of the incredible energies and high fusion points that created this rich material, veined and veiled with secret code, but it cannot be deemed scientific. There is little other choice than to classify it alongside Gurdjieff's music and his Movements as "art." The important role played by unusual concepts and images in his book confirms this classification. In other words, for the time being we can conclude that the tangible parts of Gurdjieff's legacy—his books, music and Movements—comprise artistic expressions.

NEW QUESTIONS ABOUT COHERENCE

The versatility of the parts of Gurdjieff's legacy makes these artistic expressions unique, but this versatility also instantly poses new questions. Are they the work of a talented individual who has not been able to formulate a clear, uniform vision? Is this oeuvre incoherent, or not? During the period in which he pursued writing, composing and physical movements, the chronology of Gurdjieff's life has clearly delineated periods, but this does not mean that there is coherence among his works. Does this coherence exist and, if so, from what is this evident?

These are not rhetorical questions. If indeed there is no coherence, each part of this legacy could assume a life of its own. And this is exactly what is happening on a large scale, but this is certainly not what Gurdjieff had intended. A free interpretation of Gurdjieff's music has recently made it into the Top Ten of a classical music chart, and the majority of those presently practicing his Movements, or what they believe to be as such, have never read any of his books. It is even doubtful if they are actually interested in Gurdjieff's ideas at all.

My motivation for writing this book is to reply to the question of coherence in Gurdjieff's legacy with a straightforward, heartfelt *Yes*, and my answer is based on four solid reasons:

- Gurdjieff's works complement each other
- they all share a ritualistic character
- they all share a hidden content
- their common source is the same: his teaching.

I will explain these four reasons in order.

Complementing Each Other

Gurdjieff's books, music and Movements should be seen in the light of his basic idea that thoughts, feelings and the body constitute the three main functions of the human and that, consequently, he tailored his Works for each of those functions respectively—*a trichotomy which gives the works a complementary character.* Just words, sounds or movements separately were not enough for him.

A Ritualistic Character

Gurdjieff's creations in the three artistic disciplines can be seen as a *Gesamtkunstwerk* and that explains their ritualistic character. The idea of a *Gesamtkunstwerk*, in which different arts intermingle to evoke a new vision, was first introduced by Richard Wagner and greatly influenced Russian Symbolism. This is not to say that Gurdjieff's work displays any affinity with Wagner's work. In fact, it is difficult to imagine a greater difference. However, one particular element in the idea of the *Gesamtkunstwerk* has a very strong presence in Gurdjieff's oeuvre.

To explain this, it will be necessary to dwell briefly on Symbolism, a cultural development from the last decade of the nineteenth century and the first decade of the twentieth.

Symbolism had a marked influence on the intelligentsia, in Belgium, France and Russia, but was not exclusive to them as it also formed a seedbed from which many other esoteric systems sprouted. Symbolism was a reaction to the increasing industrialization of the nineteenth century, and more especially a reaction to the tarnishing of the old, classical model of humankind by more modern, scientific developments. Galileo had already robbed humankind of its central position in the universe, but now Darwin undermined the divine origins too. Finally, the notion of humans as at least the lords and masters in their own castles was unmasked by Freud. We are subject to vital forces outside the periphery of our perception, in the subconscious.[1]

Symbolism preached the return to the realm of the spirit, to the restoration of human dignity and emphasized the singularity of each individual's personal experiences. In whatever form Symbolism expressed itself, two characteristics stand out again and again. First, that this deeply individual mysticism is usually experienced as tragic, and secondly, the belief that artistic expression is essentially a religious act, meaning that all the arts should together form a liturgy enabling the human to evolve into a higher form of being. It is this last point, the liturgical and ritual element that forms a useful clue. Gurdjieff's legacy can be seen as the result of a major effort to create an entirely new ritual in which essential questions are approached not only through a mental effort, but a ritual that simultaneously stimulates and mobilizes the sensitivity of the body and emotional life.

Shared Hidden Content

Another argument for regarding Gurdjieff's different artistic expressions as one single entity is the fact that they all have a hidden content,

1 This, in a nutshell, is what Sigmund Freud wrote in an article about narcissism, dating from 1917.

and this is very typical for everything regarding his teaching and his work. The word "esoteric" is usually used as a synonym for a deeper, hidden meaning, although the original meaning of this word is "that which lives inside a human being." The esoteric plays a role in all religious, spiritual and mystical systems and Gurdjieff's works are no exception. Secrecy, concealing information or taking gullible souls for a ride has nothing to do with it. This is not esotericism but deceit. A useful alternative word for esotericism is "inaccessible."

The inaccessible in Gurdjieff's work can be understood in three ways:

1. First, the geographical inaccessibility of the sources of his knowledge
2. Second, an insight can be inaccessible because it is cast in another, less obvious form, such as allegorical stories or hidden in a traditional art form.
3. Finally, a lack of preparation or a lack of knowledge can create a barrier.

Let me comment one at a time on these three forms.

As a young man, Gurdjieff was convinced that somewhere on earth an old form of knowledge still existed and he went looking for it. Whether or not he succeeded in finding it is unclear, but his idea is less otherworldly than it might at first seem. The existence of ancient forms of culture in remote areas certainly seems plausible. In contemporary ethnological musicology, "uneven distribution" is a recognized phenomenon. This accounts for the continued existence, in geographically or culturally remote areas or communities, of music that cannot be found anywhere else anymore. A farmer who grew up in the Appalachian Mountains in North America could bellow out a song that had crossed the ocean with his ancestors and had been preserved in his remote village, but long forgotten, in Europe.

Gurdjieff grew up in an environment where stories, myths, music and dance were passed on without losing any discernible vitality. Not just his native soil, but also his travels through the East must have brought him into contact with an enormous divergence of traditions and arts that originated from the ancient past, and had not been swept away by the "tidal wave of mud," a term with which he referred to Western civilization. He suspected that their folkloric form was just a cloak for real knowledge, purposely disguised in the distant past. In the case of myths, this was obvious, but traditional music and dance could contain information too, and about anything at all: a historical incident or bread recipe. Important knowledge could also be found in customs, habits and folklore, a secret codex transmitted from one unsuspecting generation to the other in a deceptively innocent form, waiting to be deciphered some day in the future. This form was akin to a time capsule, having a very long lifespan and protected from misuse. Gurdjieff used the word "legominism" to describe this form. In the future, only those who could interpret the codes could obtain access to the secret, others could not. "Those who know, know. Those who do not know, do not know" was one of Gurdjieff's cryptic statements that would not be out of place here.[2] It is consequently logical that Gurdjieff's own artistic works have a deeper heart of insight hidden under their artistic cloaks.

The Common Source

Finally, consider the inaccessibility caused by a lack of knowledge or resources. This is the meaning of the old adage that states that "something cannot be given that cannot be received." This is true for everything. A layperson cannot perceive the structure of a building in the way an architect does, nor can an untrained ear absorb music as a musician's. It may seem dogmatic, but I believe the significance of

2 Solange Claustres, one of Gurdjieff's pupils, remembered this statement by Gurdjieff during an interview published in *Bres*, number 186, 1997 (see footnote in Preface). Quoted with kind permission from *Bres Magazine*.

Gurdjieff's works and his teaching can only be understood by putting them into practice. To the extent that people attempt to apply the content of his books, music and Movements, his doctrine will gradually unfold. His works must be understood as a single work of art, created in different areas, but fed from a single source and energized with a single force: his vision of fate and the potential of the individual considered within the scope of a vast creation. Gurdjieff's legacy provides the material in the form of a ritual. This ritual puts his teaching into practice in order to test it, study it and decode it, like in a laboratory. His legacy also provides the material as in a workshop, in which, in quiet contemplation, his books are read aloud, his musical compositions are listened to and his Movements can be practiced. Books, musical compositions and Movements are the liturgical elements of his works.

As noted previously, the bulk of Gurdjieff's teaching, in the form of explanations to his immediate circle of pupils, was given from 1912 to 1924. Not that he was no longer active as a teacher after this, he continued to teach until his death, but he made use of entirely different means. The clear argumentation, by means of which he displayed his daring vision during the period prior to 1924, was definitely confined to the past and was replaced with personal conversations, readings from his books, his music and his Movements. The Movements could be described as his final, regular and structured form of education.

Like a continent split by a fault line, in 1924, the year of his car accident, the rationally accessible part of Gurdjieff's teaching was divided from everything that followed. His biographers and pupils offered various reasons for why this happened. The opinions vary markedly and are no more than surmise and speculation. More likely, he realized that spiritual ideas cannot be conveyed rationally, or through employing rationality alone, and for this reason he later hid them in his works of art, his "legominisms." One way or another, it must be emphasized that it is impossible for anyone to form a complete picture of Gurdjieff's teaching without knowing his pre-1924 expositions. The same is true for the comprehension of his books, music and Movements. The study of a fragment of Gurdjieff's legacy, isolated from his teaching, will produce a distorted picture and only deliver results that have little or nothing to do with the content and with Gurdjieff's actual objective.

The odd thing now is the fact that his teaching, understood here as its rational part, unlike its irrational part formed by his works of art, is the source of his legacy as described in the opening lines of this chapter, but that it is not named as such, nor can it be. *It has reached us solely through other people's testimonies.*

3

GURDJIEFF'S CONVEYANCE OF HIS TEACHING

True contact between two people can only occur at a unique moment in both their lives.

– Jan Foudraine[1]

Verbal instruction, as it is known in esoteric literature, existed long before the written word was used. And, in the preliminary phase as a teacher, Gurdjieff expounded his teaching through conversations with small groups of students, passed on from person to person, in this way of the spoken word.

Within Gurdjieff's family circle, as well as in the region where he was raised, the spoken word had a central role. This region, present-day northeast Turkey, was populated with Greek immigrants who had settled there centuries earlier: Kurds, Turks, Armenian immigrants who had settled more recently from the Caucasus, and the original Anatolian population. Religion and culture intermingled freely: Greek and Armenian Orthodox, the Jewish faith, and a plethora of cults and rituals, some originating from the Mother Goddess culture with roots reaching as far back as the Neolithic era, the dawning of humanity. In all these cultures, the spoken word, not the written word, was the most important medium. Storytellers

1 Jan Foudraine (1929-2016) is a Dutch psychiatrist who became known through his book Wie is van Hout (1971) in which he took a critical stance against the psychiatry of the time. The quote is from a television interview a few years later, concerning the primary relation between psychiatrist and patient. His statement seems to me to have a relevance of a far greater scope.

and singers were living links with the past. Characteristically for this region, the written word arrived here relatively late, which is borne out by the fact that the first pictorial reading book for children in Kurdish dates from 1920.

What a difference from our Western-European society, where books and libraries are the main pillars for the conveyance of knowledge. This is important with regard to practical and applicable sciences, yet the question is to what extent esoteric knowledge can be stored within such a framework. It is interesting to note that in the Jewish religion it is not permitted to record in writing some of the holy concepts and insights! This indicates that the written word cannot embody the soul, the living content that insight provides. It is as if the written word has lost some substance, has been reduced, in the way in which a photograph or film distorts actual human form, or a compact disc changes live music.

In any case, verbal communication has a dynamic that is missing when we read, as an answer can be given immediately, and if something is not properly understood an explanation can be offered using other words. These are the advantages, but there is another factor at play that can be disadvantageous. One of the hallmarks of person-to-person communication is that the recipient of the message partially determines what can be conveyed. This varies from person to person, dependent on his or her ability. This means that Gurdjieff's teaching can now only reach us after two variables regarding its conveyance have been taken into account.

- Firstly, the quality of the students determined what could and could not be discussed.
- Secondly, those students passed on the message in their own manner, based on their impressions, understanding and verbal ability.

Factor in the problem of language. When Gurdjieff started his teaching he did not speak a single Western European language, and this is exactly the time when he framed his teachings in logically structured words, so his words had to be translated.[2]

There is one, great, notable exception to the perception that our present knowledge of Gurdjieff's teaching is limited to the words and interpretations of others. In a diary, kept by the Russian author Pyotr Demianovitch Ouspensky (b. Moscow 1878, d. Lyne, UK 1947) from 1914-1921, *everything* that Gurdjieff told him and the group of students to which he belonged was recorded meticulously. Following the death of the author, his widow passed on the diary to Gurdjieff, who, and various sources agree on this, confirmed that it contained an exact account of his words, and he subsequently gave permission for its publication. The diary was published in 1949, prior to Gurdjieff's death and the publication of his own book, under another title, *In Search of the Miraculous*. The original title was more descriptively accurate: *Fragments of an Unknown Teaching*. The original diary can be found in the Yale University Library.

This account of Gurdjieff's teachings eliminates the second of the aforementioned variables. After all, he confirmed that it was a correct representation of his words and thereby authorized this version of his teaching. That the first variable was not eliminated is apparent from the jargon that Gurdjieff had to employ in order to be understood by the Russian intellectuals of the time. These were mostly words and concepts already used by Petrovna Blavatsky (1831-1891), the founder of Theosophy, such as "astral," "school" and "initiates."

These kinds of vague words are a source of confusion, but are still common in current interpretations of Gurdjieff's teachings. But Nietzschean concepts, too, which had a great influence on the

---

2 Olga de Hartmann provides a typical example of an incorrect translation that has taken on a life of its own. One of Gurdjieff's most cited statements is a qualification of the people that follow his teaching, i.e., "The Sly Man." In her book *What For?*, an unpublished autobiography, Olga de Hartmann proposes that this translation is absolutely incorrect and it should be "the intelligent man." Russian was her mother tongue.

thinking of the intelligentsia of the time, and especially on Ouspensky, appear in the following quote that dovetails into Gurdjieff's ideas, as a good example of this: "A fact that people don't want to accept is that a thought comes to us when 'it' sees fit, not when 'I' desire it. It is a distortion of facts to state that 'I' think, no 'it' thinks and there is no certainty that 'it' is actually 'I.'" Nietzsche wrote this in 1885 in his book *Jenseits von Gut und Böse.*

A NEW "MAN"?

The diary, *Fragments of an Unknown Teaching,* is the vital key to Gurdjieff's world of ideas. At the same time, it is the cause of some stubbornly held misunderstandings which I will discuss further on in this chapter. P.D. Ouspensky was an author with an exceptional gift for philosophy, physics and crystal-clear writing. The word "thinker" maybe describes him best, but a thinker who did his utmost to live according to the consequences of his thoughts.

Ouspensky met Gurdjieff in Russia shortly before the Russian Revolution, a remarkable period of scientific and cultural development. In the atmosphere of the times, smoldering with new ideas, nothing seemed impossible. An entire constellation of artists and scientists worked together towards the creation of a grand utopia, releasing in their respective areas of expertise one revolutionary development after the other. Mendeleev developed the periodic table of elements. Tsiolkovski, the father of space travel, designed rockets to colonize space. Kandinsky and Malevich, at the same time, crossed the boundary into abstract painting, while the composer Scriabin experimented with the mixing of sound and color. In the midst of this creative explosion, a plethora of philosophical and artistic systems came to be, most of which have lain unnoticed to this day.

Gurdjieff and Ouspensky met in St. Petersburg, the cultural capital of Russia, at the time home to famous composers and painters including

Rachmaninoff, Stravinsky, Prokofiev, Chagall, Kandinsky and Roerich, and the writers Gorki and Blok. St. Petersburg was a city with great disparity between its rich upper class—infatuated with everything to do with Eastern philosophy, magic, theosophy, Buddhism and secret societies—and a poverty-stricken majority who lived in ghettos that were literally bursting at the seams, due to a constant influx of immigrants, and in which one in four children did not survive the wretched conditions.

Besides the bohemians, who out of boredom were initiated in one teaching after another, St. Petersburg also accommodated another elite, worthy of their name, formed by a group of Symbolic poets and theoreticians. The most important of the Russian Symbolists, the "high priest," was Vladimir Solovyov, a fascinating historical figure who can, in many respects, be considered as Gurdjieff's predecessor. Many ideas that would later play a role in Gurdjieff's teachings were originally expressed in Russian Symbolism. An example of this is the notion that the human comprises three independent functions: mind, feeling and body. They also saw a need for building a bridge between Eastern intuition and Western science.

Vladimir Solovyov predicted that a "new man" would arise, equipped with higher spiritual and physical capacities. He would be able to not only look forward but also backward, with a new appearance, a different face, and speaking an entirely new, universal, language. Solovyov and the Symbolists of St. Petersburg believed that a breakthrough would occur in the near future from which humanity would arise with a higher consciousness. The simultaneous revolutions in art, science, and Russian society were, according to them, indications of this. They also shared in the Wagnerian concept that art would have to form a liturgy to assist humanity in its evolution to a higher form of being. The painter Malevich left the faces of people in his paintings blank, awaiting the facial features of the "new man." However, these silent witnesses of the "Great Dream," as this era could be referred to, waited in vain. They will never speak the universal world language. The difference between the ideal and reality led, after the Revolution, to a suffocation of the avant-garde. "Art is a dangerous disease, just like religion" was already a slogan in 1922. The period before the Revolution was, however, a unique creative highpoint. Most of the literature, philosophy, occult and mystical contributions were never translated and as a result never reached the West. Thanks to Ouspensky, Gurdjieff's teachings did not share in this fate.

THE CONTRIBUTION OF OUSPENSKY

Ouspensky was already a successful author when he met Gurdjieff in St. Petersburg in 1915. His book, *Tertium Organum*, written in 1911, had earned him international regard. The title stands for a new logic, a third form, next to the first two that Aristotle and Bacon had proposed, yet one that actually preceded them; a paradoxical logic named "intuitive logic," associated with a higher form of consciousness. In this first book, Ouspensky crystallized the fascination of the era with the fourth dimension. It deeply influenced the Russian avant-garde, who saw Ouspensky as their mouthpiece. His ideas continued to spread. The Surrealist painters Gordon Onslow Ford and Roberto Matta also drew inspiration from them several decades later.

Gurdjieff left a deep impression on Ouspensky, because he appeared to possess practical knowledge, devoid of speculation, of a type Ouspensky had never previously encountered. Gurdjieff spoke about facts that he himself had verified, and he did so in a dialect akin to that used by an illiterate Caucasian farmer, rather than a prophet revealing a cosmic vision. In a phenomenal feat of memory, Ouspensky recorded literally word for word how Gurdjieff had explained the complete system of his teachings. In every meeting, Gurdjieff introduced surprisingly new and original concepts, until finally the structure of one of the greatest all-encompassing visions of humanity and the cosmos was revealed. Gurdjieff did not promise great wealth; quite the contrary, he suggested to his students that they were nothing more than machines. The body, thoughts and feelings were nothing more than the cogs, levers and springs in a complicated mechanism that an impulse: birth, jolts into motion. Such an impulse then powers the mechanism until the springs wound at birth, like clockwork, unwind, eventually losing their power: death.

His vision denied that one possesses individuality, a will or a soul. This could be acquired, yes, but only through great effort and voluntary suffering. A human life did not come into being to serve humankind, but as a part of organic life on earth that, in totality, generates a substance that nourishes the moon. The sun, planets, earth and the moon are not dead masses competing pointlessly, but are living growing organisms. The moon will become the earth, and the earth the sun. This is reminiscent of the vision of the Russian Symbolist composer Scriabin who lived around this time. He was so convinced that one day the sun would wrap its fiery arms around the earth that he devoted an amazing composition for the piano, *Vers la Flamme*, to this belief.

After spending seven years at Gurdjieff's side, while his following of students in Russia was still sparse, Ouspensky slowly lost his faith in Gurdjieff, but never in the ideas he had learned from him. He stayed true to them and passed them on to his own students. He believed them to be fragments of a hidden knowledge that was kept somewhere in its totality. He called that "somewhere" a "school," and he lived in the hope and expectation that this "school" would once again cross his path. It never happened. Shortly before his death, with one foot in the grave, Ouspensky shocked his countless students with a complete renouncement of all he had formerly taught them. "No system exists" was one of the blows with which he axed his own life's work. After his death, his widow advised the bewildered students who were left behind to go to Paris and contact Gurdjieff, something that Ouspensky himself had always forbidden, punishable by excommunication. His relation to Gurdjieff and his teachings was split in character and his life seemed to bear the mark of a difficult-to-describe, inescapable, tragedy.

Ouspensky wrote numerous books. His final book, *The Wondrous Life of Ivan Osokin*, published shortly before his death, is a fictional tale in the form of a fable describing the depressing idea formulated by Nietzsche of the circular course of human existence, which relentlessly repeats itself in every detail from birth through to death. A theme closely linked to his fascination for memory and memories.

Perhaps I have dwelt for too long on the tragic aspects of Ouspensky's life; the following may help to redress the balance. Long ago, I spoke to several people who had known Ouspensky personally, and I listened with great interest to their recollections of him. In 1996, during a dinner at the home of the very elderly Mrs. Van Oyen, we were talking about Ouspensky. When I alluded to the tragedy of his life, she looked at me sharply and declared: "This was not my experience of Ouspensky at all and even less so my opinion. I always found him uncommonly invigorating, with great spirit, knowing exactly the direction he wanted to head in." At the time, Mrs. Van Oyen was the last person alive that had not only been one of Ouspensky's students, but one of his personal acquaintances.[3]

The break between Gurdjieff and Ouspensky is still a topic that can cause friction among the circles that are interested in their work. Usually, a side is chosen through portraying the other in a bad light. This is all beside the point. Since their deaths, the names of these two men have been inextricably linked by the avalanche of essays that

3 Together with her husband, Mrs. van Oyen (D. van Oyen-van Zijll de Jong, 1907-2004) established the Dutch branch of the institute "School for Philosophy" that Ouspensky had founded in England. After her husband's death, she led this "School" for many years on her own. Under her inspirational leadership this grew to become a large movement in the Netherlands with thousands of students in the 1960s and 1970s.

have been written about the subject. Ouspensky's diary remains the only authorized account of Gurdjieff's teaching, described in a readily comprehensible manner.

The meeting between Gurdjieff and Ouspensky was a determining factor in the future of Gurdjieff's "Work." It was a wondrous meeting and difficult to ignore the impression that Gurdjieff spoke, as it were, through the medium of Ouspensky. Their meeting seemed to initiate a process in which Gurdjieff was able to utilize Ouspensky's analytical talents to reveal the structure of his teachings. This almost medium-like process was repeated, a short time later, with another of Gurdjieff's students. However, this time in the entirely different discipline of music.

LOST IN THE WRITTEN WORD

As previously noted, the contradiction that Gurdjieff proclaimed his teachings through the spoken word, but that only the written version still exists, has persistently caused confusion. The written word strips what was said of the circumstances in which it was spoken, of its intensity, and of the presence of the speaker and those for whom it was intended. Because of this, the logical coherence of what Ouspensky wrote can be followed without understanding the actual content. This is such an essential point, certainly where the content of Gurdjieff's legacy is concerned, that I would like to illustrate this with an example from my own experience.

As I reflect on my life, I see a stream of images in which new images appear brightly as the previous image disappears into the dusk of the waiting room of memories, perhaps forever. Once in a while, one image appears brighter than the other and hovers for longer in my mind's eye. These are often events in which I met people for the first time, people who would come to play an important role in my life. I realize that these meetings, more than anything, determined the course of my life. Although it is difficult to comprehend, these meetings appear to hang "in the air," induced and guided by an unknown force which has been given the inadequate label of "coincidence." They seem to be part of a pattern that I believe has been independently fixed, well in advance of the events. After these meetings, the events appeared to follow the pattern that had been set out in advance, much in the way that one film image inevitability follows the next out of the projector, and as if I remembered something I could never have known.

In such meetings, words played a role, but they were not an important or determining factor. The words were only confirmations of what had already been felt by both parties. They floated on the surface of the mysterious dynamic of the contact, like pieces of wood on water. They originated from this exchange, but what really occurred can never be experienced, reduced or found again by others, in the words alone. This explains why love letters read by those for whom they were not intended are so boring and predictable. Not so for those to whom they are addressed. For them, they are a magical formula, the talisman, which keeps the flame of love burning.

Ouspensky's diary, however sublimely written, cannot transmit the real substance of Gurdjieff's teaching, and the illusion that all can be understood is so widespread that a warning is not a superfluous luxury. The many code words in this book, such as "self-remembering" and "identification," are all too easily weighted with subjective content coming from personal associations. The desire to discover a new point of view, ultimately the reason people pick up such a book, cannot be fulfilled. On the contrary, after the experiences stemming from the personal past have mastered these neutral code words, the circle closes and all new impressions become hermetically excluded.

I have spent quite some time during my active life listening to and participating in conversations about Gurdjieff's teachings, and this left me with the impression that the code words mentioned were just empty concepts that were moved *ad infinitum* to and fro on the chessboard of superficial logic. This kind of mental time wasting was not new to me. I had experienced it before in a different spiritual setting, in staunch Protestantism in the north of the Netherlands. The elders of the church spoke with each other about holy texts in code words made up of other code words! Sitting in a circle, one of them would propose: "Doesn't Josiah 4, line 2 say…"; the sentence would not be finished. After a short silence, another participant would answer, "…yes, but in Ecclesiastes 6, 1 it states clearly…"; this sentence would also not be finished. The conversation would continue in this manner. They were very good people, but the confusion of an uninitiated listener like myself is to be excused in such an exchange. I think that many people, who participate in a discussion about Gurdjieff's teachings among a group of "insiders," for the first time will suffer the same confusion.

OTHER DOCUMENTS

Besides Ouspensky's book, another document attempted to present Gurdjieff's explanation of his teachings in his own words. This document, the "Constantinople Notes," comprises some seventy pages of text. It was originally written in shorthand in 1921 in Constantinople, the present-day Istanbul, by Boris Ferapontov, one of Gurdjieff's students. The sentences are difficult to read in places and the subjects are jumbled, but it demonstrates that Gurdjieff sometimes formulated his ideas differently and provided different examples. They even weave chronologically into his explanations reported in Ouspensky's book. At this time, Ouspensky was staying in Constantinople and it is likely that he influenced this shorthand report. These notations, still unpublished today, can be regarded as a supplement to Ouspensky's book.

After Ouspensky's departure, Gurdjieff continued to teach in conversations with his students and through lectures for larger groups. Others attempted to record these lectures, which took place prior to

1924, in writing, but they did not possess as phenomenal a memory as Ouspensky. In addition, their reports lacked the comprehensiveness, the span of tension that the entire teaching in all its facets contains, which Ouspensky had documented so integrally in his diary. The major part of this last category of lectures, recorded in writing by others, remained unavailable until, in 2014, *Gurdjieff's Early Talks* was published.[4]

THE ORAGEAN VERSION

The period described by Ouspensky was only the start of Gurdjieff's first phase of his teaching. The feast was yet to begin: in the Prieuré, Gurdjieff's estate in Fontainebleau near Paris, a "new Ouspensky" took the stage—one who, just like his predecessor, was a gifted writer—in the person of Alfred Orage (1873-1934), a literary critic. Of all of Gurdjieff's pupils, Orage had the closest personal contact. When Gurdjieff learned of Orage's untimely death, he wept at the passing of his "super idiot"—in Gurdjieff's opinion a very positive evaluation—and he wiped the tears from his eyes with his balled-up fists. Orage was the only student whom Gurdjieff, during his life, so trusted with his teachings that he instructed him to spread his teachings in America as a sort of "ambassador." For eight years, Orage performed his task with a great deal of verve and enormous dedication. It was Gurdjieff

---

4 *Gurdjieff's Early Talks 1914-1931,* 2014, Book Studio. This compilation consists mainly of a collection of lectures more commonly known as the *Black Book,* because of its black cover. It is not clear who is responsible for these texts. Just a part of them were published before under the title: *Views from the Real World. Early Talks of Gurdjieff as Recollected by His Pupils*. E.P. Dutton & Co. Inc., New York, 1973.

Additional a dozen or so lectures are included coming from the estate of Thomas de Hartmann and thought to have been recorded by his spouse Olga de Hartmann. One of these lectures bears the title: "The study of psychology. Man the machine," London 1922, Chicago 1924. In this lecture Gurdjieff attempted to summarize his teaching as concisely as possible. I believe this to be a key text.

The *Constantinople Notes,* however, remain unpublished.

himself who, in 1931, unexpectedly and with unscripted drama, put an end to the activities of Orage.

There can be no doubt that what Orage taught to his groups in America largely originated from Gurdjieff, but the gifted pedagogue that he was, he could not have helped but frame the teachings with many of his own examples. Orage's teachings in America are preserved in a book, *The Oragean Version*, written by C. Daly King—a psychologist specializing in the physiology of the brain—with the intention of keeping the interpretation of Gurdjieff's teaching, by Orage, for posterity. He limited the edition of his book to one hundred numbered copies and expressly forbid any further dissemination.[5] It is difficult to over-emphasize the importance of this book as a productive study of Gurdjieff's ideas. It encompasses all his teachings, but the author wrote it independently of Ouspensky's work, of which he learned only after he had finished his own report. However, there is a remarkable, direct relation with the work by Ouspensky, because before Orage gave up his literary career and travelled to Fontainebleau to join Gurdjieff, he was a loyal attendee of Ouspensky's London lectures.

The content of Ouspensky's diary and *The Oragean Version* only partially overlap. The diary sketches every aspect of the teachings. Orage's version is a method in which, with great precision, greater than any other book or document from the extensive library of literature dedicated to Gurdjieff, the first steps describing the practical application of his teachings are explained. It also includes elements that are entirely missing from Ouspensky's diary, including a diagram that compares the possible development of the human against a

---

5 C. Daly King, *The Oragean Version*, was privately printed in a limited edition of 100 copies: New York:1951, 289 pages, with Index. This text has been republished by Magisteria, Bucharest, 2014, and by Daath Gnosis, 2014. Eureka Editions, Utrecht Holland, plans another release, not yet published, with a Foreword by Paul Beekman Taylor. The text can also be downloaded from the Internet in pdf format. I have studied the Internet text and confirm that it is an authentic rendering of the original publication, as I have a direct copy of one of the original prints from 1951 in my archive.

diatonic scale. This diagram, not included by Ouspensky, seems to me to be the most important of Gurdjieff's teachings.

~

Ouspensky's diary, *Fragments of an Unknown Teaching*, nonetheless remains as the only report Gurdjieff authorized, one of the cornerstones that supports his teaching. One of two cornerstones to be exact. The other cornerstone is the first book in Gurdjieff's trilogy, *The All and Everything*, titled *Beelzebub's Tales to His Grandson*.

4

THE *STRUGGLE OF THE MAGICIANS*

Gibbon was right when he wrote that history is little more than the register of the crimes, follies, and misfortunes of mankind. He forgot to mention the existence of an invisible force that undoes these crimes in the long term.[1]

– Leibovitch

Following his car accident in 1924, Gurdjieff started writing his trilogy *All and Everything*, of which *Beelzebub's Tales to His Grandson* was the first part, but this was not the first time he had put pen to paper. Around 1920, with assistance from Ouspensky, he wrote a script for a ballet: The *Struggle of the Magicians*, which portrays a trial of strength between "black" and "white" magic. This ballet was a first attempt to introduce a greater public to his work and showed the most important elements of his teaching in miniature. The different circumstances in which, and the intention with which, he "really" started to write years later are dramatic. In 1924, his main aim was to record his entire teachings for posterity.

---

1 Edward Gibbon (1737-1794) was the author of *The Decline and Fall of the Roman Empire* (1776-1788), probably the most authoritative history book ever written. The quote that history is little more than the register of the crimes, follies and misfortunes of humankind originates from this book. Ouspensky made the same statement, but quoted—consciously or unconsciously—Gibbon. The remark by Leibovitch, the Israeli philosopher famous for, among other things, his criticism of his country's government with regard to the occupied territories, was made by him in a television interview around 1990. He was already very elderly and due to his illness, *ankylosing spondylitis*, a disease that completely fuses the spine, he could hardly walk. The entire interview left a deep impression on me of a truly learned man.

Although only a first step, it is important to examine Gurdjieff's ballet in detail, because it embodied a number of aspects that are characteristic of his spiritual work, not just at that point in time, but right through his life until the end.

A performance of this ballet was never given. The fact that Gurdjieff and his students at the time did not have a permanent base certainly played a role here. Political tension and the aftermath of the civil war in Russia forced them to stay constantly on the move. But despite this, wherever they were, they worked dutifully on the ballet. Apart from the writing of the script, scenery was painted, costumes designed, dances practiced and music composed. Gurdjieff did not dwell on the fact that in the end there was no performance; he believed that people should work born of a love of the work itself and not for the results.

What remains of this ballet? The script, a few sections of painted scenery and a couple of designs for other pieces of scenery, as well as half a dozen pieces of music. That is all, although it must be said that the music is among the most beautiful that Gurdjieff ever wrote.[2] Besides, probably one Movement that is still known, which also illustrates the struggle between good and black magic, originates from this

---

2 De Hartmann's interpretation of a few of the most important pieces from this cycle can be heard on the CDs: *The Music of Gurdjieff/De Hartmann*, three disc set, Triangle Records, P.O. Box 452 New York, N.Y. 10021. The sheet music was published by Schott in: *Gurdjieff/De Hartmann, music for the piano*, volume IV, ED 7844, 2005, Schott Musik International, Mainz. There is something strange about this sheet music. The original composition of the third and fifth fragment was consigned to the addenda by Schott, while de Hartmann's improvisations took their place in the cycle. De Hartmann's free interpretation of the theme in the third fragment in particular—the accompanying music for Gafar's and Zeinab's hypnosis by the Good Magician—is very beautiful, but still, it remains an unusual, i.e., unfathomable, procedure for such a leading musical publisher like Schott. The original composition for the third fragment is important in a historical sense, if only because it bears witness to Chopin's great influence on de Hartmann's approach to Gurdjieff's theme.

ballet.[3] A recent study has revealed that another important Movement, "The Great Prayer," could also originally have been created for this ballet. There is a point in the script at which the Good Magician draws back his workshop's huge curtain and the rising sun becomes visible. At the sight of this marvelous spectacle, he and his pupils fall to their knees in respect. This would have been a splendid moment in the story to demonstrate this long and solemn Movement.

If we want to imagine what this ballet must have looked like, the script provides us with the most secure footing. This script was first published, most likely illegally, in Cape Town in 1957. After this, it was regularly reprinted. It is set in a city flooded with Eastern atmosphere, and tells the tale of the fight for Zeinab's unblemished soul, a beautiful and noble young woman. The rich good-for-nothing who wants to seduce her, named Gafar, is initially turned down, so he calls upon the help of the Black Magician. Fortunately, the Good Magician sees through this sly move, and blocks it before it is too late. Through his supernatural powers, the Good Magician hypnotizes the two main characters and destroys the Black Magician's plan once and for all.

Time has faded this story, but luckily the script had more to offer. This ballet was to be the first presentation of Gurdjieff's mission to the public at large and it had a distinct program objective. At three points in the story he displays, simply and clearly, actual themes from his

3 This is Movement number 25 from the European "39-series," identical to number 34 from the American "46-series." Both these series contain Movements that Gurdjieff gave at the end of his life. Number 25 is the odd one out in this series. It contains theatrical elements that are characteristic of Gurdjieff's earlier Movements, such as prescribed facial expressions. The gestures of anger and aggression made by the Black Magician's pupils under the expulsion of piercing screams are nowhere else to be found. The question remains to what extent this Movement has reached us in a historically reliable form. The section in which the "black magic" is portrayed is in a faster rhythm, but in my opinion it should be played simultaneously with the slow rhythm of the "white magic" and not separately afterwards. I base this opinion on my musical analysis. If this is indeed correct, the Movement demonstrates that both processes take place in a person simultaneously.

teaching. The concise sentences in which his vision is encapsulated are in marked contrast to the magically laden atmosphere of the story and in that sense they form guiding beacons to crucial points of Gurdjieff's teaching, dispersed in the story's old fashioned orientalism.

- In the first act, a whirling dervish enters the stage who, in the opening line, sings about the triple and sevenfold aspects of the divinity of nature.
- Then, later in the piece, the Good Magician declares to his pupils, while they gaze at the heavens through a large telescope, that a person who knows himself knows the entire cosmos, including God.
- At the end of the story, as the conclusion, Gurdjieff's most powerful statement comes in the form of a solemn incantation by the Good Magician against humankind's mechanical endeavors, the sole medium from which evil can propagate itself.

As a basis for a ballet, the story also had the objective of showing a large number of dances. A passage in the script must be mentioned in connection with this because it must have been a spectacular scene: a dozen dancers from different countries—Tibet, Georgia, Caucasus, Baluchistan, Persia, India, Arabia and other Eastern countries—represented in traditional costume who, one after another, performed a dance from their country of birth. These solo dances would, according to the text, express the soul of these nations. Gurdjieff's pupil Alexander de Salzmann created a beautiful scenery design.[4]

The dances that would later be known as "Movements" are present early on in the story, as the Good Magician's school is revealed. It is explained in the script that these "holy dances" were traditionally an important subject of study in all the Eastern esoteric schools. They express a specific knowledge and induce a harmonious state for the

---

4 On page 203 of Gurdjieff/ De Hartmann *ORIENTAL SUITE*, the complete orchestral music 1923-1924. Gert Jan Blom, 2006 Basta Audio Visuals, The Netherlands.

performers. This concise statement would be explained in more detail during the theatre performances of the Movements in 1923 and 1924.

It is nothing less than a cultural disaster that, for the twelve solo dances, Gurdjieff's choreographies and music have been lost.[5] Everyone who understands something about Gurdjieff's background, his knowledge of ethnological dances and music, as well as his ability to distill the essence contained in them, must tear their hair out at this irrevocable loss. In the time that this ballet was being learned and practiced, and also during the initial phase of the Institute in Fontainebleau, solo dances were still an important part of the Movements. Unfortunately, this component was quickly lost, probably because—apart from a single exception[6]—his pupils did not possess the required skills. Undoubtedly, the solo dances would have been a positive addition and would have invested the group dances with more character, boosting their strength. History intended it to be that, of the Movements, only the group dances survived.

That the *Struggle of the Magicians* did not culminate in a performance of the ballet did not mean that Gurdjieff let go of the idea. On the contrary, after he had settled in France and finally had time and space for the rehearsal of a large theatre performance, he took on the organization of three major theatre performances:

- the first one dedicated to Movements,
- the second one to Eastern music played on his collection of authentic Eastern instruments,
- and finally, a third performance dedicated to techniques like hypnosis, thought transfer and other paranormal skills that he learned in Eastern monasteries.

---

5 From the six pieces of music that have survived from the ballet, "A Tibetan Dance" probably stems from the third act, the section of the ballet in which these solo dances would have taken place.

6 Lily Galoumian, for whom a solo dance—a traditional dance from the Caucasus, the "Lezginka"—was planned for the theatre performance in 1923-1924.

Only the first of these performances actually took place, in Paris in 1923, and in a number of American cities in 1924. Once again, following the loss of the dances and music from the ballet, we can only regretfully shake our heads when we consider what unique material would have been demonstrated in the second and third performances, but due to Gurdjieff's car accident it was pushed aside to reside in the domain of eternity.

MAGICAL ACTIONS

More than likely, the three theatre performances that Gurdjieff had planned were to be an expansion of the key points in his ballet, as though this ballet were being examined under a magnifying glass. The major role of dance and music was already clear in his approach, but his plans also display that the multiplicity of magical actions from the *Struggle of the Magicians* was more than just a superficial theatrical device. The ballet script contains dozens of magical procedures, and two of the most significant that are described in great detail concern the transfer of energy from person to person; this is exactly what Gurdjieff excelled in throughout his life. Someone, who was present at Gurdjieff's famous "last suppers" in his Parisian apartment, once told me how much the occasions were characterized by the transmission of Gurdjieff's energy to his pupils. This took place especially during the stating of what type of "idiot" someone was: Gurdjieff's resolute qualification of his dinner guests during a series of "toasts" that never seemed to end.

All the descriptions of the magical actions in the ballet are worth studying in more detail. This is certainly true for the rite with which the Good Magician counteracts the powers of his evil opponent. At each end of a table stands a barrel, one of the barrels is larger than the other. They are connected with a copper bar. After drinking the magic potion, two male and two female pupils raise their hands above the smaller barrel. The Good Magician extends his wand, while muttering spells, over the larger barrel, at which point sparks fly between his wand and the barrel. Nine candles are arranged around the barrel, of which six are burning. Slowly the rite reaches its climax. Suddenly, the remaining three candles ignite and the symbol above the Magician's chair lights up, which is followed by a resounding retort that breaks the power of the Evil Magician. The magical props such as kettles and wands described here can be seen as the predecessors of the complex and surrealist-like equipment that will make its entrance later in *Beelzebub's Tales to His Grandson*.

The role of magical procedures in Gurdjieff's teachings, especially the inner-self exercises that he taught individual pupils in his later years, is seriously underestimated. Whatever the source of Gurdjieff's knowledge, it is certain that he distilled this from a number of methods that can be described as "magical rituals," but in contrast to our familiar magic they do not originate from a flight of fantasy or a diseased mind, but actually have their origins in extremely ancient traditions.

As already said, the ballet clearly demonstrated Gurdjieff's interest in magic, dance and music, and this all set in an Eastern atmosphere, in which hidden powers are utilized in a trial of strength. In this first piece of Gurdjieff´s creative work, his distillation of evil is remarkable. Here it has a human form and shape, personified by the Black Magician, who is called in by Gafar, because he cannot manipulate the situation to his egoistical aims. Later, in his major work *Beelzebub's Tales to His Grandson*, evil shifts shape. It no longer has a human form; it is more an impersonal result of an organ implanted in humanity, preventing humans from observing reality.

THE WAY OF STRUGGLE

Remarkably, the first word to flow from Gurdjieff's pen was "struggle," the opening word in the title of his ballet. This word is typical to describe Gurdjieff and his teaching. It is difficult to see his discipline as anything else than a "struggle" with "something." Here, arms are not raised to the heavens and prayers rattled off that evaporate into nothing; no, here "something" is being fought: the passivity that has become part of us all. Gurdjieff has written his own role as a crusader against the powers that bind Western people to slavery. The confrontation was violent and only one could survive: it was either *tsjikk*—the snapping sound that a louse makes as you crush it between your thumb nails—for the Western world, or *tsjikk* for Gurdjieff. The question remains if the struggle in the ballet can be considered the conflict that takes place independently in every living person, in which all the protagonists from the script are facets of a single individual, or if this drama is to unfold on an even larger scale? Is there a link between Gurdjieff's performance and his teachings, with an intervention in our world that could be compared to the supernatural measures of the Good Magician in the ballet?

Yellow Sound and *The Victory Over the Sun*

Finally, it is interesting to lay this ballet alongside two other revolutionary pieces of theatre from the first decade in the twentieth century, which originated in the extremely creative atmosphere of the Russian avant-garde. These two other pieces are: the *Yellow Sound* by Kandinsky and *The Victory Over the Sun*, a collaborative production by the Cubo-Futurists.

The *Yellow Sound* was a piece of theatre designed by Kandinsky. In his opinion, the world was on the threshold of a new era of great spirituality and he sought a monumental synthesis of all the arts. His *Yellow Sound* was a preparatory experiment to create an "Art of the Future" in which opera, ballet and drama were one. Thomas de Hartmann wrote the music for this and it was published in 1912 in *Der Blaue Reiter Almanach*, one of the most famous books on art from the twentieth century. Thomas de Hartmann was also actively involved in painting parts of the scenery for the *Yellow Sound,* and night after night he accompanied the dancer Alexander Sakharov with piano improvisations that were to be incorporated in the fifth act, which was dedicated to dance. This experience was to be of great advantage to de Hartmann later on when accompanying Gurdjieff's dances. Just as with the *Struggle of the Magicians,* the *Yellow Sound* was never performed. It was the 1970s before a reconstructed performance took place in the United States. Attempts to reconstruct Gurdjieff's ballet have been undertaken, but unfortunately without success to date.

The opera *The Victory Over the Sun* was performed, in contrast to the *Struggle of the Magicians* and the *Yellow Sound*, even if it was limited to the premiere in December 1913. This opera is undisputedly among the top pieces of theatre that have relevance for the philosophical and artistic movements in Russia of the time. Characteristically, the heroes of this opera were the "men of the future," who conquered an "infinite" universal space.

The music was atonal and composed by Matyushin. Malevich took care of the scenery and costumes. The opera's libretto, according to the press a scraping together of "absurd sounds," was written by Kruchenykh, who had previously argued that, "for the description of our future completely new words and completely new combinations of words would be necessary." This new language would have to extend further than the logical intellect, it had to be "trans-rational." The "absurd sounds" focused upon by the press were nothing more than his personal version of this new "trans-rational" language. Kruchenykh based them on the sounds that little children make, and had studied the sounds of members of Russian mystic sects while they were in trance and "speaking in tongues."

Placing these three theatrical works side by side, we see the extent to which two of Gurdjieff's pupils contributed to them. Ouspensky's musings over the fourth dimension had a direct influence on the libretto of *The Victory Over the Sun*. The Sun had to be conquered because it had refused to travel to the fourth dimension. De Hartmann had scored the music for the *Yellow Sound*. This confirms the leading positions of these two men in the avant-garde and spiritual art of the time, long before they had met Gurdjieff and together contributed to the *Struggle of the Magicians*. Later on, these two key figures would make an invaluable contribution to the design of Gurdjieff's teachings and his music.

~

The importance of Gurdjieff's first step to the written word, in the *Struggle of the Magicians,* bears no resemblance to his second step, four years later. His circumstances and objectives in these two steps are equally incomparable.

5

BEELZEBUB'S TALES TO HIS GRANDSON

No path is so steeped in mystery as the path that leads within: here resides eternity with all its worlds, the past and the future.

– Novalis

Gurdjieff wrote three books. The first bears the title, *An Objectively Impartial Criticism of the Life of Man,* and with a subtitle, *Beelzebub's Tales to His Grandson*. This latter title is the most commonly used. The second and third books are: *Meetings with Remarkable Men* and *Life Is Real Only Then When "I Am."* These three books have been combined under the title, *All and Everything*.

Beelzebub's Tales to His Grandson is the first book from this trilogy and a key work in his multifaceted legacy. It is perhaps his greatest achievement, but as is typical for most things related to the author, Gurdjieff, this hefty book that looks like a little fat bible, produces at first sight a life-sized question mark, rather than a new and clear picture suggested by the collective title, *All and Everything*.

A PRETENTIOUS TITLE?

The two words that comprise the title of this trilogy allude to the universal principle, the "All," and the multiplicity of phenomena that originated from this, the "Everything." Modesty does not seem to be the most obvious character trait for this author. Such modesty in this case is not possible, because the objective of his work is to achieve a tremendous synthesis of the creation and everything that this brought forth. The idea, that an individual could bring this about, verges on the visionary. It would even be highly suspect for a person to harbor such a belief. "Lunacy," people call this. And indeed, it is a well-known phenomenon in psychiatry that a lunatic is obsessively involved, his entire life, with never-ending calculations of the solar system, descriptions of the origins of the universe, or bizarre diagrams of the development of all life forms since Adam and Eve. Yet, this summary covers the subjects in Gurdjieff's book. *All and Everything* is an anachronism, and neither the subject nor the way in which it was written has any relationship with current literary or scientific forms of expression.

We need to go back to the time of the Renaissance to find the spirits who professed to know everything, and who could challenge the entire world of science to a debate about a random subject. In our times, no one has a clear picture of even a miniscule part of the current reservoir of knowledge, which doubles each year. Attempts to achieve a synthesis from all the data generated to date, staggering in their extensiveness and variation, cannot bank on much support. After all, the current scientific climate gives preference to accuracy of details above vagueness over everything. Yet, a universal synthesis is described by Gurdjieff in his bold and lonely attempt to turn the tide. The stakes were high, typical of the man and his life. It was all or nothing.

His efforts appeared infectious, because fifteen years after the publication of *All and Everything,* a previously mentioned pupil of Gurdjieff, John Bennett, published the fourth and last book from his *Dramatic Universe* and, in doing so, rounded off a heroic attempt to complete a summary of all human knowledge, experience and values.[1]

---

[1] J.G. Bennett, *The Dramatic Universe*, Hodder & Stoughton, London: Part 1, 1956, *The Foundations of Natural Philosophy*; Part 2, 1961, *The Foundations of Moral Philosophy*; Part 3, 1966, *Man and His Nature*; Part 4, 1966, *History*.

Another fifteen years on, the book, *De Compositie Van De Wereld* (*The Composition of the World*), appeared, written by Harry Mulisch, a famous Dutch author.[2] In this book, he introduced the musical octave as the principle element that is expressed in a predictable pattern in the development of each individual, as well as in the development of all humankind. This principle, which he called "codex," is not abstracted or derived from world phenomena to arrive at a manageable categorization; no, it preceded this. Just as, "In the beginning was the Word," so is the "codex." Gurdjieff's belief regarding a "Law" is the same, and therefore I will get back to *The Composition of the World* later on in this book.

People can shrug their shoulders about these three books, of which Gurdjieff's work was the spearhead, or simply ignore them. But this cannot undo the fact that they were written and confront us with an inescapable dilemma. Humanity will have to either take such attempts at synthesis seriously, or—for eternity—be condemned to isolation with regard to the multiplicity of autonomous scientific developments, of which not a single soul comprehends the cohesion.

WHY THREE BOOKS?

In the first of the three books that Gurdjieff took upon himself to write, he had the aim of destroying all the reader's ideas and convictions. In the second and third books of his trilogy, material would be provided with which reality could be experienced as faithfully as possible and not in an illusionary manner.

In the second book, *Meetings With Remarkable Men*, important sections were left out on purpose by the author and, following an autobiographic introduction, the third book, *Life Is Real . . .*, contains

2 Harry Mulisch, *De Compositie Van De Wereld,* De Bezige Bij, Amsterdam, 1980. In as far as I have been able to ascertain, this book has not been translated into English.

only the representation of several lectures given by Gurdjieff, before ending with a newspaper quote, the purport of which is difficult to grasp. These latter two books give the impression of being unfinished, and thus the whole idea of the structure and underlying relations of Gurdjieff's three books, his "triptych," is weakened. Only the external form of the triptych is kept intact, and then with difficulty. There is a clear disparity between the first book and the two latter ones. It all looks like the little creatures I used to watch swimming in stagnant pools—in the Brabant of my childhood, we used to call them "fatheads," a good name because they only seemed to consist of a fat black head and a very lively tail. I think I was told they would grow into frogs.

The first book, *Beelzebub's Tales to His Grandson,* does not give the impression of being unfinished. On the contrary, it is a rounded-off volume that is entirely independent. This argues in favor of this being his most important book. The two latter books were likely written to be read out in a ritual manner, and were probably never intended for publication. Also, it remains to be seen to what extent the published versions of the latter two books were complete.

THE MOST IMPORTANT WORK?

In a previous chapter, the question was discussed to what extent Gurdjieff's multifaceted legacy has a clear core in one single element, the linchpin around which the rest rotates. Could *Beelzebub's Tales to His Grandson* be this central axis?

To answer this question, let us focus immediately on a historical document: a circular prepared and signed by Gurdjieff, dated the 13th of January 1949. This is a date with a dramatic and ritual impact: the date of his birthday in the year of his death. In this letter, he announces his decision to publish the first part of his writings in order to make a start with the transfer of his ideas to the entire human race of the time and of the future. The remarkable thing is that Gurdjieff wanted to make his book available free of charge to anyone who could benefit from reading it. To be able to bear the cost for this, he asked his pupils for financial support, and he appointed three representatives who would assist him in this project.[3] Although in his circular letter he speaks of "the start of the transfer" of his ideas, *Beelzebub's Tales to His Grandson* will not just be distinguished as the first. In fact, it will also be *the only* part of his multifaceted work that Gurdjieff himself will formally confirm with the explicit wish that it be published and released. He does this without restriction, or without fear or favor, in writing, and seals this declaration with date and signature. This is not the case for *any other element of his work*: not for his teachings—by which I mean the verbal instruction ending in 1924—nor for his music or his Movements.

This point is one of the bones of contention from which a lot of the later conflicts arose between heirs and pupils, and even among the pupils, regarding the dissemination of Gurdjieff's ideas after his death. In the vacuum after his death, opinions differed strongly about the publication of all his other works that, actually, in quantitative terms form the majority of his legacy. This problem overshadowed his teachings as represented by his pupils, along with his music, his Movements and of course his two other books. Therefore, it was to take a long time before the second and the third parts of his trilogy were published. Interested people outside the closed circles of Gurdjieff's pupils had to wait a decade before they could read the second part, and then another twenty years before the last part.

Gurdjieff's historical circular, from the 13th of January 1949, confirms the importance that he himself attributed to the work. There is no doubt that this book has a key position in his legacy. In *Beelzebub's*

---

3 These were three people who each represented a country: René Zuber, France; Lord Pentland, America; and John Bennett, England.

Tales to His Grandson, his own voice resounds. Still, although the version of his text was authorized by him, it was unfortunately changed on several points in later translations.[4] Here, the man himself is speaking, and he speaks without any reservation to anyone who is interested in his "objective criticism" of humankind.

THE CRITICAL DECISION

What moves somebody to write a book that is, whichever way you turn it, to become a new Bible? What is going on in an author's head when he names his book, *All and Everything*?

If an answer could even be given to these questions, we have to look for them in the dramatic moment at which Gurdjieff decided he could *only* continue his teaching in book form. This was the most crucial decision in his career as a teacher; the moment in which everything would change irrevocably; in which his Institute would be disbanded, and with that, the individual approach for every pupil, which the Institute considered of paramount importance. The spoken word and personal contact with his pupils would no longer form the heart of his method. No, from this moment, the written word was central, and was directed to the future, bypassing his pupils of the

4 In the first translation into French, dating back to 1956, the translators already permitted themselves a degree of creativity. In a new French translation from 1990, the number of deviations from the original text grew considerably. It was not stated who was responsible for the new translation, only that it had been performed under the auspices of Jeanne de Salzmann, who had died before the publication of this new version, and whose native language was French and not the Armenian and Russian language in which the original text had been written. Because there cannot be any doubt about the fact that the English version, which appeared in 1950, had been authorized by Gurdjieff, this new translation has been cause for indignation, even with Gurdjieff's immediate pupils. There was even talk of an attack on the authentic text. This new version creates confusion because this translation, in turn, served as a source for a new English translation. People buying the book nowadays can therefore only find out with great difficulty whether they are getting access to the authentic or the amended text.

time. This decision was taken at the end of the summer of 1924, when he fully recognized the consequences of his car accident that had taken place shortly before this.

This accident occurred in the early hours of a spring day in 1924, on a country road between Paris and Fontainebleau, when Gurdjieff drove his car, fortunately without passengers, into a tree at full speed. In a comatose state, he was taken to hospital where there were fears for his life. Despite the expectations of the doctors treating him, he did not die from his injuries, but it did take months for him to recover to any degree. At that time, he realized that the consequences of his accident would force him to change his life dramatically. So, he did. Within two months he dissolved his Institute, once and for all.

YES AND *NO* AND THE GREAT LAWS

In Gurdjieff's life, a life-sized "yes" had met with a life-sized "no." For years, he had explored the corners of the Earth in search of knowledge, and he sifted through the knowledge with the sieve of his own experience, like a gold digger separates the gold dust from the wet sand in a stream. His entire life was aimed at transferring this knowledge, but due to his accident he no longer had the time and energy to accomplish this.

This "yes" and "no" were masses of stone hitting each other with a bang, of which the echo will resound far into the future. In the light of the shower of sparks, he saw that his only option was writing everything down in a book, so that in this way his work would at least be conserved for future generations. It must have been an unbearable moment when he sat down in the autumn of that year to write the first line of his book. Maybe he did not write it down himself, but expressed it aloud, so that his secretary, composer de Hartmann's aristocratic wife, Olga Arkadievna de Schumacher, could note it. His gaze might have wandered outside, just before that, through the large, glazed doors of his country house. He will not have paid any attention to the multicolored autumn décor of the trees lining the path to the terrace. His gaze will most likely have been captured by the small houses, situated on the edge of his estate, where the colony of Russian exiles lived—dependent on him for everything, but who now he would no longer be able to support.

Was he himself not an exile? Did he not remember the songs from his native area, repeating over and over again that a life in exile was the worst fate God could burden one with? For him, it was not the place where he lived at the time, France, that was the country of his exile. Rather, it was the entire Earth, a planet so far removed from God in the wasteland of the universe that even God's will could not reach it. But, even in this remote corner, he knew that the same principles of creation reigned as in the proximity of God, and that all the creations and every individual life was subjected to this reign, in the same way that the veins of the autumn leaves that drifted down to cover the drive to his country house represented the shape of the tree that produced them in miniature.

At that moment, he must have been overwhelmed by the sense of inescapable fate, experiencing the full intensity of the principles that he called the "Great Laws." These patterns/principles attest that every impulse should evoke an opposite reaction, through which both forces sap each other as in a lethal embrace. This "death grip" can only be broken if a third, independent force mixes with the contrasting ones, and a new construction comes into being, the result of three forces that relate to each other as positive, negative and neutralizing forces. These characteristics are not statically linked to one of the three forces, but can be adopted in turns by every separate force, like a moving, revolving triangle. Only then, from the birth-contractions of every phenomenon, on whichever scale, can something new arise. After birth, the creation must travel a road consisting of seven steps, formulated as such far back in antiquity by Pythagoras and Plato.

After his intense experience of these Laws, Gurdjieff composed the first sentence of his epos. The start of the sentence was, "It was in the year 223 after the creation of the world . . ."[5] He could not have summarized the creed of his teaching in more compact terms. The number 223, that is written in black and white here, is not arbitrary; it consists of 3 numbers that add up to 7. The number 223 is also the 49th prime number, 7 times 7. This number is represented in his first sentence as a moment in time, but it expresses the numbers 3 and 7 that symbolize Laws in Gurdjieff's teachings that have no time, that are of all times. The symbolism of these numbers reminds us of the Pythagorean tradition in which numbers do not have an independent meaning, but describe the structure of creation. In much the same way, the ten figures of the Sephirot in Jewish tradition should not be seen as separate, standing in a line; rather, they have an interrelationship, like the "flame has with the piece of wood that it burns," to quote a poetic statement from the latter tradition.

The number in Gurdjieff's first sentence refers to a timeless experience, liberated from the tyranny of a chronological time in which one second after another flies by irrevocably. It is a call to experience the eternal in the temporary, like in the song by a cantor in the synagogue where the believers have gathered around the secret of the Torah; or in the singing of the muezzin at daybreak; or in the ringing of the church bells in our cities. He invokes the hourglasses of a slow time in which individual lives, generations and centuries submerge. A few years later, he would revert back to this figure in one of his most impressive compositions for piano, "Prayer and Despair," a title that could recall the difficult time he had gone through. The serene motive

[5] G.I. Gurdjieff, *All and Everything*, London, Routledge & Kegan Paul, Limited, 1950. Page 51. The quoted sentence was the first sentence from the book. The preface was only written later on. This was described by Olga de Hartmann in her as yet unpublished autobiography, *What For*.

of this piece of music, representing the prayer, lasts 7 strokes, divided over 3 measures: 2 of 2 counts, 1 of 3. The first measure, in turn, is divided into 7 beats, and this division is spread over the entire composition as concentric circles, which is, despite its apparent romantic sound, a hermetic, mathematical formulation of the numbers 3 and 7, equally as precisely constructed as a Swiss timepiece.

The genesis of Gurdjieff's book, *Beelzebub's Tales to His Grandson,* is his effort to free himself from the impossible contradiction that occurred in his life, the "yes and no." The solution he found was writing his book. The result would be less than he had envisioned of his teaching, but better than the half-hearted attempts for which no time or energy was left. Sitting in Parisian cafés, or wherever he may have been, jotting down thoughts on bits of paper wherever he was, it would take him more than eight years to write—eight years, before this "third force" took on a satisfying form for him. But this didn't mean that the work was over; Gurdjieff kept working diligently on the text, rewriting it time and time again, after trying it out on all kinds of different people. Gurdjieff died eight days after the printer's proofs of his book were delivered to him.

THE TALE UNFOLDS

The reader does not have a lot of time to pause at the first sentence of this work, at Gurdjieff's ingenious numerical invention, because immediately a monumental epos unfolds that is situated in an immense planetary space. The main character of the story, the devil Beelzebub, returning in a spaceship from his place of exile to the planet from which he came, nears the Earth during this return journey. This planet has aroused the curiosity of Beelzebub's grandson who, together with Beelzebub's following, is also aboard the spaceship. Beelzebub has often studied this planet and its inhabitants through his telescope, and has previously paid it a number of visits.

During this particular long trip, he tells his grandson everything he knows about it.

Earth appears to be a planet of doom, a freak of nature full of abnormalities. The leitmotiv in the story to his grandson is of a particularly horrifying nature, compared to which a typical horror-film scenario is an innocent bit of light reading. As Beelzebub recounts the tale, a cosmic disaster took place there a long time ago: a part of the Earth had broken off and was hurled into space; this part, known as the Moon, had to be brought into harmonious relationship with the other celestial bodies. The special energy required for this re-establishing of relationship had to be provided by the organic life on Earth, including humankind. To spare humans the knowledge that their life was merely intended to repair some kind of cosmic imbalance that had become unsettled through no fault of theirs, an organ was incorporated into humans, called the "Kundabuffer," which hid this horrible truth. After restoration of the planetary order, this organ had become superfluous and had been removed again. Unfortunately, in the meantime, the unrealistic dream-world that people had lived in, for generations, appeared to have become anchored so deeply in their being that the effect of the Kundabuffer organ had become an independent force—a situation that still continues. The awful repercussion is that humans, in the embrace of the effect of this organ, attribute characteristics to themselves such as "individuality," "will" and a "soul," and consequently do not see that they have to make an effort to develop these. This would be a fully desperate situation if it were not for "His Endlessness," who sent messengers from time to time—like Jesus Christ, Buddha, Lama or Mohammed—to awaken the inhabitants of Earth, the "creatures with three brain systems," from their hypnotic sleep. The method for this awakening was often repeated, by these various messengers, invariably in the same words: conscious effort and intentional suffering. One of these messengers is Ashiata Shiemash, in whom many think they recognize a Gurdjieff alter ego.

I read all of this for the first time in 1964, and although I understood virtually nothing from the book, the aforementioned leitmotiv kept me occupied. In the evenings, I worked in a bar in the center of Amsterdam. While I automatically poured the coffee and beer, and obliged the customers with off-the-shelf answers, some of the images from the book had an oppressive effect on me. Like that of Chapter 18, which depicts a square full of people who have all suddenly died.[6] As the book recounts, their deaths created a strange sort of substance, which, I imagined, ascended from the square as a cloud and was subsequently absorbed and digested by cosmic entities, whatever they may have been. What a nightmare!

There actually was a large square in the area close to where I worked. The Dam Square in Amsterdam is a central point in the metropolis. Due to Gurdjieff's powerful description, it did not take much effort to suddenly perceive the wriggling mass of people on the Square quite differently from a distance. All these people, rushing to Central Station or disappearing into the alleyways of the Red Light District at night, would die one day. What would be left of their lives? A mere series of experiences of the most varied types strung to the chain of time?

The Square, which I could see from the bar, transformed in my perception into a concentrated point of an immense volume of human experiences. That all these experiences could serve one particular objective was not impossible. That it could be a purpose that was not even suspected by these people themselves, and in which they had no share, was ominous. Was Gurdjieff a prophet who called out a warning in these pages? In that case, I did not need anything else from this book; I did not have to understand anything else. I had been warned, and had every reason to thank Gurdjieff.

---

6 From Chapter 18 in *Beelzebub's Tales to His Grandson*, "The Arch-preposterous."

In the other direction, opposite from the Square, the former Jewish quarter extended. This was that part of the city whose inhabitants had been systematically exterminated by the German occupying force during the Second World War, and a neighborhood that had become a horrible scar in our city. This awareness made my thoughts even more oppressive.

Beelzebub's Tales to His Grandson leads us through the earliest history of humanity via Atlantis, Egyptian culture, Babylon and Greek antiquity . . . all the way to the middle of the twentieth century. Such a broad brushstroke must make an historian's hair stand on end. And, to the extent that these episodes can still be traced, I do not think we have any other choice than to dismiss Gurdjieff's theories as myths. Still, a fundamental assertion from the book, on which his theory described above is based, and one that was considered an illusion in Gurdjieff's time, was more recently acknowledged as a scientific fact. The Moon is indeed part of the Earth. It was torn from it by an enormous physical force. This was probably generated by a centrifugal force at the time the Earth was still liquid. Since 1960, however, there has been no doubt that the Moon consists of material from Earth. A certain amount of prudence is therefore called for in the assessment of Gurdjieff's visions.[7]

THE DEVIL AND A SPACESHIP?

A devil as the main character is not the first thing one expects from a book by an oriental spiritual teacher, and certainly not a devil who

[7] A more recent scientific explanation was that a proto-planet came so close to Earth that this tore sections off the Earth, which first formed a ring around the Earth before these sections amalgamated themselves to form the moon. This view comes close to Gurdjieff's version. In the March 2014 issue of *Nature*, a most prestigious scientific journal, it was explained that there actually was a collision between Earth and another planet about the size of Mars. This enormous impact hurled matter into orbit around the young Earth, which eventually formed into the moon. Gurdjieff's vision, taken in his time as a form of lunacy, has now been confirmed by science.

travels around in the universe in a science-fiction-like spaceship. However, the character Beelzebub, as well as his science-fiction-like environment, show similarities with familiar themes from the Russian cultural climate at the end of the nineteenth century. For example: the devil, not unknown in European literature anyway—thanks to Milton and Goethe—played a major part in Russian Symbolist literature and painting under the related name "Demon." This word comes from Greek, where it means "soul" or "ghost." The Demon entered Russian literature in a novel with the same title written by Lermontov, who was a Russian equivalent of the French *poète maudit*, in 1838. Far from being the malignant tormentor from religious phantasies, this Demon is a soul condemned to have knowledge that makes him lonely and desperate in the realm of the mortals. Later, in a poem from 1904, the poet Voloskin described the Demon as "an angel doomed to knowing."

Even more obvious is the relationship between Gurdjieff's space-travel scenario and similar phantasies from the nineteenth century. This theme had already been established in European romantic and mystical literature—the Swedish mystic Swedenborg wrote a book about the interplanetary trips of ghosts and angels as early as the nineteenth century; but the theme got a new lease of life in Russia, and one that would have far-reaching consequences. A library assistant from Moscow, Nikolai Federov, wrote *The Future of Astronomy* in 1880, arguing in favor of emigration to other planets for the simple reason that, after Judgment Day, the Earth would be too small to accommodate all the people risen from their graves. However naive his vision may have been, it was a precursor of the current concern for the Earth's overpopulation, and for the evanesce of its natural sources of energy. His ideas were a great influence on the cosmic messianism of the Russia of the time, and on Tsiolkovsky, the pioneer of Russian space travel. This demonstrates how the surreal world of dreams and visions can be related to the most advanced forms of engineering.

Interplanetary space was a familiar theme, a beloved retreat, in Romantic literature due to the "liquid rest"—as the Romantic poet Shelley described it—that would exist between heaven and earth; and Gurdjieff's choice is very appropriate in that sense. *Beelzebub's Tales to His Grandson* attests to a distant observation that is infectious, and one that stimulates a form of awareness that beholds the world without being destroyed by it.

TWO REMARKABLE PARALLELS

Gurdjieff's Tales and Mark Twain Letters

By far the most striking, even astonishing, analogy between Gurdjieff's book and those produced by other authors during his lifetime is the essay, "Letters from the Earth," by Mark Twain (1835-1910). This text was written in 1909, but only published after his death in 1939, a decade after Gurdjieff had finished his own book. I came across Twain's essay only accidentally, and have never heard or read any comment on it in relation to *Beelzebub's Tales*. The title, "Letters from the Earth," refers to letters written by the Archangel Satan to his colleagues Gabriel and Michael, noting his observations about the curious proceedings of earthly life and the nature of humans. Satan had been banished to the Earth by the Creator, who did not particularly like his wit, sharp tongue and criticism. Once on Earth, he began to study organic life on that planet "under his microscope." This theatrical setting is identical with Gurdjieff's, but that is only the beginning of the analogy. Twain's description of the Law of Creation, in Satan's view a "stupendous idea," is remarkably similar to Gurdjieff's. Even more astonishing is the following description by Satan of the phenomenon "man" found in Letter VI: "The human being is a machine. An automatic machine. It is composed of thousands of complex and delicate mechanisms which perform their function in accordance with laws devised for their governance, and over which man himself has no authority, no mastership and no control."

To call Twain's text a "parallel" or an "analogy" of Gurdjieff's work is an understatement. It seems more likely that the two authors, independently of each other, were open to one and the same vision that "came to them." Twain's intelligent and razor-sharp essay *ends* after just 19 pages, and leaves not much leeway for hope. For Gurdjieff, this vision is only the *beginning* of an epos whose unfolding takes some 1300 pages, and in which the human's possibilities are clearly indicated again and again.

The common ground, noted here between Gurdjieff's book and the cultural products of the time, is not intended to cast doubt on the quality of his work. Whatever is thought of it, *Beelzebub's Tales to His Grandson* is original. Such originality is the clue that always helped me to assess the value of written or spoken words, even to the extent that an absence of originality in design casts severe doubts on the quality of the experience from which the work has resulted.

Gurdjieff Tales and Wölfli's New World

A French television film, made in 1978 by the Institut Gurdjieff, states that André Breton called Gurdjieff's book, "one of the three or four masterpieces of this century." This is incorrect. Breton's statement refers to Adolf Wölfli's work, also quoted in his article. It is interesting that Breton's sharply-focused intuition chose to quote Gurdjieff and Wölfli in succession in his article. If ever the saying "extremes meet" was applicable, it would be here.

Adolf Wölfli lived from 1864 to 1930. Barely twenty years old, he ended up in a psychiatric institution where he, as diagnosed "schizophrenic of unsound mind," would remain interned until the end of his life. He also spent most of his time in isolation. In the loneliness of that cell, Adolf Wölfli created his life's work, steadily working year upon year. He wrote, drew and composed music on sheets of wrapping paper that, after his death, had formed a meter-high stack of about 25,000 pages of prose, an uncountable number of musical compositions and 3,000 drawings. In these drawings, Wölfi's head often appears amidst labyrinths, with dark circles under his large eyes, depicting his grief. From this central point, the absolute sovereign oversees his creation, but is also its prisoner.

In his writings, Wölfli relates how he leaves the Earth with his ever-growing "Avantgarde" (*sic*) of "Nature Explorers" and visits star after star with his "Airship." After having worked uninterrupted, Wölfli is canonized by "God=father" and, fulfilled with this Omnipotence, the "Holy Adolf" decides to create a new world.[8] Wölfli reached for heaven by creating for himself, with unimaginable perseverance, a more beautiful world than the hell in which he lived.

There are many similarities between Gurdjieff's first book and Wölfli's, such as: travelling through the universe in a spaceship with his retinue; an eventual recognition by God who, just as in Gurdjieff's book, is described with an entire series of capitalized words over and over again; his made-up words and numerology. Both books have a mystical text in which, as under a false bottom, a lot of autobiographical material can be found. Is it not remarkable that a man who travelled through the East for dozens of years, looking for ancient teachings, writes a book that has similarities with that of another man who barely set foot outside his isolation cell? Despite the major difference between the life and the personalities of these authors, their resemblance is that they both view the Earth from a great distance. Not just their works, but also they themselves have put themselves outside of this, a choice that is accompanied by an irrevocable loneliness, similar to that of death.

---

8 The first parts of Wölfli's texts appeared in 1985 and 1991, with the publishers Fischer and Hatje, edited and clarified by Elka Spoerri and Max Wechsler of the Adolf Wölfli Stiftung.

A MYTHIC EPIC

The form of this book is that of a narrative. This is in keeping with the tradition of the storytellers, such as his father, whom Gurdjieff remembered well from his native area. Such storytelling made him feel at home; the traditions of Western literature were unfamiliar to him. His book is a modern variant of old story-cycles, an ominous version of *One Thousand and One Nights*, but this time without women playing a significant role.

Hearing stories is different from reading a book. Any child who is read to knows this. The presence of the storyteller, the voice, the sounds of words, all this richness is lost in print, which is why his advice is to read the book as if you are being read to.

The story is a mystic epic from which, like a genie from a bottle, a cloud of events and thoughts ascends, and in which all the events have a metaphorical meaning that can be interpreted in more ways than one. Here is an alchemistic mixture of myths, symbolic incidents, analogies, allegories, old sayings, proverbs, formulas from religious sources . . . and all this interspersed with made-up words.

Gurdjieff's intention was to summarize his entire teachings in this book, so that they would be saved for future generations. But he buried them so deeply that they remain hidden, as if covered by an invisibility cloak. Readers wanting to become acquainted with Gurdjieff's teachings will frequently be disappointed. The book seems like a giant jigsaw puzzle of which the picture on the box-lid is missing.

WHY THIS DIFFICULT STRUCTURE?

Gurdjieff did not commonly repeat himself, but one thing he kept coming back to is that there are no words for higher insights or knowledge; that words only suffice for simple facts of a practical nature. This is not new. Philosophers such as Kant and Fichte have worn their pens out on this theme. The poet Novalis went one step further. In his view, words are an isolated medium devoid of contact with reality. He asserted that this does not apply for mathematical or geometric formulas. These only exist in pure form in the mind, without antitheses in our physical world. This is why they are less confusing than words that suggest a non-existing correlation with reality. This thought, that one would not expect from such a Romantic poet as Novalis, will be convenient for the description of the Movements later on.

Gurdjieff consciously does not opt for a clear and logical text. He cannot! In his conviction, a superficial mental understanding destroys the possibility of further development. However, one is tempted to try to understand this mysterious text logically. (It became clear to me a long time ago that "thinking" about this book does not produce much.) Moreover, every mental interpretation of such a mystical text as this one remains guesswork at all times. The interpretation will never be confirmed or denied with authority. The author is no longer alive and, even if this were the case, he would never lend himself to such confirmation.

I have read this book several times, but only when it was being read aloud in our small study circle did I establish contact with the text. For me, the days in which Gurdjieff's writing method—his never-ending sentences and his own made-up words—caused aversion are over. In particular, the daily ritual in which my life-partner, Christiane, and I read the book to each other has gained profound meaning for us. We experience it as a real benefit that this book can be interpreted in more ways than one. This enables us to freely reflect on its contents. Of course, entire sections still remain locked to us; but regularly, it is as if we hear the voice of the author speaking to us directly. I consider it a privilege that the book revealed itself to us in the autumn of my life. There are still many sunny days in this autumn, and the opening might be a reward for the long years in which we have tried to put Gurdjieff's teachings into practice and have performed his music and Movements. In more general terms, it seems as if *Beelzebub's Tales to*

His Grandson can only gain real meaning for the reader after a very gradual, extended study.

This book need not count on a positive reception in literary, philosophical or religious circles. As noted earlier, the French author, André Breton, the founding father of Surrealism, is an exception. He did Gurdjieff the honor of mentioning his book and quoting from it in the very last article he wrote, "*L'écart absolu.*"[9] This title can be translated as "Away with it!" and relates to radically swiping all science, philosophy and social achievements of our culture off the table to be able to forge new paths, comparable to the way that the legends surrounding Christopher Columbus assert that he avoided all known ocean routes, thus enabling him to "discover" America. Gurdjieff's book has the same intention, and it is therefore understandable that Breton quoted him.

GURDJIEFF'S PUPILS REACT

This book has certainly been perceived as a problem by several of Gurdjieff's pupils. Ouspensky, for example, refused to read it. The confusion caused by Gurdjieff's intervention in writing a book lives on today, lending his book a controversial character. His teachings have been broken in two—into two distinct phases, so to speak. His book, clearly addressed to future generations, bypasses all his pupils. While another part of his teachings *was* handed on in direct contact with his pupils, these were not his entire teachings. Why else would he have taken the trouble to write his book? This demonstrates one of the issues involved in conveying spiritual teachings, for both teacher and pupils.

~

[9] Breton's article appeared in the catalogue of the 11th International Surrealist Exhibition, no date. Breton signed the article in Paris, 16th of October 1965.

I want to conclude this chapter with a sentence I heard a long time ago, in a completely different context, from Don Byas, a famous American jazz saxophonist who had come to live in Amsterdam. He sometimes played in the only jazz club that Amsterdam had at the time, accompanied by fellow Americans on tour in Europe. Of course, I made sure I had a first-row seat, to not miss one note of this master. At one time, I had a chat with him between two sets. I knew he had played with Charlie Parker in the same orchestra in Kansas City. Parker, whose musical genius had created the post-war melodic architecture of jazz music, was sixteen years old when he joined this orchestra. I wanted to hear from Don Byas how he had experienced playing with such a revolutionary musician.

Don Byas sat in front of me, all relaxed, drinking beer from a bottle. We were both slanting on our seats in order not to soil our shoes in a puddle of beer lying between us on the wooden floor. Byas took my inquiry much more seriously than I had thought. His face gained a calm, pensive expression while he took the time to go back in his memory. He answered: "When that kid took his horn to his mouth, it was as if the sun rose early in the morning." We kept talking. I asked him if Parker's melodic revolution had not caused the harmonic development of jazz to fall behind. Though this might have been true, it must have sounded fairly far-fetched coming from me. Byas looked at me in a good-natured manner and fiddled with the reed of his saxophone. He then uttered the sentence that was not only an answer to my question, but is also applicable to the controversy surrounding Gurdjieff's book. "My son, don't you worry about that. If his genius wanted it that way, it simply means there was no other way."

6

GURDJIEFF'S FINAL YEARS, HIS DEATH AND THE SUCCESSION (TO THE THRONE)

I live alone, out of time, I am going to a sun lost to your eyes.

– Text produced during a psychic séance, author unknown

In the early thirties of the previous century, Gurdjieff had completed his first book and the ideas for his second book were in an advanced state. Up to the beginning of the Second World War, they were read aloud regularly to small groups of pupils. Things had gone quiet around Gurdjieff, and the silence would become impenetrable for the outside world in the following war years. It is encouraging that, despite this, a description of Gurdjieff during the occupation of Paris can be read in a book written by an outsider. The very fact that the author was not one of Gurdjieff's pupils, did not even know his name, and was not interested in his teachings, means her description offers us a neutral and historically reliable picture.[1]

The central character in this book describes how her mother died during the war years, lonely and hungry in a small, unheated room in Paris. That, nevertheless, she died in peace was thanks to a "bizarre Armenian trader" who continually managed "right under the nose of the German occupiers" to provide her mother with food. He did not just give her food, but his love too. Following the death of her mother,

[1] Josephine Saxton, *Group Feast*, Doubleday, New York, 1971.

she visited the Armenian man from time to time, and spoke with him in a small room packed with food that he shared with all the poor and old people in his neighborhood. He also played moving music on his small harmonium. Upon his death, many people in the neighborhood in Paris wept, and later, when she thought of him, she was overcome by piercing and inexplicable grief.

The picture this sketches is so remarkable, as if we are offered a glimpse in passing, not a staged event, of the goodness of a man who, during these hopeless years, did what he could to alleviate the suffering of others, without expecting anything in return. We see a picture of Gurdjieff without a mask.

POST WAR, NEW WORK

Gurdjieff's pupil Jeanne de Salzmann provided an important new stimulus for the work of her teacher, just a few years before the Second World War.[2] She gathered together a number of pupils, who in turn she entrusted to Gurdjieff, and this relatively small group was destined to become the core of the later Institut Gurdjieff, from which Gurdjieff's work was continued after his death. The arrival of these new pupils also encouraged Gurdjieff to take up his Movements again in 1937.

After the war had ended, a new flood of visitors came to Gurdjieff's modest apartment in the center of Paris—pupils from earlier phases and especially Ouspensky's pupils, after his death in 1947. Gurdjieff's final years had begun, and Gurdjieff would not have been Gurdjieff if he had not developed several new teaching methods. These concerned

---

2 Jeanne Matignon de Salzmann, born Allemand, 1889-1990. Wife and later widow of the painter Alexander de Salzmann. She studied piano and musical composition at the Conservatoire in Geneva, and later Eurythmics with Emile Jaques-Dalcroze in Hellerau. In 1919, the couple de Salzmann met Gurdjieff in Tiflis, Georgia, after mediation by Thomas de Hartmann. Until Gurdjieff's death, Jeanne de Salzmann remained at his side.

his renewed approach to the Movements and a typology called "the science of the idiots." The latter was exclusively practiced during ritual meals, Gurdjieff's "last suppers." After his passing, they were discontinued. According to Gurdjieff, twenty-one different types of idiots had been described in this five-thousand-year-old science, a series that ran from "the ordinary idiot" to "our God." In this series, everyone could climb or descend, but the most decisive step and the condition for progression was the transfer from an "objectively hopeless idiot" to a "subjectively hopeless idiot."

During his final years, Gurdjieff regularly undertook short trips through France accompanied by his pupils, to cities with ancient cathedrals, but also to spa towns like Vichy or to the French southern coast. Each trip was a succession of unexpected events and problems, and Gurdjieff continually trod on the participating pupils' most "painful corns." He never missed an opportunity to test them in difficult practical situations. Just as a pupil once told me: "Upon returning home after a couple of days, it was as though you had been away for months, so intense had the flood of impressions been."[3]

In the final months of 1949, Gurdjieff knew better than anyone that his days were numbered. He formulated his approaching departure in a way characteristic for him, through explaining that he was going on a journey, "this time further than New York." Eyewitnesses have told me that Gurdjieff made a sad impression during his final months, convinced that his work had already been damaged in parts through a lack of understanding. He believed that the core, the substance, would disappear within four generations. In a final dead lift, he doubled his efforts to pass on the Movements, the mysterious calligraphy of movements untainted by words, in which he summarized his teachings for the final time, until he collapsed during a Movements' class and the

3 A well-written record of this trip can be found in: Michel Congé, *Inner Octaves*, Dolmen Meadow Editions, Toronto.

end was announced. He died on the 29th of October 1949 at 10:30 in the morning and was buried, following a liturgical ceremony at the Armenian-Orthodox church, on the 3rd of November, in the family gravesite of the small churchyard in Fontainebleau-Avon, where his wife and mother were buried.

DEEP RIFTS

Gurdjieff's death was a hard blow for his pupils, but the definitive silence of his absence created two unavoidable and acute problems: the legal legacy of his books, music and Movements, but most especially the form in which his work should be continued and by whom. Jeanne de Salzmann had taken this task upon herself, and most of Gurdjieff's other pupils considered this an obvious decision. After all, she had been Gurdjieff's pupil for more than thirty years, was completely dedicated to him, and her efforts in the final years of his life had provided him with a new group of pupils. She had also been his chief support throughout this period. No other pupil could match the degree to which she was considered the "spiritual legatee." In the years 1950 and 1951, Jeanne de Salzmann established the Institut Gurdjieff, currently still the most important organization, with many international branches, dedicated to the study and dissemination of Gurdjieff's teachings.

Not all of Gurdjieff's pupils supported her initiative. Striking by their absence were the good writers among the ranks, like Fritz Peters and Katharine Hulme. Other pupils established their own, mostly small, groups. They remained on good terms with Jeanne de Salzmann, but maintained their independence, like Rina Hands in England and Annie Lou Staveley in America. The situation was also complicated because pupils from earlier phases of Gurdjieff's teaching had built up organizations or formed groups. Ouspensky's school in England was long established and still played an important role in the dissemination of the ideas Gurdjieff set out during his first phase in Russia. The version of Gurdjieff's teachings as Orage had instructed in America was also still practiced. The greatest proponent of this was the chemist Wim Nyland, who had worked closely with Orage.

This is only a rough sketch of the channels in which Gurdjieff's teachings were continued after his death. In the next section of this book, I will clarify this picture for the transmission lines that are of importance for the Movements.

Then, regarding the second problem, the legal settlement of Gurdjieff's legacy: The rights for his books, his music and his dances went directly to his family. Gurdjieff had children, but none of them bore his name and this excluded them as legatees. The legal legatees, his family, sold "all musical and choreographic works" by Gurdjieff to the company Editions Janus through a legal document, dated the 2nd of October 1950, which was signed by the three legatees. The proceeds from these works were to be divided into three, for the benefit of three different parties: Gurdjieff's legal heirs, Thomas de Hartmann—as co-composer of Gurdjieff's musical body of work, an obvious interested party—and the company Editions Janus. As an appendix to the contract, a list was drawn up of tape recordings of Gurdjieff playing the harmonium in his final years, and an overview of his musical compositions from the period 1923 up to and including 1927. The choreographies were not specified in any more detail in the appendix.

The list of the compositions is far from complete, and demonstrates that even the small circle of relations and pupils did not have a clear picture of the extent of Gurdjieff's entire musical repertoire at the time. They had never been collated systematically. The manuscripts were scattered here and there, with pupils, with de Hartmann and his spouse, and also with Gurdjieff's family. The incompleteness of the list of compositions is nevertheless not a single, incidental error, brought about by the difficult task of producing a complete list within a year of a composer passing away; it is a structural phenomenon in taking stock of this legacy. To this day, it has remained an area characterized by gaps and voids, through disintegrated or censored fragmentation, and through incorrect or incomplete information. To acquire a complete picture of any specific part, a researcher must have access to authentic sources of information and be blessed with the patience of a saint. Only then will a cohesive picture slowly begin to emerge, like with a puzzle, piece by piece. More than eighty years since the composition of Gurdjieff's and de Hartmann's music, there is still no catalogue of works. This incredible fact says it all.

That the catalogue of music is incomplete in the document mentioned is not really so important. More important is that the sealing of this apparently reasonable contract ignited a conflict that still smolders. As noted, Jeanne de Salzmann was an important pupil for Gurdjieff and the founder of the Institut Gurdjieff, but she was not a legal heir, although Gurdjieff was the father of her son. The company Editions Janus, to whom the rights for the music and choreographies were sold, was only an independent entity in name; its policies were determined by Jeanne de Salzmann. Her position as "spiritual legatee" was already strong, but through this contract she also acquired a vote in the management of the legal rights of Gurdjieff's legacy.

De Hartmann, who would only live for another few years, supported de Salzmann. He led a withdrawn life in Canada and was mainly involved in composing. His support was understandable, because he knew de Salzmann from his earlier Russian years. The relationship among the three parties to the contract—Jeanne de Salzmann and Thomas de Hartmann on one hand, and Gurdjieff's family on the other—did not improve when, shortly after this, a rift occurred between Jeanne de Salzmann and John Bennett. Gurdjieff's family turned to John Bennett, and the task of mediating fell to him, a thankless task that would serve to enlarge the split between him and Jeanne de Salzmann.

More and more, Gurdjieff's family felt short-changed, and Sylvie Anastasieff, the spouse of Gurdjieff's nephew Valentin Anastasieff, did not shy away from publicizing a notice of complaint, with a razor-sharp, acid-dipped pen. The shrill social contrast between the Institut Gurdjieff, which enjoyed a great heyday—financially too—under the skillful management of Jeanne de Salzmann, and the poverty-stricken circumstances in which Gurdjieff's own sister Sophia found herself was no surprise.

The contract sold the rights to "all musical and choreographic works" by Gurdjieff. How the word "choreographies" should be legally interpreted formed a never-ending and legal tug-of-war. The court had to intervene to resolve this matter. There are no choreographies signed by Gurdjieff, so they reasoned, and as such it cannot be proven that the Movements, as they are now practiced, are of Gurdjieff's creation; consequently, they do not fall under the legal protection of this contract.

A DIVIDED POTENTIAL

The aforementioned rift between Jeanne de Salzmann and John Bennett was a catastrophic occurrence, and the current situation for the Movements is closely connected with this, as will be demonstrated later on in this book. This rift divided the potential of Gurdjieff's pupils in the same way that a guillotine separates the head from the body of a person. The head on one side of the blade, the body on the other. The "head" in this example represents John Bennett, a brilliant theorist who also had a great name as a scientist outside the Gurdjieff tradition. He was the only Gurdjieff pupil who had been able to undertake attempts at synthesis of Gurdjieff's teachings and science—a matter that had always been close to Gurdjieff's heart—and most probably the last to embark upon such an awkward venture. Certainly the "body" represents Jeanne de Salzmann, her lengthy experience with Gurdjieff, the way in which she had taken on his work and passed it on in a practical and passionate way, and most especially her knowledge of the Movements.

These two prominent pupils of Gurdjieff both influenced me, and their break disturbed me. I suffered from this in a way that a child is embarrassed by his parents' arguing. A type of cynicism, based on a caricature of the difference between male thinking and the female instinct for reality and physical connection, was reinforced in this split and caused me pain. Not just me: disagreement among Gurdjieff's pupils has not gone unnoticed by many, and throws the value of his teachings into doubt. This was an understandable response, because the struggle among pupils is really the last thing to be expected following the death of a spiritual teacher. After all, was his work not aimed at rising above a world of discord? It is worth noting, however, that the unity of world religions is generally cosmetic. This so-called unity usually results from the violent removal, or slaughter, of groups who have held different opinions within that religion.

Two reasons have been mentioned in this book that explain why, here again, the legacy of the spiritual teacher caused disagreement. First, the uncertainty of the publication (or not) of the legacy, with the exception of Gurdjieff's first book; and second, its unfortunate legal division. But, even during Gurdjieff's life, disagreements with important pupils like Ouspensky and Orage led to definitive splits and, in the light of this, the rift between John Bennett and Jeanne de Salzmann appears to be the continuation of a tradition, however unfortunate this may be. In addition, not one of Gurdjieff's pupils was equally skilled in word, music or body movements as Gurdjieff himself, so each pupil inclined toward one of the three areas. The deeper roots from which this all originates are the continually different forms into which Gurdjieff poured his teachings, and the change to his method of conveyance: the change from verbal instruction to the written word.

Despite the ideological differences and disputes among Gurdjieff's pupils, the way in which his teachings are instructed to new generations display great similarities. The most striking characteristic is working in what is called a "Gurdjieff group."

7

REGARDING "GURDJIEFF GROUPS" AND THE DISSEMINATION OF HIS TEACHINGS AFTER HIS DEATH

The past never dies completely
– Constantin Brăiloiu[1]

Gurdjieff's works took different paths after his death. His books have been translated into increasingly more languages, but are read less in Western countries than used to be the case. They are no longer available in German, and in other countries they only remain available through financial support. In contrast to this, his music has experienced a new lease of life, thanks to musicians who are not part of the traditional Gurdjieff groups. His Movements have gained unprecedented popularity, but we will get back to that in the second part of this book.

What has become of the teachings? It is often suggested that Gurdjieff's teaching has superficially influenced many contemporary writers, psychologists and scientists. Whether or not this is true, and to what degree, is difficult to ascertain, because these teachings insinuated themselves without direct reference into the works of others. Certainly Gurdjieff is no longer an unknown in the contemporary, esoteric-oriented "supermarket." It is not easy to witness, at least not for me, how a proud and spectacular doctrine, with which the "mechanical man" could acquire a "soul" for himself, must now be satisfied

1 Founder of the Institute for Comparative Ethnomusicology Research in Geneva.

with a modest place on the shelf between oil for foot massages and the latest report on conversations with aliens.

The most important medium within which Gurdjieff's teachings survive is the "Gurdjieff groups," the name for organizations where these teachings are instructed. These groups, of which three are mentioned in the previous chapter, are to be thanked in that they make the teachings accessible for a new generation of students. There are, of course, many more Gurdjieff groups than the three mentioned. A primary distinction in this multiplicity is whether the group adheres to the line of transmission that can be traced back to Gurdjieff, or not. An authentic group is a group that is led by a person who has studied under a teacher who, in turn, was taught by Gurdjieff. This is called a "direct line of transmission." In my view, a person who has appointed himself as a teacher, but was never a pupil, has no authority.

The moment that I first came into contact with one of Gurdjieff's pupils was a decisive experience for me. I saw myself from the perspective of the evolution that had taken place in this other—this teacher—and consequently, I understood that these teachings were of a far greater order than I could ever have imagined. The terrain of speculation and theories was behind me, from that moment on. This is why I believe that Gurdjieff's teachings can only be passed on through person-to-person contact.

A multitude of Gurdjieff groups have come into being, a labyrinth which an outsider would have difficulty navigating. The criterion of direct transmission provides a support, but is by no means a guarantee. Spiritual development balances on a fine wire and there are no certainties.

The Gurdjieff groups are considered from within as "research groups," but by the outside world they are often labeled as "sects." The word "sect" is correctly used if it is an organization of people who adhere to a religion or way of life that has not yet acquired a powerful social position. The dangers of belonging to a sect are generally well known, so I will refrain from summing them up, and limit myself to details that I have personally observed and experienced.

Gurdjieff's teaching is intended for those who take part in society, but who often retire as a group in social isolation. It is difficult for the members of the group to find the balance between their convictions and socially-accepted views. To escape this problem, the social contacts outside the group are reduced, and members limit themselves to mixing with people with the same convictions. The world religions that have undergone a centuries-long social integration process make it a lot easier for their followers. A degree of isolation is unavoidable for such a group, yet this does not have to be a problem. This becomes a problem if the opinions of the people who think differently are no longer respected, and are experienced as hostile. When such attitudes are present, this is a sign of weakness within a sect or group that can quickly degenerate into a feeling of superiority towards others. "There is no intelligent form of arrogance," according to the writer Louis-Ferdinand Céline, and he hits the nail on the head.

A problem closely connected to this "arrogance" is that people who leave the group are considered "traitors." Not only are their decisions not respected but, on the contrary, they are treated with suspicion. Forms of aggression toward those who turn their backs on the group are caused by doubt and uncertainties that every right-minded person undergoes from time to time, but that the members of the group suppress and subsequently project onto the black sheep who leaves the group. Finally, it is striking that there are few Gurdjieff groups that are involved in social tasks. A sub-program in which the needy, down-at-heel and oppressed in our society are assisted would not be out of place, and in this respect there is enough to learn from the example of Christianity through the centuries.

A problem of a different nature is that the leaders of groups, since Gurdjieff's death, cannot match his authority. Gurdjieff constantly changed his course and continued to add new creative elements to his arsenal of educative methods. A group or organization cannot do this. They are focused on the maintenance of what was previously imparted by the initiator of the teachings. This lends little flexibility to the position, and yet, to provide the group with stimuli, these organizations often seek salvation in adding new elements to their educative program, such as Zen meditation or rituals from Sufism or Eastern philosophy, depending on the preference of the person leading the group. Because it is generally left unclear that these additions do not originate from Gurdjieff, they eclipse the teachings and form a source of confusion. This phenomenon plays a role in all the traditional groups I know of, and I find it difficult to understand. In light of the tremendous wealth of Gurdjieff's ideas and rituals, these additions are completely unnecessary, especially because these groups profess to represent Gurdjieff's teaching, and profile themselves as the guardians of this legacy.

There is little contact among the different traditional organizations or groups, but there is uniformity in the activities. There are weekly meetings, in which experiences are exchanged regarding an exercise previously assigned by the leader of the group. In addition, weekends are organized, usually in a country house that belongs to the organization, in which the group performs practical physical work, instructions are given for Movements, and Gurdjieff's books are read aloud. The day is usually begun with what is called a "morning exercise," a led-meditation session in which the leader of the group verbally instructs the members in an inner-self exercise. This sum of activities is a contemporary cocktail of elements from the various phases of Gurdjieff's teachings. However, this does not apply to the led "morning exercises," an element that only came to be after Gurdjieff's death.

The transfer of spiritual teachings from teacher to an institute or organization is a necessary step for preserving the teachings for posterity, but it is fraught with risk in the form of sociological laws that are wholly foreign to spiritual teachings. A structure must be built with rules that, in an unfavorable situation, start to lead a life of their own.

An example and warning for all that can go wrong was provided by the social democrat Karl Kautsky: "The growth of Christianity could only take place through denying its very own principles."

There are so many different groups that adhere to Gurdjieff's teachings that it is not possible to make a general statement about them all. It is like observing a silent street at twilight—doors everywhere, behind which people live. Behind some doors, children are raised harmoniously, behind others they are traumatized for life. It would be a good thing if you could see by looking at a charismatic leader of a Gurdjieff group if he was "good" or "bad," but unfortunately this is not possible. Besides being in a direct line of transmission from Gurdjieff, the other thing to look at in determining the strength or accuracy of a group leader is his or her presence of being, or obvious embodiment of the principles of the teachings. Book study of the teachings is not the issue here. Rather, in this context, genuine study is synonomous with "who one is," which includes that individual's practiced attention, allowing one to see themselves clearly, honestly, without pretense. Moreover, it includes that individual's strength in being able to bear what is honestly seen. One cannot escape this essential demand merely by relying on what one *hopes* to be, what one *imagines* as a future possibility, if one is not living from that context presently. Such an image of oneself is but a will-o-the-wisp, and bound to lead in a wrong direction. In fact, the very first step, guided by such a false idea, is often a step in the wrong direction.

MOTIVATION FOR JOINING A GROUP – A PERSONAL NARRATIVE

How does a person come to the point that he or she joins such a group? In response to this question, I can only relate my own experience, which is naturally intimate, and could therefore suggest that I have a misplaced interest in myself. That is a risk I am willing to take, because spiritual experiences are always personal. Teaching is given form in everyone's life, which is sometimes illuminated in a flash, as when lightning strikes in a landscape. The following memory describes such a moment.

After leaving secondary school and signing up for university, I was suddenly overcome by a strong urge to write. Together with a friend, I had taken up residence in an apartment in an old house. There, on one long white wall, we hung a large collection of old clocks that we had picked up for next to nothing at a flea market. In the spaces that remained between the clocks, we wrote sentences from poems that we considered poignant enough.

Yielding to the urge to write, I settled myself at my typewriter, among the nervous ticking of all those clocks, to write about why I was alive. I found myself in a situation not far removed from that of a medium who opens themselves to receive thoughts and sentences from the spirit world. The sentences that appeared were unraveled as if from a spool, and I was unclear whether they were within or outside of me, but these sentences were not influenced through the reading of spiritual literature. Up until this point, I did not have even the slightest interest in books on these topics.

The sweat poured from my body as I hammered out the title of my essay: "The Animals in Their Place." I can no longer remember clearly what had moved me to write such a title, but I believe that it was a vision of two wild animals, each in its own cage, in a circus. These two caged animals symbolized the two main elements of my existence as I experienced it. One of the animals was called "within me," the other "outside me." Only when these two animals could leave their cages and live in peace together would my life have found the form it was supposed to have. At the conclusion of my epistle that, by now, had taken on the significance of a program for my life for me, a few lines appeared that I can remember word for word. I believed that I would have to be reborn, that after the first physical wrestling, with which the body acquires a place on Earth, a second birth should follow "under unmoving white clouds." In one way or another, that I can no longer feel, these "white clouds" fitted in the vision I had of this second birth.

After I had finished my essay I felt relieved and, in an unusual way, myself. This feeling returns to me from time to time in my life. A feeling that I am very close to the person I actually am.

I still experience the separation I described between reality in myself and the world beyond me as a mysterious polarity. The Earth is overrun by the ever-expanding mold of humanity, of which each cell experiences the world from its "own perspective." Two questions with which Gurdjieff once opened a conversation with pupils can be traced back to this polarity. The first was: "What is this life that has been given to me; what is it exactly?" The second question was: "Do you need the sun?"

Gurdjieff's teaching, in which a human had to be reborn, also dovetailed into my life program that I had written down for myself. What also motivated me to start studying this teaching was the description by Ouspensky, in his diary, in which he related the phenomenon of "self-remembering." This was the first explanation that convinced me of several experiences I had previously undergone, in which my perceptions both of myself and of the world around me suddenly changed. It was as though I had awoken in another world, larger than I could have imagined and that I perceived as completely new, however, without losing contact with myself. I was no longer in a central position from where I viewed life around me, but was only a small part of everything around me. Amazed, I noticed that what I used to call "myself" was not a stable entity at all, but something that changed second by second.

What I have written here about myself is true, but it is not the whole truth. I, too, was trying to escape myself when I joined such a Gurdjieff group. I came to realize this fully, much later, after I had left the group. I, too, had taken a first step in the wrong direction. Attempts at self-development are fraught with such trial and error.

HOW LONG TO STAY IN A GROUP?

Opinions on this issue differ markedly within the traditional groups. John Bennett worked with the principle that students devote themselves to the study-community for an entire year, and after that return to their lives under their own steam. The Institut Gurdjieff assumes a long-term participation, actually for the rest of your natural life.

Anyhow, I have experienced a large number of group meetings and still participate in a group that I attempt to coordinate. I have not been tainted by whispers that I am a "leader" or someone who is "on the Path." I became immune to that virus as the result of an event that took place long ago. During one of the first meetings that I experienced, the group leader read a passage from *In Search of the Miraculous*, in which Gurdjieff described the astral body of man and how this manifested itself in Christ during the Last Supper. After reading, the group was invited to ask questions. I knew the passage that had been read aloud, one of the most remarkable in the entire book. That afternoon—a beautiful autumn day in which the sun sparkled on the water in the canal, which I could just catch a glimpse of through the windows—a new visitor had joined our small group. He was much older than all the others, with grey, almost white, hair. An Indonesian by birth, he was tall and encircled with the dignity and calmness characteristic of his culture. In these types of groups your status is quickly raised to "friend," which was apparent from the question that the group leader put to the new visitor. "Does our new friend have a question perhaps?" The leader's voice sounded confident, because he could not have anticipated the thunderbolt that was about to strike from the clear sky above as a result of his invitation.

"Yes," answered the old man, "I have a question."

A couple of seconds passed. "Okay, yes, would you like to share it with us?" responded the group leader.

"Certainly," answered the visitor; and while he fixed his dark eyes on the group leader, without moving a muscle, he asked: "Do you have such an astral body?" and again here followed a short pause: "Yes or no?"

I comprehended this "yes or no" addition all too well. In Ouspensky's description of Gurdjieff's teachings, there are no words like "perhaps," "a little" or "could be." Water boils at one-hundred degrees, not at ninety-nine degrees centigrade. In the stifling silence that followed this question, we all "heard" the second question from the old man that had not been asked (he was too kind to pose it) with a clarity as though word after word glided over our heads: "If you do not have such an astral body, how can you teach us to acquire one?"

This related incident is not meant to put our group leader in a bad light; he was the last person who deserved this. This event demonstrates how difficult a task it is for the leaders of Gurdjieff groups to pass on these spiritual teachings. The old man's question cannot be answered, because it is a textbook example of a paradox created by words. If someone has read about an astral body, he imagines something based on associations from the past. If later on he observes a new development in himself, he will measure this against previous associations. As a new experience of reality can never be explained with words that stem from past associations, he is put on the wrong track, which will cause a distortion or denial of the new experiences. Someone who experiences new inner developments is therefore more likely to use other words, or those of his own creation, which is exactly what Gurdjieff did throughout *Beelzebub's Tales to His Grandson.*

ADDITIONS TO TRADITIONAL WORK

The aforementioned "new elements" added within the traditional Gurdjieff groups are likely to have been included, in part, through the efforts of those groups to release themselves from subjective associations from the past with the hope of new insights. These efforts have likely been in vain, however, because rituals from other cultures, of which little is understood and the language even less, place an even greater burden on subjective interpretations than the explanations by Gurdjieff, which excel in their precision.

Human history can be compared to a hair plait, in which different strands are woven together. One of these strands is the search for the hidden meaning of life that embraces more than the tangible world, and can continue to exist after the passing of the physical body. I have reached an age in which I have experienced the dying process in an ever-increasing number of people with whom I am linked through family ties or friendship. I have been struck by those who, through their practice of a religion or Gurdjieff's teachings, have sought a deeper meaning in their lives; at the moment when they are standing face to face with the inescapable fact they are about to die, they have left a different impression on me than those that have not been so involved. Doubt does not prey on them in the way it does on others, and some even exude great strength in this phase of their lives. This does not mean that they are not suffering. Suffering comes to everyone, and there is no remedy for it. But, this experience has taught me that the search for a more comprehensive meaning of life can be of great support in the most difficult moments in a person's life. I am certain that many people involved in a religion or sect have found the place that is good for them. By no means has this blinded me to the wrongdoings and cruelties that are performed in the name of "ideals," but I focus on my own experiences with people I have known well and who were precious to me.

I attach great value to the clarity of the opinions I have expressed above, and would like to reemphasize that my underlying principle is as follows: Wherever someone stands, as an individual, as a participant in an isolated group or as part of a world religion, he or she may have found the place that is the best imaginable place for them.

A FINAL CAUTIONARY NOTE

I was once told a story about Gurdjieff by one of his students (now deceased) whose reliability I trusted. The story relates to the dangers as well as the possibilities of the groups formed around his Work. I share it here, fearing that I might very well be the only person who knows this story at the present time, and feeling a responsibility that, if I don't tell it, it might be lost. As usual, in this story he expresses himself in a seemingly innocent, childlike way. But the message is as sharp as a knife.

In a nutshell: During a discussion with a small group of people in his apartment, Gurdjieff suddenly amazed (and shocked) everybody by announcing that he had really seen the Devil himself, some time ago. With much theatrical play, he described how, in the middle of the night, he happened to be in the park and saw the Devil sitting there on a bench. Approaching him, he saw that the Devil was looking very bad: pale, skinny, in short . . . like a tramp. He was really a "poor devil," Gurdjieff noted, and at that remark the audience was greatly amused and produced a roar of laughter. But, Gurdjieff added in a suddenly very serious tone, "Last night I saw him again. But now he was dressed very smartly, and looked quite healthy and strong. Was very good humored too. I couldn't refrain from asking him: 'Devil, what in the world has happened to you that made your life change like that?'

"The Devil kindheartedly told me, in a whisper as if to conceal a secret: 'My good man, you will not believe this, but to my good fortune people are starting to participate in your 'groups.' This is the best thing that happened in my life, because they work and their souls grow. If their souls have become bigger and fatter, then it is my time to take them as my food. See how excellent my health has become."

~

I do not pretend to understand Gurdjieff's symbolism, but have the strong intuition that, in the spiritual realm, after a certain time, a difficult choice presents itself: either your ego takes everything you worked for and degrades it, or you go on the road purifying yourself from this "ego." I take his story as a warning of what will happen in the first case.

8

THE FLIP SIDE

. . . and so the Kingdom of the Dream with all its visitors was destroyed as a result of the battle between the visionary Patera and the pragmatist Bell. Only the blue-eyed original residents lived on . . .

– Alfred Kubin

While working on this book, I noticed that what I write is always the outcome of a struggle. On one side, I have the wish to assist the reader's understanding of complicated subjects, but unfortunately, this wish often mingles with the dubious desire to be appreciated by others for what I am not. On the opposite side, another, usually unconscious, force is active: to avoid and repress all that confuses me and therefore seems unfitted to write about. Actually, since the most valuable information is often hidden through avoidance and confusion, I have decided in this chapter to give free rein to what I might have liked to repress in myself. Hence, it is called "The Flip Side."

Some years ago, I found myself in conversation with an international group of managers who invited me as a "Gurdjieff expert" to meet with them because they were working for a media giant on a project about spirituality. We met in a penthouse in Amsterdam, the kind that only the wealthiest people can afford. The air was heavy with a smell that my earlier experience as a jazz pianist identified as originating from hashish. The presence of bodyguards made it clear that, since that time, much had changed in the social profile of its users. Between people interrupting each other's conversations, rattling printers and bleeping mobile telephones, I was introduced to the chairman of the committee. He spun his chair around, gave me a penetrating stare, as far as was possible through the smoke, and asked me without standing on ceremony, if people were mistreated in the name of Gurdjieff. This question took me by surprise and my response was an indignant denial.

The conversation was continued during dinner, when I related much about Gurdjieff, but internally I was preoccupied with the question of whether I would have to pay my own bill at this expensive restaurant. During dessert, I noticed that the woman opposite me was staring, as though in a trance, at the back of a spoon. "She is very psychic," someone whispered to me, "but also stinking rich and she pays for the lion's share of the project."

When I finally arose to bid the company farewell, the woman looked up from her spoon and said to me: "Gurdjieff's secret is in his jacket, a yellow jacket."

I left the building and entered into the city night, with this bizarre message still resounding in me. The facades of Amsterdam's old houses were all around me. They were shrouded in darkness and appeared to be leaning forward under their century-old burden. To me, at that moment, they were like silent witnesses of a struggle within me. The labyrinth of canals and streets appeared jumbled under the inexorable arrangement of the stars. The black mass of water in the canal moved, because Amsterdam was emptying its intestines, the canal network, in the river IJ, which occurs every night through a complicated system of locks.

I had lied.

I knew all too well that in Gurdjieff's good name people were mistreated. For example, I knew of the psychological torment of an old woman by a Gurdjieff organization, and the disgusting rape of another woman, which was related to me by someone whose word I had no reason to doubt. The perpetrator of this act has this on his conscience, despite continuing to pontificate about Gurdjieff, surrounded by admiring pupils, like a charlatan is by gullible villagers.

The penetrating question that was put to me earlier that evening turned slowly towards me in the dark of the night. The neutral words, "Are there people who…?" faded and became "Are *you* being mistreated…?"

One night, after giving a concert of Gurdjieff's music in the Amsterdam Concert Hall, a splendid moment in my life, I arrived home to receive a call from a "high authority in Gurdjieff's work" who accused me of being a "thief of holy music." I have been insulted, threatened and accused, year in year out, because I have taught Gurdjieff's dances to others. I have been pained to continually see the faces of my friends—those I knew from the very beginnings of the Gurdjieff groups—who have taken their own lives. They form a silent procession of those who *sought*, but did not *find*.

Arriving home after this meeting with the media personae, I slept restlessly for the remainder of the night. I dreamt that I was walking along a never-ending avenue and was met with an unceasing, cutting wind.

The night sees what remains hidden in the day. In this case, those who attempt to live in due observance of Gurdjieff's teachings, and those who believe they can represent it, still remain ordinary people, in all their capacities, however sublime or macabre. The most diverse activities take place in association with Gurdjieff's name, and diametrically-opposed organizations continue to bear his flag.

The dissolution of Surrealism offers us a historical example of how to avoid a flag no longer covering the meaning. Following the death in 1966 of their source of inspiration, André Breton, the most important theorists in this movement at the time announced, through Jean Schuster, that Surrealism no longer existed. Schuster explained that the continued existence of Surrealism, devoid of Breton's inspiring strength, could only lead to *historical confusion*. The novelist Julien

Gracq added: "In Breton's presence everything was new or reborn, everything glowed. . . After him all that could follow would be dull thinkers of pointless plans." The dissolution of Surrealism was a courageous decision. The Surrealists never lacked courage.

In connection with this, it is relevant to mention that, after Gurdjieff's death, a representative of his family, Mrs.Sylvie Anastasieff, made an effort to avoid a type of "historical confusion" in Gurdjieff's case. She stipulated by court order that the use of his name was forbidden by any institute whatsoever! Obviously, this was meant to protect his legacy against false claims of authority by organizations that officially carry his name, thereby suggesting a direct relationship that might not exist at all.

No one seems to observe this court decision, but it does exist. This edict reminds us of the fact that, when Gurdjieff's name is used by institutes or individuals advertizing certain methodologies or practices—as for example in "Gurdjieff's Teaching" or "Gurdjieff's Movements"—it always remains open to question *if* the direct relation with his teaching or Movements, suggested by using his name, actually exists.

What is being passed on as the "Gurdjieff Work" could, in many cases, not be representative of the teachings of its founder. Fifty years have now passed since a personal disciple of Gurdjieff told me: "Poor Mister Gurdjieff . . . His work is dead." The intensity and the honest sorrow accompanying this statement hit me like an unexpected blow out of nowhere, and my only response was, "But why?"

The answer was given after a long silence: "They have taken the feeling out of it!"

All those years I have carried this experience as a heavy load, which has made my shoulders sore. The positive result of this shock was that I was stimulated to observe and study, as well as I could, the expressions of feeling in those involved in Gurdjieff's Work and those participating in other so-called "new religious movements."

Unmistakably, ideologies of any kind have the potential to modify human feeling, deforming it into either ecstasy or suppression. Agreement about an ideology gradually takes the place of sympathy and trust, and disagreement is the form wherein antipathy hides.

In Chapter 6, I quoted Gurdjieff's own pessimistic expectations about the future of his teaching, no doubt based on his direct awareness of the psychological forces within us that defend our illusions with the ferocity of wounded animals.

But is it already dead *now*?

How can that be?

For me, this question evokes a flood of associations, each carrying a wave of emotion, that seem to raise my body temperature and involuntarily lift my head up toward the sky, as if the answer could be found in the clouds slowly pursuing their way over the city's landscape.

Is not each sincere effort a victory over death and the beginning of a new life?

Let me respond by relating one of my associations. The Zagros Mountains form a chain of 2000 km in the Near East. Since the beginning of time, nomads travelled back and forth on the old mountain paths with their herds, from summer to winter pastures. Those who died during these difficult and long journeys were buried alongside the road under large stones. On one of these stones four words in the Turkish language were carved:

Hayat biter Yol bitmez

All life must end, but the Way never ends.

9

GURDJIEFF'S TEACHINGS

Truth is a disease. Only for as long as we live in the selfishness of our lives do we feel well.

– Jan Gerhard Toonder

Dying to not have to die.

– Teresa of Avila

Everyone interested in Gurdjieff's Movements should ask the question, "What are his teachings all about?" Unfortunately, I cannot offer an adequate answer. I could summarize some concepts from these teachings that are apparently logically interconnected, but I have no desire to put myself and others on the wrong track. It would only serve to provide an illusion of comprehension, nothing more. Above all, it is not a single question, but a tangle of questions, such as:

- What intention lies beneath these teachings and what means are employed?
- What results does this teaching deliver?
- How does it differ from other esoteric systems?
- What is new about it?

In fact, we need to start with answering another question: What does the word "teachings" mean here?

THE "SCIENCE" OF HIS TEACHINGS

Reference is often made to a "Gurdjieff system," as though this is a series of exercises in an ascending degree of difficulty that will deliver a predetermined result. However, the objective of Gurdjieff's teachings is growth of the inner self, which cannot be acquired through the dedicated practice of a series of instructions and exercises, similar to the monthly installments of a repayment contract. Neither can the teachings be considered scientific, in the usual sense of the word. But, in order to make this distinction about science, I will return to an example taken from my youth.

I return in memory to a building that I can picture as if I saw it yesterday, as though I entered it but never left again. When I saw this building for the first time, I thought it a monstrosity, like a caricature of the laws of perspective. Here I spent my youth, because my education, in accordance with the practices of the time, had been entrusted—in other words "turned over"—to a religious order, in this case the Jesuits. The members of this monastic community were extremely rational, but they had been brought together and dressed in the black monks' habit through a religion. Whether or not the intellectual schooling that they fired at me was worth their efforts I do not know. What I do know is that a few insights remained with me after leaving this school, which event could be compared to the experience of a cat being suddenly thrown into a square bathed in sunlight after years of living in a dark warehouse. One of the insights I received concerned a definition of what is science, and what it is not. "Science," I was told, "only exists when the results of an experiment, performed in controlled conditions, can be predicted with certainty." Many current sciences, such as psychology, sociology, economics and even parts of medicine, do not comply with this norm. This rigid definition, originating from physics, is nevertheless useful because it warns us that the results from practicing spiritual teachings, which can be described as a "self-experiment," are far from predictable. On the contrary, anything is possible, even the opposite of what was intended. It is in this sense that Gurdjieff's teachings are *not* scientific.

Here, we are faced with the unavoidable, larger-than-life contradiction of rational-irrational. In oversimplified terms, the rational camp investigates a candle through analyzing the wax and the wick, without the notion that this could deliver light and warmth. The irrational camp circles the flame like a blinded moth, without knowing how it comes about. It is precisely this contradiction that Gurdjieff wanted to bridge. He demanded a critical attitude; he demanded that observations had to be collated first, from which only later conclusions could be drawn. Here, his teachings touch the sciences (like psychology, economics, etc.) that do not comply with the strict, aforementioned standard, but are still referred to as "empirical," because they are based on observations and probability calculations.

Gurdjieff's teachings are not limited to thoughts, but also target feelings and bodily functions. His teachings have little in common with philosophy, which gives the impression of wanting to crawl through a hole in a wall that only allows the head passage, and in which the body and shoulders get stuck. Gurdjieff's teachings are first and foremost pragmatic. "Work as an artisan out of love for the work and not for the result," were his words.

In the previously mentioned book by Ouspensky, *In Search of the Miraculous*, these teachings are presented as a series of facts. It was certainly not Gurdjieff's intention that these facts were to be accepted without question. No, their authenticity and usefulness had to be put to the test. All his statements: concerning the three centers of man, the self-remembering, the rebirth, and the place of the human in the cosmos, can be seen as *hypotheses*. Studying these teachings comprises the collection of one's own material, day in day out, year in year out, which ultimately confirms or disaffirms these hypotheses.

This material must not be influenced or come from others. In his study groups, Alfred Orage provided a description of a simple test. "Ask yourself a question and then examine which insights you have acquired to answer this from solely your own efforts. That is, only from yourself and not any other associations that have littered your path through the opinions of others, books or education."

AN INSIGHTFUL DREAM

To serve our purposes—to better describe the bridge that Gurdjieff's teachings construct between religion and science—I will share some images that originated in the domain of my own visions and dreams. One night, even as I worked on writing this chapter of the book, the recurring dream that visits me every couple of weeks happened again, early in the morning. The beginning was vague, it was still too dark, but I can remember that I was visiting a person I knew, who was lifting his boat onto a trailer behind his car. His words were inaudible, but apparently he was planning to go sailing. A dangerous enterprise with such a small boat. Following this visit, I headed homewards and wandered through a residential neighborhood in the city that I only knew from this dream. This area was on the coastline, and on my left I saw, between the houses, the mass of water in an ever-increasingly brighter light. Close to home, I saw that the sea had become turbulent. Large waves with foamy white crests tumbled over each other. That was not all; the sea had broken through and flooded the city. To continue on my way, I sometimes had to wade waist-high through torrential rivers and streams that swept flagstones and pieces of timber along through the streets. In the distance, an angry sea raged, which had acquired a hellish, bluish, hallucinatory color. At the door to my house, where the water slopped against the door, my dream ended.

In this dream, I had no fear. Peculiar, if you know anything at all about the dangers of the sea. On the contrary, a strong feeling of peace and relaxation came over me, as though the sea welcomed me with its infinity. After waking, I did not feel exhausted, as is often the case after other dreams, but instead bursting with energy, as though the sea had shared some of its strength with me, in the way that it leaves shells behind on the wet beach.

The meaning of this dream is perfectly clear to me. The water is the truth. The city and houses are the temporary dwellings that will sooner or later be overwhelmed by the sea. The two signs in the dream, the water and the houses, do not just symbolize the contrast between eternity and the temporary, or irrational and rational, but also the difference between a spiritual and a scientific discipline. All spiritual systems, including that of Gurdjieff, focus on the water, not on the city. A choice has to be made: you go out on the water in a boat, or you stay at home. Gurdjieff's teachings tell you what you must do once you have reached your decision to be on the water, and how to attain the other side. The objective of the teachings is to get to the other side, but I will let Gurdjieff talk about this himself.

THE OBJECTIVE OF THE TEACHINGS – ACQUIRING A SOUL

At the end of the first chapter of *Beelzebub's Tales to His Grandson*, a short and funny anecdote is related. It is set in the Georgian city of Tiflis, early in the morning. The storyteller has to extricate himself from an exciting book, *About Dreams and Magic*, and has to set off to work. His job is the operation of a steam-whistle that will awaken the city's population from its sweet dreams. On his way to the tower to which the steam-whistle is attached, he witnesses how a dogcatcher attempts to catch a dog. Wagging its tail, the dog has just spotted an interesting bitch on the other side of the street. At the very moment the dogcatcher is about to throw out his net, the dog is startled by the sound of a church bell and runs away. The dogcatcher calls out, "What a time to sound the church bells!" This dogcatcher, it was explained earlier in the anecdote, had to catch dogs that were not wearing the "metal badge for the city of Tiflis" around their necks, which showed that the owner had paid the dog license. His only focus was on the ones that did not have such a "passport"—this word was Gurdjieff's. Those that were caught were carried away in a "solemn ceremony" along a long dark tunnel to a machine in which they were destroyed, and from which, after their deaths, a "special kind of fat" appeared that was presented respectfully to the city's patriarchs.

This anecdote is a fine example of the deceptively innocent way in which Gurdjieff conceals his teachings. The operator of the steam-whistle, Gurdjieff, has to perform a hard intervention to awaken the people. Through the sounding of the church bell, the dog narrowly escaped the fate that normally would have befallen it. Many of its kind would not escape this fate: to be killed, in order that from their bodies a substance could be extracted that would be of use to the "fathers of the city," in other words to higher organisms in the cosmos. Only the dogs with a "passport" did not share this terrible fate. This passport is the "soul" that, once it has been formed, protects us from falling foul of an equally anonymous and merciless law, but transports us to a safe haven on the other side.

The consecutive stages that lead to the acquisition of a soul are simply depicted by Orage. This explanation is absent from Ouspensky's book, and is therefore, for that very reason, worthy of mention. The possible development of humankind is put on a par with the diatonic scale.[1] "Do," "re" and "mi" are the body, the feelings and the thoughts, followed by the important link "fa" to higher thoughts and feelings: the notes "sol" and "la." Here, the insights are revealed upon which religious revelations are based. The next note, "si," is the step that can bring about the octave—the rebirth through a transformation

1 The scale called "diatonic" is the normal major scale that can be found by playing on an instrument the following notes: c-d-e-f-g-a-b-c. It can just as well begin at every other tone, but the two half-tones have to come between the third and the fourth, and the seventh and the eighth note. In Orage's example the notes are called do-re-mi-fa-sol-la-si-do.

of the sexual energy. *The function of the note "fa" is an essential difference between Gurdjieff's teaching and other spiritual systems.*

This scale describes human evolution in two parts: the part as it has already taken place, and the part that still has to take place. The notes "do," "re" and "mi" symbolize what a person is given at birth—a physical body, feelings and thoughts—and, in their sequential order, also the long evolution that led to the creation of humankind. All the notes that follow have to be acquired by the individual, nothing more is given.

The three human centers that have already been given can deliver exceptional achievements. The body can climb mountains, the feelings can inspire great works of art and the thoughts can form science. But, with none of them are we able to perceive ourselves through the eyes of a neutral and unbiased observer. The note "fa" is the decisive transition to the higher possibilities and stands for "self-knowledge," the mysterious elixir of life of Gurdjieff's teachings.

THE NUMINOUS "FA"

Many words that have become commonplace in these teachings describe a process that needs to take place here, such as "self-remembering," "self-observation," "attention" or "alertness," but "fa" cannot be described with mere words. Perhaps it is not such a bad comparison to visualize this consciousness as a peculiar light and the blue of the seawater in my dream as described above. In the note "fa," a different form of consciousness is encountered. This announces itself in the moments at which another light falls upon us, from another space, and from which the individual sees himself /herself as they actually are, a sobering and sometimes alarming experience. These moments of truth are always brief.

The point from which observation takes place appears to be some distance from us—it is a diffuse point that is not centralized in the brain, but that can adopt multiple positions from which we can see ourselves as a whole. This self-knowledge has nothing to do with introspection; it comes from a different source that our will cannot influence, and even less so our fantasies of ourselves. It has nothing to do with self-criticism or improvements that we would like to or should make. This consciousness observes things as they are, quietly and without labeling. This is the door that provides access to what Gurdjieff meant by "awakening consciousness."

The forms of consciousness that are accessible for individuals are: sleep, awakening dream state, awakening consciousness, and a fourth, the awakening to the actual world, as it is. Ouspensky was right when he said that the third form of consciousness had remained unknown in Western philosophy and psychology.

If this third form of consciousness, symbolized by the note "fa" in Orage's example, is of such imperative importance for any further development, you would expect that even though it is absent in Western philosophy and psychology, it would have been described in Western literature. This is indeed the case, but it is no coincidence that this has taken place almost exclusively in the autobiographies written by authors with a strongly developed ability for remembering.[2]

AN ANECDOTE ABOUT SELF-REMEMBERING

For a final description of what is meant by self-remembering and how this can be evoked in us, I will let Gurdjieff say it in his own words. This regards an anecdote that, as far as I am aware, is not recorded

[2] In my opinion, the first part—say for the sake of argument the first hundred pages—of the book *Voyage Au Bout De La Nuit*, published in 1932 (English translation, *Journey to the End of the Night,* published by New Directions, 1952) by Louis-Ferdinand Céline, offers an almost unsurpassable example of the description of "self-remembering." Fragments of great power can equally be found with many other authors, in Dutch literature, for example, with Simon Vestdijk.

elsewhere in literature.[3] In the final Parisian years, a rumor circulated that Gurdjieff would answer all questions on a certain evening. On that particular evening, his apartment was packed to the gunnels, and indeed Gurdjieff asked those present who among them had an important question. Many questions were asked, especially the classics, about life and death, the soul, etc. Amongst the crossfire, an old lady sitting in the back row vied for attention, but she only managed this when Gurdjieff demanded silence and gave her an opportunity to speak. "Mr. Gurdjieff," she began, "I live in a house that is a distance from the road. As I walk along the dark path that leads to my house in the evening, I am always terrified." All those present, completely immersed in their own profound questions, thought that she was crazy. But, following all the other questions, Gurdjieff focused his attention solely on the old lady, and her question was the only one he answered: "Madam, I can help you," he said. "The next time you are walking home in the dark and you are overcome with fear, I advise you to say the following words to yourself: *'May I be here?'*" After this, he stood up and left the residence.[4]

~

The scheme of possible development from the Oragean version (using the diatonic scale), and the emphasis on the concept of self-remembering as sketched above, cannot fully represent Gurdjieff's teachings, in which visions, systems of thought, works of art and practical approaches

---

3 Unfortunately, in this book I must follow the same procedure as James Webb applied to his book *The Harmonious Circle*, and omit my sources in several cases. For the sake of completeness, I guarantee the authenticity of this and all my other citations, which I have attempted to reproduce word for word. It is up to the reader to take me at my word or not.

4 The anecdote was related to me in English, but it is likely that the language spoken that evening was French. Gurdjieff had the habit of—in whatever language—speaking a type of "compact" or "summarized" language in which the word order was different from normal and anything unnecessary was omitted.

are blended into one organic whole. However, both Ouspensky and Orage should be given due credit for their intellectual and intuitive firmness that kept this version of Gurdjieff's teachings in its pure form and safeguarded it from other influences.

ANOTHER VERSION OF THE TEACHING?

Do the words "this version of Gurdjieff's teaching" that I used in the previous paragraph imply that another version exists as well?

Yes indeed! And certainly not an unimportant one. Gurdjieff's own description of his teaching, found in his first book, differs so much from the Ouspenskyan and Oragean versions that it does not seem to be the same teaching at all, but an entirely different one. In *Beelzebub's Tales to His Grandson,* the teaching is directed toward the acquisition of conscience, which has to be brought from our sub-conscious into our waking existence.

How can this difference be explained? Could it be that these two versions—one put forth by Ouspensky and Orage, the other by Gurdjieff himself—describe *successive stages,* and that the methodology of the first version *is only a preparation for the next step,* which will show us how much the results of the organ Kundabuffer determine our own life? Could it also be that the first version is overemphasized by the predominant characteristic of our society to make mental efforts—rather than those of the feeling and the body—that consequently serve as *an excuse* not to enter the second stage? To be honest with oneself leads everybody, without exception, to great suffering, but I hope and pray that this suffering will be the dawn of true conscience.

I cannot answer the above questions, but we can assume that each version reflects the oneness of Gurdjieff's teaching, like two crystals reflecting the same source of light into another color spectrum.

10

THE TWO RUDIMENTARY ELEMENTS

The composition of the world.
– Harry Mulisch

Gurdjieff's teachings are characterized by two laws: the "Great Laws" of Three and Seven. The existence and meaning of these Laws cannot be confirmed or explained in a logically constructed train of thought. They can only be experienced once our inner self has acquired access to the unknown worlds, described in the previous chapter as "sol" and "la" from the scale of human development, and in this unknown area, logical, physical or mathematical concepts are no longer applicable.

The most ancient shrine in my native region was a medieval cathedral: a subsided grey stone mass in a marshy landscape, decorated all round with ornaments, holy statues and grinning devils' heads. My mother's hand guided me there once, and inside we were cloaked with the silence of a grave. Through the twilight, a shaft of light fell upon the worn stone floor before us from a stained glass window. "God lives here," said my mother, as though this was the most normal thing in the world. Filled with awe and reverence, I looked around in an attempt to catch a glimpse of his presence in the dark spaces and vaulting.

I experience exactly the same feeling when I open my mind to these Great Laws in a process that is called "contemplation." In the meantime, I have learned that, depending on my own strengths, I will see as little as ever. The energy that is bundled in these Laws, like a very dense cloud that drifts on the edge of our atmosphere, can only reach me if I first discard my illusions concerning myself, in the way that a devout Muslim does with his footwear before entering the mosque. This is the price that must be paid: the note "fa." A high price, because it is difficult to see how and who we are. It is only with tremendous tenacity and effort that we can create the conditions in which our "self-observations" can be given space, and even then we do our utmost to avoid having to look into this merciless mirror. How strange, in actual fact, that we cannot see ourselves without fleeing from this; sooner or later, it will become clear to us who we are, or, as will be the case in the last moments of our lives, who we were.

Gurdjieff first explained a scant sketch of the Laws of Three and Seven to his pupils in the period up to the end of 1924, but subsequently fleshed them out in fine detail in his books, his music and his Movements. All his works are focused on demonstrating and explaining these Laws in continuously different forms, although at first sight it will not be evident, because they are concealed in an artistic form. The first impression people get of an artistic expression is what is referred to as "programmed art," something quite usual in the history of music. For example, a composer imagines thunder, a galloping horse or the Last Judgment, or whatever, and then proceeds to express this in sound. Nothing is further from the truth in the case of Gurdjieff's statements regarding the Laws of Three and Seven. Gurdjieff was not an author, composer or choreographer in the ordinary sense of the word, but he understood these art forms *inside out*.[1] He *experienced* the Laws he expressed, and this was the creative source for his books, music and Movements. This idea might well evoke great opposition, because the inspiration for works of art appears to have been reduced to just a few inconsequential numbers, as in the case of programming a robot. It is therefore important to emphasize that the *inner experience*

[1] I owe my thanks to Michel de Salzmann for this insight, who, incidentally very briefly, informed me about it in a personal conversation dating from 1965.

of these Laws is of a very high order and opens an entirely new chapter for the possible evolution of humankind.

Although these Laws cannot be placed in a rational framework, the logical explanation of these principles, attempted by everyone who has felt called upon to do so, has taken place frequently since Gurdjieff's death, and has recently culminated in numerous writings about the enneagram, a geometric symbol that incorporates the Laws of Three and Seven. All these explanations depend, without exception, on mathematics, physics or other scientific elements –numbers, geometric forms or physical-vibration relationships—and are deceptive, because they incorrectly suggest that these Laws originate from these areas or could be derived from them.

THE LAW OF THREE

Gurdjieff was very reserved when he spoke about this Law, and his practical examples could be counted on one hand. He stated that a moment of creation, at whatever level, can only occur when a "third force"—like a breath of life—counterbalances the tension between a positive and a negative pole. An alternative word for this reconciling force is the "designing force." This principle can be traced back to the Trinity principle in Christian teachings, or the Trimurti of the Vedic tradition, but this does not mean that this Law is simple to observe. Gurdjieff believed that we are blind to the third force, because it is easier to see duality.

I can add to this explanation of Gurdjieff's that the one-dimensional line, at which on one end an angel stands and at the other extreme a devil, has become a prototype for Western culture, as well as for the duality of body and soul. Considered from the Law of Three, a positive force can never, under any circumstances, win from a negative in a definitive dual, as we are led to believe in the old Hollywood westerns. The negative factor cannot be destroyed by the positive opposition, but has to be observed and lived through, which results in the evocation of a neutralizing force that transforms the duality into a force-field of three factors. Could it be that, through the complete acceptance of the irreversibility of our death, a new insight is generated that rises above the duality of life-death, as the epigraph of the previous chapter, a quote from the holy Teresa, suggests?

The subsequent explanations offered for Gurdjieff's theories by interpreters of this Law did not serve to help me. Some examples borrowed from physics are unmistakable, but their brief explanations of a law that subjects the entire creation to its structure convinces less than Hegel's Dialectic, which is sometimes considered as the most "imposing intellectual construction that has ever come from a single pair of hands." Hegel asserts that the trinity comprises the reconciliation of opposites that transform into a synthesis. This cannot assist us, however, because this logic does not permit a variability of the factor "consciousness"; it only recognizes statements, formulated in words, which are true or untrue. It is difficult to deny the existence of variables in conscious states; there is too much evidence to the contrary, but they are gladly swept into a pile with hallucinations, and this is not completely without foundation. Even so, this is where the secret hides that provides access to this Law, which is a testimony from a state of consciousness that is completely unusual to us. This other and rare quality of consciousness explains why this Law lies at the roots of many religions and philosophical systems, and archaic forms of it can be found in almost every culture. But, at the same time, this all-encompassing principle has remained inaccessible, and will always remain so, for a logical thought process expressed in words.

Words . . . I see how they slip away from my thoughts and are replaced in my mind's eye by another image from my childhood. The black earth of the field, from which, in the furrows, germinated grain grew. It was a warm day, the earth was being worked and, along the side of the field, lay thermos flasks with cold tea, from which we were allowed to take a swig from time to time. Along the edge of the woods, the profile of small farms with their red roofs and whitewashed walls was visible. Modest accommodation, but they were rooted in the landscape. The heat of the sun was heavy on everything, like a large, silent bronze bell in which time stood still. A child experiences, in such a moment, his or her young life as a beautiful promise that will be fulfilled in the future.

But does life keep its promise? To find the answer, I need only look at the faces of the people in the U-Bahn, my fellow travellers. That says it all. It sometimes occurs to me that they, and equally so myself, are waiting all our lives for this promise to be fulfilled. We are waiting for that which in our youth was perhaps reality for just a moment, to return and remain in our possession. Spiritual teachings have the capacity to break through this passive decline, as the neutralizing force between the promise that life had made and its unavoidable volatility.

THE LAW OF SEVEN

About the other Great Law, the "sevenfold," Gurdjieff explains that every stimulus and every initiative must undergo predictable stages, each with its own characteristics. The scale in major demonstrates these stages: do-re-mi-fa-sol-la-si-do. The new "do" is the octave note of the first "do." Thus, this Law is often also called the "Law of Octaves."

"Octave" stands for the number eight, but the reference to "sevenfold" describes the seven distances between (or separating) eight notes, which must be covered before the basic note can reach the next, the higher, octave. However, this Law is not so much about isolated, stationary landmarks, but more about the development of one characteristic (or stage, or phase) into another. Each distance between two notes is like a path or way to walk upon until the next landmark note is reached. This is a gradual process, expressed here in terms of physics as vibrations that become higher, thus producing a higher sound.

This Law depicts a predictable process that follows after an initial impulse has been given, whether this impulse be of a physical, chemical or a psychological nature. The impulse has to reach the octave step by step, much as the notes of the major scale are struck one after the other on a piano.

Gurdjieff describes two variations of this Law. The first one as a chronological process in *time*. This version was explained at length by him, as quoted by Ouspensky in *In Search of the Miraculous,* and when Ouspensky writes about this Law he means the Law expressed by a chronological process. This second variation of this Law—the one "outside time"—does not appear in Ouspensky's book, but solely in Gurdjieff's own work. He refers to the Law of Seven existing outside *time,* where the notes become frozen force-fields that keep each other in balance. Gurdjieff gave various examples of this second variety, such as opium that comprises seven components that in turn each comprise seven parts, or that of the human face of which the form is determined by the dimensions of seven parts of the body. The co-existence of these two varieties of the same Law, seemingly so contradictory, indicates that we are dealing here with an organic phenomenon that is difficult if not impossible to understand by logical means alone.

Gurdjieff's most important example encompasses nothing less than the entire cosmos and is referred to as the "ray of creation" in Ouspensky's diary. This ray runs through the octave from top to bottom as follows: "do"—the Absolute, "si"—all worlds, "la"—all suns, "sol"—the Sun, "fa"—all planets, "mi"—the Earth, "re"—the Moon, "do"—the Absolute. This construction has come about logically from determining, from the bottom up, the composition of the surrounding worlds for each link. This appears similar to the Pythagorean creation of the worlds based on numeric relationships as explained in Plato's *Timaeus*. The numeric calculations of the creation in Plato's *Timaeus* are so complex that "even the Demiurge who created the world gave a sigh of relief once the creation was complete." If these calculations are carefully computed, a series of numbers are generated that relate to the notes of the octave in the same way as the vibration numbers do in Gurdjieff's Law of Seven. In other words, a series with five whole and two half-increments of tone, located in exactly the same places.[2]

It is striking that Plato believed that the creation of the world also took place based on this same scale, but the way that Gurdjieff arrived at this scale is different. For him, there was no question of complicated calculations. Rather, the diatonic scale occurs because a line—in other words a phenomenon or process—is first divided into seven equal segments, and after that into three. The "milestones" from the first division of seven are now shifted in such a way that two of them converge with the "milestones" from the division of three.[3] This could explain why Gurdjieff called the Law of Three the "second Great Law," as though the creation itself is related to the Law of Three, which deregulated the harmonic and balanced division of seven from before the creation through the creative stimulus of the Law of Three.

SUPPORTING SHOCKS

An essential part of Gurdjieff's theory of creation remains absent in Plato's and cannot be traced back to any other tradition whatsoever. Gurdjieff claimed that no single stimulus can progress in the right direction without supporting shocks being administered from the outside. If this is not the case, the progress of the stimulus is at the mercy of coincidence, and runs out of steam . . . or in the opposite

2 In the book, *Plato's Cosmology* by F.M. Cornford, London, 1937, this calculation is made and the author came to the conclusion that this led to number relationships that are equal to those of the diatonic scale.

3 This is a brief summary of what Russell A. Smith derived from the chapter "Purgatory" from Gurdjieff's first book. He published his findings in *Cosmic Secrets*, The Dog: Texas, 1993. He explained this to me personally, and without his instruction I would never have been able to understand this.

direction. His example of this is the Inquisition that tortured and killed its victims out of "love for their dearest."

The supporting shocks have to be given in two fixed places, where the vibration number is not increased by a whole note, but only by half a note: that is, in the intervals "mi-fa" and "si-do." The position of the interval "fa-mi" in the ray of creation, which octave declines (goes from top to bottom, or from higher octave *do* to previous *do*) could answer Gurdjieff's question about the meaning of life on Earth. Life on Earth is the stimulus from outside that is administered to the "ray-of-creation octave" at this "fa-mi" interval. The extremely thin film of organic life that is wrapped around the planet must secure the stimulus from the Sun ("sol") and all the planets ("fa") in the direction of the Moon ("re"). This second-to-last component of this staggering column of creation, the moon, devours all the life on Earth like a hungry predator.

Other octaves have less incredible dimensions than the ray of creation for Gurdjieff. He sketched a picture in which stimuli simultaneously propel and are tangled together in every area. One octave serves as a jolt for the other. In this way, the absorption of nourishment, breathing and experiencing of impressions are three octaves that set each other in motion with clockwork precision.

This "intervals and jolts" (intervals or shocks) component in Gurdjieff's Law of Seven is a mysterious and crucial addition that comes out of nowhere and is completely independent. In Gurdjieff's eyes, the knowledge of the intervals is the difference between barbarianism and culture.[4]

THREE TYPES OF OCTAVE

There are three types of octave, of which two types have already been mentioned: the ones that exist "outside time" and those "inside time."

---

[4] This statement by Gurdjieff can be found in the unpublished "Constantinople Notes."

This last category can also be split into evolving and involving processes. In accordance with his picture of the world—in which nothing can maintain its position but is ever evolving or degenerating—Gurdjieff assessed processes as "increasing" or "declining," positive or negative.

The third type of octave is an exception that does not fit this division. The ray of creation is the octave that is separate from all the others. It is the only declining octave that is not assessed negatively by Gurdjieff, but, as appears from a single remark from him in Ouspensky's diary, is *creative*. This "creativity" is analyzed in a less than reassuring way by Mulisch in his book, *The Composition of the World*, previously mentioned in Chapter 5.[5]

MULISCH AND THE GREAT LAWS

The Composition of the World is a remarkable book in many ways. First of all, as a result of the unavoidable fact that an almost identical principle to that of Gurdjieff's Law of Seven is fleshed out. The author has also given this book an uncommonly great personal slant. Mulisch knew intuitively that he could not die in peace if he had not written this book. He has now died, but I doubt if there has been anyone of such a literary status who has attempted to understand the rudimentary elements of the Law of Seven. It is illustrative to lay his vision over Gurdjieff's and to hold them up to the light together.[6]

An obvious explanation for the similarities between both the visions could be that Mulisch was consciously or unconsciously inspired by Gurdjieff's ideas, which, after all, had been published thirty years previously. When I asked him about this, Mulisch himself waived any influence from that quarter away, for the simple reason that Gurdjieff was completely unknown to him when he wrote *The*

5 See footnote 2 from Chapter 5.

6 Here I refer to my article in *Bres* 179, 1996, "Did Mulisch Know Gurdjieff?"

Composition of the World.[7] Above all, he mentioned that 1949—coincidentally also the year of Gurdjieff's death—was the year in which one of the "rudimentary elements" (the "Law of Seven" in Gurdjieff's cosmology) became clear to him. He discovered the rudimentary elements in a moment of ecstatic insight in which he saw that the two tones from an octave are equal and at the same time unequal.

In the first part of his book, he employs this fact to resolve Zeno's paradoxes. These are ancient problems—such as "Zeno's arrow" that remains stationary in the air, because it cannot be in one place and at the same time in another—with which this philosopher demonstrates the impossibility of movement and, in doing so, undermines the entire system of logic. New solutions for this monstrous paradox have continued to be offered in the form of complicated calculations, but it has never been negated. Even the physicist Leibniz could see no other solution than that "God continually destroys and recreates the world" so that the arrow can move. This first section of Mulisch's book dovetails into the first axiom of the "New Logic" as formulated by Ouspensky in his book *Tertium Organum*: A is equal to A and A is also equal to "Non-A."[8]

Mulisch presents many octaves in his book, but here we have to limit ourselves to just one: the historical development of humanity. The capacity to allow equipment and machines to serve us takes its toll in that humankind loses itself in these extensions. In this drain, emotions and gods transfigure to become technical achievements: Notre Dame is empty, God now flies above it in the form of an airplane. The individual degenerates to nothing more than a guard for machines, the "ultimative," while here and there some "people" wander around ghost-like, much as nomads from a previous era wander.

7 Personal conversation with H. Mulisch, c. 1995.

8 P.D. Ouspensky, *Tertium Organum*, London: Routledge & Kegan Paul, republished 1965, page 223.

The difference between Gurdjieff's and Mulisch' visions is that the first perceives the possibility of evolution within the descending octave of the ray of creation and Mulisch does not. The great flow descends, but Gurdjieff believed that a small stream can return, "can challenge God."

Despite their heterogeneity, Mulisch and Gurdjieff both are of the opinion that a rudimentary element itself is the primary reality, and that even people are no more than the manifestation of the operation of this Law. People cannot just employ these formulas as and when they please. Mulisch compared this to the robbing of a royal tomb after it had been discovered, through which the archaeological value is lost forever.

I have pondered this statement at times when I have been confronted with musings on the enneagram, or about supporters of the psychological theories regarding it. Mulisch told me himself that he was not able to understand this symbol. "I just couldn't fathom it," he sighed.[9] This statement from someone of his literary and philosophical stature should serve as a warning for not interpreting the enneagram too lightly. Gurdjieff said that this symbol could only be understood by those who had danced the enneagram-Movements. My own experiences have confirmed this. Not that I now understand this symbol, far from it, but it is as though you come into contact with a secret. The deep silence that practicing the enneagram-Movements has evoked in me, time and time again, is so different from the mental effort required for deciphering the enneagram, that the craving to do this has left me. The word "enneagram" is absent from Gurdjieff's own writings—it only occurs in Ouspensky's book—but in his Movements this symbol plays a major role, if not the singularly most important role.

---

[9] Personal conversation with H. Mulisch, c. 1995.

11

MUSIC BY GURDJIEFF / DE HARTMANN

Hear the melodies in the way in which the stringed instruments of love exhale them. These are the true Psalms of David. Do not dwell on the future or the past. Live now. That is the secret of peace.

– Omar Khayyam

Gurdjieff's life was intertwined with music from his earliest age: with his father's singing, an *ashik* with an in-depth knowledge of old ballads; with Greek-Orthodox liturgical music, and with Greek, Armenian, Kurdish, Turkish and Persian traditional music. During his travels, he studied the music of religious communities and immersed himself in Central-Asian folk and ritual music. More important to him than the emotional value of all this music was the fact that the vibrating sounds of the long-necked string instruments, the monotone song of the monks, yes even his little harmonium that accompanied him to the end of his days, comprised vibrations in which universal patterns could be studied. Music was an essential ingredient of his teachings. And its significance is still overlooked, even among circles interested in this discipline.

From the beginning in St. Petersburg and Moscow, to the end of his life in Paris, he was musically active—on guitar, piano and harmonium. He could write music in the usual Western fashion, but elected to have his music noted by his pupil Thomas de Hartmann, an already famous Russian composer with good contacts with the artistic avant-garde, especially with Kandinsky, who considered him as his best friend.

Gurdjieff's works were written in musical notation by de Hartmann, his "court composer," in a historically unique collaboration. Gurdjieff indicated the themes through singing or playing the piano with one hand, and de Hartmann immediately made a sketch of the melody and of a simple harmonic and rhythmic accompaniment. Gurdjieff then indicated if this idea corresponded with his intention or not. This was a source of tension, and the differences of opinion were anything but slight. Gurdjieff's habit of making continuous minute alterations to, for a Western ear, monotone Eastern melodies, contributed to this.

De Hartmann knew nothing of Eastern music when he met Gurdjieff. The fact that nevertheless, in a short period not lasting two years, hundreds of compositions could be created is difficult to conceive. It is especially astonishing if you consider that the traditional music from all sorts of cultures appears to have been faithfully represented, and that Gurdjieff's own work is of such a high quality. This is completely separate from the fact that the many pieces are of such a precise mathematical construction, different from Bach, but no less complex. How is this possible?

Thomas de Hartmann wrote a biography, but unfortunately he died at just the point at which he was to begin the chapter about Gurdjieff's music. Previously, he had indicated that he always felt connected to Gurdjieff through some kind of magnetic attraction, also throughout their years of separation.[1] It is this magnetic force that played a role in their collaboration. Not limited to musical exchanges, it was as though a simultaneous transfer of energy took place, of which Gurdjieff was the source and de Hartmann the receiver. This

---

1 De Hartmann never saw his teacher again after their separation in 1929, but still felt a magnetic attraction. This was written by Thomas C. Daly, personal pupil of de Hartmann and heir to the "de Hartmann Estate," in a personal exchange of letters with Gert Jan Blom and the author.

also appeared to have taken place in an earlier collaboration between Gurdjieff and Ouspensky. It was not just Ouspensky's logical and memorization abilities that produced *In Search of the Miraculous*. The energetic force from Gurdjieff irradiated Ouspensky in the same way as this happened with de Hartmann several years later.

Noting down music in these circumstances was an ordeal for de Hartmann. In a literal sense too, as the task was like a test that he was subjected to by his teacher. If Gurdjieff was contented with the first sketch, this was then arranged for piano solo by de Hartmann. His spouse, Olga de Hartmann, then rewrote everything neatly. The result is exceptional music in which Eastern folk music and that of remote monastic communities was made accessible to us through de Hartmann's arrangement. He was always modest about his role. He said of this: "I only picked up the Master's handkerchief."[2]

The fact that Gurdjieff employed Tibetan singing bowls in his early period in St. Petersburg has remained almost unnoticed. It is not known if this was only for brief experiments or if it led to compositions.[3]

The stimuli that moved Gurdjieff to compose music were to provide Movements with accompanying music and, following his accident, to give musical illustrations while reading from his books, as an emotional version, complementary to the intellectual form comprising words. Gurdjieff said this literally. It means that just reading or studying his books misses out on the added value of his music.[4] The stream of compositions that took place after the second stimulus, in the years 1925 up to and including 1927, might perhaps indicate that his not

---

2 De Hartmann made this statement during a visit to London in March 1950.

3 This fact was confirmed by Prof. Dr. H. Petzold in a letter dated 18th of May 1994 and addressed to Bruno Martin in Germany. A literal quote from this letter: "As a young man, my father participated in Gurdjieff groups in St. Petersburg in 1916 or 1917—partly in Moscow—where Gurdjieff played gongs or Tibetan scales, also harmonium and piano too. My father also had contact with Gurdjieff during the period in Paris."

4 As quoted by Carl Zigrosser in *The New Republic*, 5th of June 1925.

yet realized intention to give a second major theatre performance, this time not dedicated to Movements but to Oriental music, still gnawed at him. The musical collaboration between Gurdjieff and de Hartmann ended for good by their going their separate ways in 1929, but the source of their music dried up two years before this for reasons unknown to me. It is probable that Gurdjieff's time-consuming trips to the United States influenced this.

CHRONOLOGY OF THE MUSICAL OEUVRE

Period 1915 up to and including 1924

- Six fragments to accompany the ballet *The Struggle of the Magicians,* written for piano solo.
- Forty-one compositions to accompany Movements for the demonstrations in 1923 and 1924. These pieces were orchestrated by Thomas de Hartmann for an orchestra of thirty-five musicians and later, when there were insufficient funds to pay so many musicians, transcribed for a smaller complement of five instrumentalists.[5] These compositions were first scored for piano solo by de Hartmann, so that they could be played to accompany the dancers while rehearsing the program and only afterwards were they orchestrated—an enormous task that was completed by de Hartman in just a few months. Both orchestral scores and sheet music for piano solo exist for these pieces.
- A dozen or so compositions for piano solo, the majority of which were made to accompany Movements that were not

[5] This music is recorded on the CDs accompanying the exhaustive book about Gert Jan Blom's research project: *Gurdjieff / de Hartmann Oriental Suite, The complete Orchestral Music 1923-1924*" 2006 Basta Audio Visuals, The Netherlands.

shown during the performances in 1923 and 1924, or that were created shortly afterwards.[6]

Period 1925 up to and including 1927

More than 220 pieces for piano solo. This number is an estimate, based on the comparison of two independent surveys. One of them was prepared shortly after the death of the composer for his legal heirs.

The year 1949

One-hundred-thirty-six recordings of Gurdjieff's harmonium improvisations. These were recorded with a tape recorder, in an intimate atmosphere and were not recorded as sheet music.[7]

As indicated from the list above, Gurdjieff's musical oeuvre was comprised of three parts:

- music to accompany Movements
- a relatively large collection of pieces for piano solo
- a number of recordings of Gurdjieff's improvisations on his harmonium.

Hereafter, I will limit myself to considering the second part, written for piano solo. The Movements music will be discussed in Part II of this book, and I cannot say much about the last part, the harmonium recordings. I do not recognize any structure in this harmonium music, of which the rhythm and tempi do not alternate. Even when

---

6 These are the accompaniment for the Movements Gurdjieff gave after the Performances, in the next few months before his car accident later that year. They are titled: "Exercise 1-4," "Slow Obligatory" (2 versions); "N11" (a title that possibly refers to an orchestration, which was never made, or has been lost), "Forming Two's," "Enneagram Exercise," "The Thirty Gestures," "Women's Prayer" and finally "Lost Loves." No orchestral versions of these pieces were made.

7 Gurdjieff's harmonium improvisations are represented integrally on the CDs that accompany Gert Jan Blom's book *Harmonic Development*. 2004, Basta Audio Visuals, The Netherlands.

Gurdjieff's harmonium pieces were being played back from a recording, I witnessed the force of emotion evoked among those pupils who had been present when Gurdjieff himself was alive and played the harmonium in their company. This is why I am cautious to draw conclusions from my inability to comprehend this music. It appears to me as though an infinite melody resounds here, and I believe that Gurdjieff's later piano works, those from 1926 and 1927, already announced this infinite melody.

SHEET MUSIC

Soon after Gurdjieff's death, de Hartmann selected a number of compositions for piano solo from the period 1925 to 1927, and published five music albums (Editions Janus, Paris, 1950-1955). Do not be misled by the word "composition," as these are not necessarily lengthy works, such as a piano sonata. They are pieces of, on average, three minutes in length, a collection of musical miniatures, simple and devoid of any frills. These albums were a private publication, at the time difficult if not impossible to obtain, and they are of historic importance because it is very likely that de Hartmann selected the works that were for him the most representative, and because he had prepared a clear categorization. Each album was devoted to a certain type of music. The titles were, in order of appearance: *Hymns from a Great Temple, Songs and Rhythms from the Orient, Sayid Chants and Dances, Dervish Chants and Dances* and *Sacred Hymns*.

From the titles it appears that these concerned Eastern folk music, music from religious communities and hymns. What exactly do these titles mean? A hymn is a religious song of praise, but we do not know what to think of "Great Temple." The word "sayid," [plural seids] also written as "seid," a common word in the Near East, means leader, clergyman or priest. De Hartmann intended to say something else here. In the introduction to this album he wrote that the seids were considered to be the direct descendants of Mohammed and as such they were revered. It has proven impossible to find a population that corresponds with this description. Then the word "dervish." This can have two meanings: a member of a religious brotherhood or a wandering mendicant who has given up all earthly possessions. The second is the oldest. Finally, the word "sacred" in the title of the last album. This can mean that the hymns from this album are holy, but I think that the word carries too heavy an association here. I believe it has more to do with the fact that many pieces were dedicated to religious feast days. In checking the data regarding when they were made, it appeared that this often took place on the feast day itself, as though Gurdjieff first experienced the meaning of such a feast day—Christmas, Ash Wednesday, Maundy Thursday, Good Friday, Easter—and then afterwards transformed this into sound.

The album *Songs and Rhythms from the Orient* is the most varied. It includes folk music from Greece, Armenia, Afghanistan, Turkish and Kurdish music, Persian and Tibetan melodies and songs from various peoples like the Molokans and Assyrians. The pieces of music from the *Sayid* album are interrelated, because these pieces begin with a long recitative—a free introduction—and end with a rhythmic part, a musical practice that can still be heard in East-Turkey. There are also recitatives on the *Dervish* album, but in general these later pieces are more rhythmic. The *Hymns* are slow and devoid of a clear rhythmic stimulus.

Following de Hartmann's death, his widow published three albums in 1970 (publisher undisclosed): *Seekers of Truth, Rituals of a Sufi Order*, and *Journey to Inaccessible Places*. These titles suggest musical categories that do not exist in this music; they have been given a romantic color. The only names and categorization that make any sense are de Hartmann's own. Again, these three albums were, just as those of de Hartmann himself, intended exclusively for the members of the Institut Gurdjieff in Paris and its international branches.

Between 1996 and 2005, the famous music publisher B. Schott & Söhne, which had previously published the collected works of

Mozart, Beethoven and Wagner, made the sheet music generally available through the publication of 170 compositions for piano solo in 4 albums: *The Piano Music of Gurdjieff / de Hartmann, Definitive Edition*. These publications were a mark of recognition for the services of Gurdjieff and de Hartmann as composers and form a historical breakthrough for their music. The committee that prepared these publications was thorough in its work. The albums are absolutely splendid, and all the uncertainties in the manuscripts have extensive commentary. Unfortunately, this publication, in contrast to its name "Definitive Edition," is actually incomplete. The piano versions of the music for Movements is almost completely absent, as are a significant number of pieces composed in the period of September through December 1926, the pinnacle of the collaboration of these composers.[8]

The categorization of the Schott albums does not tally with that of de Hartmann. The *Sayid* cycle has been combined with the *Dervish* dances, and the original set of nine *Hymns from the Great Temple*, as previously selected by de Hartmann, was changed to a group of ten hymns, through the addition of a hymn that was chosen by de Hartmann for his fifth album.

The nine hymns as previously compiled by de Hartmann form a conclusive whole with a mutual bond. It is even possible to allow the final note of a piece to resound in the commencement of the following one. The number nine also has a special meaning in Gurdjieff's numerical world, and not exclusively there. Is it not striking that major Western composers like Beethoven, Bruckner, Mahler, Saint-Saëns and others, wrote nine symphonies? As though nine is the last step in the

---

8 The following Movements pieces were included in the Schott editions: "Prayer Number 2," "Initiation of a Priestess," "The Big Group," and "Women's Prayer." The selection criteria—based on which these compositions for Movements were included in the recordings and not all the other accompanying music for Movements (about fifty in all)—are unknown to me.

creative process in which everything that could have been said has been? Anyway, it would have been better if Schott had, at least for the sake of completeness, stated the content of de Hartmann's own publications.

A CATALOGUE OF MUSICAL WORKS

There is no reliable catalogue of Gurdjieff's music in existence, compiled by an authoritative source, even though the music is over eighty years old. I have mentioned this surprising fact before. Such a fate has never befallen a jazz musician, and not even most composers of average ability from the nineteenth or twentieth century. That there is still no catalogue indicates a lack of understanding of the cultural value and the general importance of this music.

The work of the independent, Dutch, music-researcher Gert Jan Blom should not be overlooked here. He has recently ensured that the orchestral work and the harmonium recordings were made available to the public at large. The distribution of Gurdjieff's music owes a great deal to this pioneer. Calling upon this work of Gert Jan Blom, and the chronological list of works as stated at the end of Part 4 of the Schott publications, a practical alternative for a catalogue of works can be created.

We can begin with the forty-one works composed for the Movements, as arranged in Blom's *Oriental Suite*. To this, we add Schott's chronological list, and underneath it we stick the harmonium recordings from Blom's *Harmonic Development*. This latter overview (the harmonium list) is complete. However, the first part, the Movements music, must be complemented with a dozen or so pieces for piano.[9] From the middle section, the Schott list, a few dozen pieces are missing. The exact number of those missing is difficult for

---

9 See Footnote 6.

me to ascertain, because the titles for the same piece can vary in the different lists, and so I may have counted a composition twice. It is certain that what is missing concerns a relevant part here, and that this definitive edition actually remains incomplete in some way. I have received diverse compositions not included in the Schott publication and their authenticity is assured.[10]

SOUND RECORDINGS

In the course of the Fifties and Sixties, sound recordings were released, once again private publications, of Gurdjieff's harmonium playing and the interpretation by de Hartmann of pieces from the albums he had compiled. Around 1980, four long-play records appeared in general release and for everyone, from which it could be heard how de Hartmann had played this music. Later, these long-playing records were transferred to three CDs. This is still a small part of the total number of recordings that were made of him. To an increasing degree, from this time on, other pianists have tackled this body of works, with differing degrees of success, but not a single interpretation begins to approach the authenticity and depth of de Hartmann's playing.

De Hartmann was in the last phase of his life when his interpretations were recorded, and he was paying his own compositions more attention than the work he had composed with Gurdjieff

[10] To mention only some of the missing pieces here:

- "Fontainebleau, 5th of April 1926."
- "26th of June 1927." In this beautiful and lengthy piece the same theme is represented differently three times, through which three different moods are suggested.
- Untitled. An extraordinarily long piece, seven pages, in which a long melody is played over a continually repeated rhythm by the left hand.
- A five-page long hymn, in D major, that must be considered as one of the most beautiful of this oeuvre. Interestingly, part of the melody is repeated three times in notes of different length. This possibly illustrates the different characters of the three elements.

over thirty years previously. His performances are consequently of differing quality. There are recordings where you "see" him, as it were, frowning at the manuscripts that he most likely had not seen for many years, and playing them through gingerly, wisely skipping the difficult passages. In other recordings, he sounded so inspired that it is as though we are listening at the edge of the source from which the music came. Sometimes, he allowed himself to take major liberties with regard to the manuscripts. For example, where it says "pianissimo," he hammers the keys with a "fortissimo," and entire melodies are steered in another direction. His playing is then so beautiful, because the visible manuscript only serves to evoke his recollections from the past with Gurdjieff, during their collaborative years in the Prieuré. He experiences two things simultaneously, the manuscript and the past, such as a "Janus face" that can be seen in our old cathedrals. These sculpted heads with two faces hold symbolic meaning—a person can have simultaneous impressions of the outside world and of his inner self. The extra dimension of memories of the collaboration with Gurdjieff are inevitably missing from the playing of other interpreters.

Recently, this music experienced a new lease of life through an interpretation using authentic Eastern instruments. I have not yet been able to study this, but it appears to be a promising initiative.

MUSICAL RECOLLECTIONS OR THE CREATIVITY OF GURDJIEFF?

Which part of this oeuvre can be attributed to music that Gurdjieff heard in his youth and during his travels, and which part did he compose himself? In other words: where do the memories end and where does "Gurdjieff" begin?

Gurdjieff continued to mix historic and traditional material with his own creativity. Not just in his music, but in all his works. Where did the boundaries lie? This question can also be asked with regard to all his teachings. Are they founded on an existing but hidden tradition, or do they all originate from him?

We can address this issue of Gurdjieff's method with regard to his music, and that can have significance for the other areas in which he was active—areas where it is usually more difficult to ascertain, or completely impossible to answer, where the boundaries were. Only a sparse comparison with a traditional type of music that is still in existence can be made, because most of the original material has vanished from the face of the Earth. But where it has been found, his representation was exact. Besides, all melodies possess a natural span of tension, and nothing appears to have been invented or made more attractive. The titles speak for themselves: "The Dance of the Kurdish Shepherds," "The Tibetan Masked Dance" or "The Mourning Song of the Assyrian Women." Gurdjieff remembered this music from the nineteenth century and from the most remote places, with precision and tenderness. De Hartmann made crystal-clear notations. A treasure trove of traditional folk and religious music is stored in this collection that would otherwise have long been washed away by the increasing influence of the West in these areas.

Take for example the "Kurdish Melody" (Schott I,17). On an old manuscript, this piece bore the title "The Melody that My Father's Shepherd Played." It is easy to imagine Gurdjieff as the child hearing the shepherd, employed by his father, playing his flute as night fell, while the flock of sheep gathered together to seek shelter for the night. His memory stretches far back.

Take another piece: "The Song of the Molokans." This title transports us to the recollections of his travels, when Gurdjieff was permitted to place his luggage on the Molokans' wagons and to accompany them through a mountain pass. Perhaps the group of Molokans even sang exactly the same song. With a strong sensitivity for melody, Gurdjieff's interpretation represents how this song must have sounded. It has an unworldly peace that matched the nonviolence practiced by this sect, despite the fact that they were continually pursued and murdered.

The length and range of the Persian songs, which he could have heard in the places where the caravans camped overnight during his travels in this country, are extraordinarily long but appear to be complete (Schott I, 6 and 11). One of Gurdjieff's disguises during his travels was that of a singing mendicant. He needed a complete arsenal of holy songs at the ready, and it is likely that a large proportion of them ended up in the *Sayid* and *Dervish* cycles. We can be confident that all the folk music and the *Sayid* and *Dervish* cycles are reproductions of the music as heard by our composer. This means that more than half his works for piano are "memories."

The authenticity of the reproduction is more applicable to the melodies than to the rhythms and harmonic accompaniment. A single minimal, but effective, chord scheme is often utilized as a harmonic accompaniment, and the complex rhythms from the Caucasus as well as those from some Dervish brotherhoods do not occur in this music. It is possible that the rhythms are absent because de Hartmann was unable to understand them when Gurdjieff attempted to pass them on. De Hartman could not do anything about this; one really needs to have grown up in this kind of culture. The five scales that are used are modest for Eastern music. In any Eastern country, multiples of these are used.[11] It is more than likely that Gurdjieff did not consider the more complex harmonies and rhythms as important, but with regard to the scales I am not so certain. He simply had no choice because of the limitations of a piano.

[11] The Western major and the two minor scales are used, as well as what is known as the "Arabian scale." Seen from C, this looks like: C, Des, E, F, G, As, B, C. Exclusively for Tibetan melodies, the pentatonic series of five tones is utilized. Compositions in major do occur, but they are rare.

Gurdjieff's work has a lot in common with that of Béla Bartók's. This composer, too, devoted a lot of his work to folk music, East European in this case. He was also the first composer of renown who stated that his renditions of folk music were no less important than his own original work, a striking statement. His music is definitely more complex than that of Gurdjieff's. This was because he was far too ingenious a composer to not continually experiment, giving melodies other chords, and to approach Oriental quartertones, which he recorded carefully in his sketchbooks, with alternating melodic twists. Gurdjieff did not work from notes, in the way his famous colleague did, but was able to faithfully reproduce his musical impressions decades later. The original wealth of sounds and the many extraordinary Eastern intervals were summarized, mutated as it were, into the corset of the keys of the piano and, thanks to this, anyone could gain an impression of this Eastern folk music. This was a convincing realization of Gurdjieff's objective of connecting East with West.

It is worth mentioning that jazz music, similar to Gurdjieff's music, also results from the merging of two worlds—in this case, European harmonies with African rhythms. These two worlds met in a single city, New Orleans, and in a single moment. The amazement of those who experienced this at the time was, to use their own words, greater than if they had seen "an elephant dancing."[12] Centuries of mixing two cultures preceded this. Gurdjieff's music was different in this respect. It is the result of the will and determination of a single person.

How is it possible that a person could remember all these melodies so precisely decades later? The ability to immediately reproduce music that has just been heard is an ability many musicians possess. This natural talent usually manifests itself at an early age.

---

12 Described in *Mister Jelly Roll* by Alan Lomax, 1952 Cassel, Co. An example of good musical research.

The composer Scriabin amazed his parents when, barely four years of age, he played the music of a passing brass band on the piano. Mozart's and Felix Mendelssohn-Bartholdy's abilities in this area are legendary. But does the ability to immediately reproduce music explain why it is possible to remember it for so long? Does memory not have a lot to do with the quality of awareness at the moment that the observation takes place? Exposure through awareness fixes what we have observed in our memory; we cannot recollect a moment that was not consciously experienced. Could it be that Gurdjieff's music, most likely without his intending it so, demonstrated a quality of his consciousness?

THE HYMNS

In two cycles from this oeuvre, and possibly the most impressive, it remains unclear if they originate from an unknown source or if Gurdjieff composed them himself. I am referring to the musical fragments from the ballet *Struggle of the Magicians*, which he claimed came from an unknown tradition, and the *Hymns from a Great Temple*. In the area where Gurdjieff travelled, musicological fieldwork hardly takes place today, never mind a hundred years ago. So nothing of certainty can be said about this. Even so, the *Hymns from a Great Temple* share common ground like chapters that follow each other in a book. Their strength is that of a monument that, from deepest antiquity, suddenly opens our eyes—a sign from another world that has, solely through its improbability and anachronistic existence, managed to put into perspective everything we thought we knew and understood. We are left with the impression that, in these hymns, important things are "related" step by step. The form aspects of some of these pieces are even extraordinary for Gurdjieff's own work. It occurs to me that some musical forms could be an attempt to reproduce sounds, on the piano, of events that have no sound or make another sound. This could be unknown instruments, but also ritual gestures, or an advancing ritual step in a procession.

In the first hymn, which begins with three long notes, in the middle of the composition at three random places, strange low tones resound, which appear to have no musical function. Is this an interpretation of the gong beats during a liturgical ritual? Analysis of the piece shows that it is a depiction of the Law of Seven. Several musical reasons, such as the height of the melody's tone and the "question and answer" model, point in the direction of a sung piece of music, with a lead singer and a community that answers the song. An unknown instrument, big and heavy, hammers out seven tones, time after time, in a ritual that might have taken place to anchor the Law of Seven in the consciousness of those present. Of course, no analysis could ever replace the music itself, I provide this proposition only in an attempt to stimulate the listener to develop a vision of their own. But, even if this is just a flight of fantasy and there is no question of the mimicking of the sounds, it still seems as though the sounds in this hymn have an almost tangible strength.

De Hartmann believed that Gurdjieff had heard these hymns in one or more temples, and I suspect that de Hartmann's opinion is correct. Above all, I am of the impression that this music has been reproduced with exacting precision, note for note, and I consider it possible that Gurdjieff did indeed hear this music in certain shrines, which he did not want to specify at a later date. There is absolutely no doubt that they are the musical pinnacle of the work of these two composers.

Gurdjieff's own creativity is clear and bountiful in his hymns. A hymn is a sung prayer, and some of these pieces do indeed evoke associations with the choral singing from Greek Orthodox liturgy. Once again, these reflect memories from his youth when he sang in such a choir. But most of the hymns do not bear this comparison, and these others are the most striking. The hymns were composed by Gurdjieff himself, and if he had been influenced by other sources, they are not to be found on a map of folk and religious music. There is absolutely no influence from Western music.

De Hartmann harmonized the hymns in a traditional manner. He added three voices—the alto, tenor and bass—to the melody, the soprano. He knew his trade well and an excellent example of this is the four-part harmonization of the "Greek Melody" (Schott I, 1). But his harmonization in the traditional four voices did not always turn out so well, and sometimes a certain degree of predictability creeps in as a result of this traditional approach. Now there are many places in the hymns where the chords suddenly deviate sharply from what our musical theory would have dictated. These are Gurdjieff's own harmonies! He stepped in here, and these—for our ears—unusual sounds, are of his hand, and not from de Hartmann.

An Unusual Element in the Hymns

The following analysis of the hymns employs the technical musical terms "fourth" and "fifth," and to make this accessible to everyone I invite you to accompany me on a slight digression.

We suddenly find ourselves in the South of the United States in the year 1929, in a time when trains still had steam locomotives pulling them, thundering past endless cotton fields and plantations with their whistles screeching. They did this at set times of the day, dividing the day into recognizable time-intervals for the people who did not have watches. For the black population in the area, the train had even more significance. It embodied freedom. Trains headed north, where the cities offered employment and there was less discrimination. The sound of the trains on the journey to freedom, the rhythm of the wheels on the rails, the jolting of the wagons as the direction was changed by points, yes, even the hunger and thirst of the travellers, and especially the longing for family and loved ones they had left behind, all this was transformed into music with the same mastery as Gurdjieff did with Eastern rituals that he had experienced.

These trains had legendary names: the "Southern," or the "C and A" mentioned in the short poem, or stanza, by the blues singer Peetie Wheatstraw:

> Let me tell you folks what the C and A will do to you
> Let me tell you folks what the C and A will do to you
> It will take your woman away and blow black smoke back at you!

Here, someone who is left behind expresses his grief. The first sentence is repeated as always in blues music. The melody of both the stanzas is almost the same, but the second time it is accompanied by a fourth—two-and-a-half tones higher than the keynote from the first. This procedure, a law in the Blues, is unusual in Western music. Western music has a preference for first exchanging the keynote with a fifth, which sits a tone higher than the fourth, but has far more in common with the keynote, and consequently sounds more pleasant to the ear. In this example, it is not about something pleasant, it is about oppression and grief. This is why first the fourth is chosen—it creates tension. Only later, in the third line does the fifth resolve this musical tension. In brief: the quarter evokes tension, the fifth resolves it.

Blues music is based on the effect of the fourth and fifth on our emotions, and I provided an example that may have raised the question about what this has to do with Gurdjieff's music. In my example the train is irrelevant, but the fourth and fifth are everything. The simultaneous resounding of fourth and fifth is unusual in Western music! Not the case with Gurdjieff. In one of his most interesting hymns, "The Resurrection of Christ" (Schott III, 50), he does almost nothing else. As if to suggest that the solution—the rebirth, the fifth—must go together, taking place simultaneously, with living through the inevitability of death, the fourth. Thanks to his compositional skills, this does not result in a cacophony, but actually in a feeling of peace, an ascension from the earth.

In the hymn "Prayer and Despair," too, simultaneous resounding of the fourth and fifth play a role. The musical principle is the same, but it has a different meaning here and is more difficult to observe. In the left hand the fourth can be heard, and in the right hand the fifth. Let me clarify this. The entire piece comprises three separate sections, which are even separate on the keyboard of the piano. The middle section is without question the prayer referred to in the title. This is the formula that forms the foundations for the piece. It is of a tranquil beauty, but also a mathematical pattern in which the numbers three and seven are interwoven.[13] This formula is continually taken over by the left hand, in the lower register of the piano but not completely. In the entire piece this does not get further than the fourth: that is, the formula as expressed in the left hand gets stuck at the fourth note and cannot reach the fifth. It does not come to its natural solution and therefore gives a taste of something uncompleted, a tension evoking in our feeling an association with the experience of human sorrow.

We only hear the solution of the fifth in the middle prayer-section. High above these two parts we hear an uninterrupted melody, an infinite melody, and perhaps a predecessor of the music he would later play on his harmonium. I cannot interpret these sections as anything but, from the left hand (expressing the Earth), to the middle section . . . the formula (the situation of humans), to the right hand's melody (the promise of the heavens). Earth, humans, heavens. Desperation is expressed in the turmoil and drama of the left hand, the Earth. The heavens are the high melody, far removed from this. Interspersed, renewed each time, the prayers can be heard. Could the meaning be anything else but the solution of the tension caused by the earthly situation only being resolved through prayer—an inner prayer, originating from the experience of the Laws of Three and Seven?

---

13 For a description of this piece of music see the opening of Chapter 5.

I have limited myself to the fourth and the fifth here, but if this has aroused your interest in the emotional content of all the tones of the octave, I suggest you listen to the "Religious Ceremony" (Schott III, 21). There they are all depicted in sound. The intermediate tones in the octave each symbolize an inner development, and this composition expresses the various stages and corresponding emotions where words fall short.

As familiar as we have become with the individualization of the arts, it is unusual for us that a work professes to depict universal laws in the way in which all of Gurdjieff's hymns do. This individualization is a recent phenomenon that first began following the French Revolution. Prior to this, every scientist and artist would have considered it a strange idea that a work of art would not have had close ties with the principles that govern our own existence as well as those of the entire universe.

THOMAS DE HARTMANN

In this chapter, the role of de Hartmann, the joint composer, has been left in the shade. Thomas Alexandrovich de Hartmann (1866-1956) was from the highest circles of Russian aristocracy and as a composer he was a sharply rising star when he met Gurdjieff in 1916. Pavlova and a debuting Nijinsky, the top of the Russian ballet of the time, danced in his ballet *The Pink Flower,* performed in the presence of the Czar. His teachers in harmony and composition were also those of his older friend, Scriabin. In Munich, he made another life-long friend in Kandinsky, for whose play *The Yellow Sound* he wrote the music.

Married to the singer Olga de Schumacher, de Hartmann played an important role in the cultural life of St. Petersburg. After their first encounter with Gurdjieff, the de Hartmann couple gave up their lives in St. Petersburg and followed him through the Caucasus, Georgia, Istanbul and Germany to Fontainebleau. In 1929, a rift occurred between de Hartmann and Gurdjieff. They would never see each other again. This did not lead to a decline in the respect de Hartmann had for his former teacher.

Although de Hartmann independently, beyond his work with Gurdjieff, wrote almost one hundred pieces of music, operas, symphonies, and piano sonatas, he was forgotten less than ten years after his death. He had been joint director of the music publishers Belaieff, but they no longer reprinted his work. In an encyclopedia of music, one could only find a brief entry for him. It was not his own one hundred compositions, but the musical works for which he had been of service to his teacher that slid him back into the star gallery of classical composers. This was only possible because de Hartmann was talented, well schooled, and had a tremendous ability for musical arrangement.

De Hartmann is one of Gurdjieff's two pupils who sacrificed a glorious career to follow a then-unknown teacher with a dubious reputation. Ouspensky, to whom de Hartmann dedicated his second piano sonata, was the other. How should we view this self-denial? Is this act not symbolic of what everyone who finds themselves on a spiritual path must do? Give up a part of oneself, so that a new, larger part can take its place? Did the simplicity and tremendous clarity of the music of Gurdjieff/de Hartmann not come about because of this?

The music of Gurdjieff and de Hartmann tells us the listeners, just as all good music does, that life and the creative force from which it comes is basically good, despite the excess of evidence to the contrary that we are presented with.

12

OBJECTIVITY AND SUBJECTIVITY IN ART

The Gods reside in the realm of mathematics.

– Novalis

Gurdjieff made a distinction between objective and subjective art, between art that can be read like a book, providing the language it has been written in is comprehended, and art that comes from random associations. Objective art always has the same effect. In the case of subjective art, this is different for everyone, and in the case of an individual, the effect is dependent on his or her mood at a moment in time. The benchmark for objective art is consciousness. The standard for subjective art is the unconscious. Only consciousness is able to create. In all other cases, something happens in the artist that he or she does not understand for themselves, and is understood even less by others, in turn at the mercy of random impressions and associations.

The preceding paragraph is a summary of what Gurdjieff said on this topic, in 1915, 1916, 1919 and 1924. His explanation was simple, and he answered questions with examples of objective art referencing Eastern art and ancient rituals. On many occasions, he repeated that objective art originated from mathematical knowledge, which has nothing to do with talent and can be expressed in any area. There are no limits to its possibilities. In 1924, he was put to the test with a number of direct questions, especially about whether, with this form of knowledge, someone could write compositions equal to those of Schubert. Gurdjieff confirmed that all that was necessary was knowledge of the mathematical formula.

All Gurdjieff's early oral introductions to his ideas were later sketched out in full detail in his books, and he gave them substance in his music and Movements. The center of gravity in his writings on the subject "objective vs. subjective art" is contained in the chapter "The Bokharian Dervish Hadji-Asvatz-Troov" in *Beelzebub's Tales to His Grandson*. The human sensitivity with which this impressive chapter was written, as well as an unmistakably autobiographical passage, demonstrate Gurdjieff's heavy involvement with this subject. As always, Gurdjieff's previous verbal explanation related to his written descriptions in the way that a primitive drawing of a skeleton does when compared to a colorful anatomical print, on which not just the frame but also the muscles, organs, blood vessels, lymph glands and nerve bundles are depicted in detail.

What struck me especially about this chapter (the contents of which I shall not attempt to summarize) is that parts of the story work on your emotions: such as the dramatic life story of the dervish who grew not in external but inner wealth, or the struggle of a learned European who attempted in vain to cure his wife of cancer. Other sections provide material for mental reflection: such as descriptions of the experiments of the dervish in his laboratory. The stimulation of the physical center is not forgotten in this carefully staged history: the description of the landscape and that of the cave in which the dervish lived could be taken as being analogous with the human body and its environment. So too, the sources of energy in the cave could be taken as the sources of energy supplying the human body. I interpret this three-fold approach as an indication that there is not much point to thinking about such a subject if the emotional life and the body do not each process the theme in their own way. Gurdjieff's text breathes a mystical atmosphere and invites lengthy reflection, rather than a rational interpretation, but the latter here is unavoidable in my introduction to this particular chapter.

THE CHALLENGE OF UNDERSTANDING

The idea (expressed in Gurdjieff's concept of objective art) appears dogmatic and is often perceived as such, with the result that one person accepts it hook, line and sinker and another pushes it aside as complete nonsense. Representatives of these two conflicting views on the subject can dispute this forever without coming a step closer. I have experienced the same in my efforts to comprehend what is meant by objective art. I want to get somewhere, as if in a dream that many people have, but I am held back by invisible hands. From where I am now, I have resigned myself to the fact that there are works of art that exist which may only be "contacted" in exceptional circumstances, that is, if we find ourselves in a state that corresponds with the consciousness in which the work was created. This could come across as a flight into vagueness, and consequently I must add that this degree of understanding has not taken place without a considerable struggle for me.

For many years and regularly, for days, sometimes weeks, this topic has consumed me with the intensity of someone in the grip of an obsession. The stage of my "wrestling with an angel" was music, a field that is familiar to me and was also important to Gurdjieff. This was my first point of reference. The second contextual influence is that I have collected vast materials that mainly originated with others. With these as my platform, I have given this topic of objective art thorough consideration. I am not trying to think up "something new" so to speak—I gave up the belief in that long ago—but to clearly categorize, in an orderly manner, the many experiences I have had in music that relate to and open up this question. Just a few of these categories include:

1. Memories of proverbs, sayings, stories and legends that I have heard or read about that appear to have something to do with this theme.

2. That which has been related to me by musicians, musicologists and music therapists in personal conversations that touch on this topic.
3. Possible answers to the question of how objectivity in music could be recognized.
4. To what extent is it possible, through music, to make contact with the thoughts, feelings and sensory perceptions of people from other times and places?
5. To what extent is it possible, emotionally or physically, for one or more listeners to absorb a single musical tone, or a single chord, and in doing so shorten or lengthen it?
6. The specific emotional responses from test subjects in hearing a piece of music in the following scales: diatonic major, diatonic minor, the "gipsy" key, the "Arabic" scale, the pentatonic scale, and finally the "whole tone" scale.

The second category alone, noted above, has become so extensive that I could fill a book with it and, due to the scope of this current book, it is quite impossible for me to list its contents here. This is a pity, as I have had a great number of conversations with people who have dedicated their lives to this topic: musicologists, composers, music therapists and famous performing musicians. They excelled in the originality of their research or their immense musical talents, and I would gladly quote them under other circumstances. I did, however, write down all their statements, and where it was possible I drew my conclusions from them.

For example, I concluded that it is far more difficult to understand music than is commonly accepted. The most important spokespeople believed that the content of music is in many cases entirely misunderstood by others, due to the restriction of culture, geographical location or period. The opinion was unanimous that this applies for folk music if it is devoid of experience, since childhood, of the cultural values of the group from which it originates. With regard to classical music, Pan-Islamic classical music, the Indian musical tradition, and Javanese and Balinese court music, some believe that it is understood to a degree, but only at the expense of great tenacity and years of dedication. All their statements appear to agree more or less with Gurdjieff in his indication of the subjectivity of the listener.

A TURNING POINT, A STORY

The decisive stimulus for the collection of data that I categorized came from a story that was once related to me. My memories of that conversation go back over fifty years. It all took place in the night and in a car, the driver of which had picked me up as a hitchhiker. We crossed a mountainous region, which was noticeable from the climbing and descending of the vehicle and the endless hairpin bends. There was not much to see, except for strange dream images—like ghosts that float through a house in the night—mingling with reality from my brief moments of sleep. The driver, probably as fatigued as I was, talked to me to overcome the sleep-inducing monotony of the trip. The night and the unfamiliarity with someone you will never see again can move a person to greater openness. This was clear from the account that I heard from the driver, whose face I could barely make out. Between the sentences, which have been strung together here, were long pauses that felt in some way or another heavier than in a normal conversation during the day, as though the silences were mixed with the mystery of the night.

> *You might not be able to hear it from my French, but I am actually Greek. You just told me that you make music and I would like to tell you something that my father experienced. Unfortunately, the Greeks and Turks regularly bait for each other's blood, and in one of the many armed-conflicts my father, as a Greek soldier, was captured as a prisoner of war by the Turkish army. He was taken to a camp in an*

isolated area of Turkey. I no longer recollect how long he was there, but it must have been a number of years, at least. The treatment of the captives was not so bad, and after my father had been released he forgot about it fairly quickly. But one thing left a deep impression on him and he told me about this with tears in his eyes. Weather permitting, the prisoners were allowed to sit in front of the barracks in the late evening, to breathe some fresh air and behold the evening skies in silence. On the other side of the barbed wire were the Turkish guards. They too sat outside. They sat together on the grass in a circle, with their legs crossed and their guns resting on their laps. They spoke very little and were as quiet as the prisoners. Sometimes, one of the guards would pick up a saz and begin to play.[1] *A slow and piteous melody struck up, and whether it was because it expressed the sorrow and loneliness of the prisoners, or that it originated from the melancholy mood of the evening, it affected all the prisoners so deeply that they all, without exception, began to cry. Strangely enough, the music had the same effect on the Turkish guards on the other side of the barbed wire. They too cried. The melody persisted as the evening became the night, the precursor of the loneliness of death.*

What kind of music was this with the power to evoke the same feelings in the hearts of people who were supposed to be each other's enemies?

LOOKING TO GURDJIEFF'S OWN WORDS

Another possibility for examining the theme of "objective and subjective art" is to scrutinize the content of the words that Gurdjieff himself used, and from the range of meanings that each of these words could

1 A saz is a stringed instrument with a ball-shaped body and a long neck, usually with three double strings. It is the most commonly played instrument in Turkish folk music.

have, only to perceive the most likely intended meaning. In doing this, we relieve ourselves of all the undertones that these words evoke in us, and perhaps we will better understand the topic. Again, in this exercise, I will limit myself to music.

Gurdjieff used common words to proclaim his ideas, such as "art," "subjective," "objective," "mathematical formula," "scientific" and "consciousness." Each text with these kinds of words is a labyrinth without Ariadne's thread to lead us. To begin with, the collective word "art" in this chapter is, as I note above, limited to the word "music." There are countless types of music, and a comparison with the multiplicity of languages that are spoken on the Earth, currently more than seven thousand, does not fall short.

To create some order in this mosaic it is useful to think in terms of three types of music: ritual music, folk music, also known as ethnological music, and the types I call "cultural music," an inadequate term, but I know of no better one. This categorization must not be seen too rigidly. These three types of music are points of concentration in a field that is constantly in flux. They overlap and influence each other, and their mutual relationships are different in each culture. Even so, these three points of concentration have an essentially different core and another social function; and what is especially different is the way in which the listener responds. The inner point of contact in people is different, and it appears that each of these three forms of music cause movement in a different part of the inner self.

For example, in the case of ritual or folk music, it is the *whole person* who participates in the music, just like with national costumes, traditions, passed-down stories and dances from a certain group of the population. Everyone, child or adult, in a community in which these traditions still exist knows this music through and through, and they do not consider their music, focused on the highlights of human existence—birth, marriage and death—as "culture" or something that is separate from actual life.

Cultural music, a description that covers almost all music we hear and continue to hear, such as classical music, jazz music and all their derivatives, causes movement in a different part of the inner self. It is sufficient to limit this category to Western classical music. This has an honorable tradition; and one characteristic of it is that a lengthy, dedicated study is required to be able to play it. In the centuries in which such classical music was formed, it always reflected the social developments. It was composed by talented people who had something to add, or alter, to its form that was in step with the spirit of the times. This is a major difference from folk music, in which nothing is thought-through or changed. Unlike in folk music, in cultural music there is a division between musician and listener. The listener has now become passive and anonymous. As an individual, he sinks beneath the sea of people that populate a concert hall. Recordings are the following step in enlarging the distance between the musician and the listener.

Other characteristics from this category are that the instrumental contributions overshadow the use of the human voice, which is so important in folk and ritual music. Cultural music leans towards exaggerated expression and perhaps this is how composers and players attempt to break through the invisible wall that separates them from their listeners. Finally, cultural music, different again from folk music, is always the product of a special class or caste in society.

When Gurdjieff used the words "subjective art"—within the scope of our exercise in this chapter which is restricted to "subjective music"—did he then mean all of the categories described above? I assert that his judgment certainly does not cover two of these three forms: the ritual and the folk music. These, after all, amount to more than half of his own musical works. The man who was of the opinion that, "Everything that stems from the distant past and has remained unchanged is of value" is not about to accuse old folk music or rituals of subjectivity. Rather, he is likely referring to *the cultural form that is constantly changing*. Consequently, we can assume that the "subjective art" he was targeting is nothing more than Western cultural music, in other words "classical music." This suggests the likelihood that his idea covers more than just a qualification of arts, but is a disguised judgment of the whole of Western culture.

About "Subjective" / "Objective"

The meanings of other words, like "subjective," have to be investigated. Classical music is made by composers and musicians. Are they both as subjective as is alleged?

You need to have played in an orchestra only once to know that the countless rules you have to take into account are as numerous as the bars that keep a caged animal at bay. This is also true if a musician plays a solo. The performance of a piano sonata requires a lengthy study, and there is no end to the number of experts who will tell the pianist what he needs to improve. It appears that the performer has to forget his subjectivity to achieve as good as possible an interpretation. Clearly, it is even a difficult test for a professional to identify a soloist, based only on the sound, if single recordings of the same piece are played one after another, and each by other famous interpreters. Most people completely miss the point. This simple test demonstrates that even professionals cannot distinguish one famous interpreter from the other. That a performer demonstrates a personal subjectivity is difficult to defend. Subjectivity must be sought with the composer, who, according to Gurdjieff's indications, is influenced by stimuli that he did not understand himself, in contrast to the maker of objective music who has mathematical insight, according to a "formula."

However, it just happens that mathematical insight plays a major role in the *composition* of classical music. Let me clarify this with a recollection from my youth, when I was seventeen.

I was born in a city in the south of the Netherlands that comprised many textile factories, around which small homes were grouped for the textile workers. In one of these houses there lived a jazz musician who I had asked to help me with improvisation. Improvisation in jazz music is not much different from compositions by a classical composer, only the jazz musician does not write down what he has played and it is not his intention that others replicate his music. This jazz musician was thought of highly in the city's musical circles, which is why I visited him regularly. He must have been around thirty at the time. I sat in the small, dingy house next to his piano many times. I have seldom, in all my years, heard such a good pianist. He was not just creative, but he could also listen to a piano solo on a record and then replay it note for note, and could not understand why I could not do this. He never attained world fame. On the contrary, he led a sad and lonely existence. He played in nightclubs in Antwerp to earn his keep and hitchhiked back home in the morning with the truck drivers who were going his way. He once told me something, in his heavy local dialect, that has stayed with me. "You're playing all wrong. When you improvise, you have to hear in your head, beforehand, what you're going to play next. I can hear straight away if someone can do that or not. If he can't do it, the music is bad. If he can, the music is good."

This insight was completely new to me. As I cycled home that evening, through streets lined with the dark shapes of textile factories that in the morning would spring to life with the wail of their sirens and the rumbling of their looms, I repeated the sentence that had struck me: "First, hear it in yourself, only then do you play it." It seemed that, beneath music as I knew it, a great space had opened up, the existence of which I had no previous idea. I had only experienced music as a feeling, and now it was as though music was a magician's cardboard box, with a false bottom that had been opened.

All that could be hidden in the false bottom of a magician's box was related to me years later by my piano teacher: the composer and piano virtuoso Wolfgang Wijdeveld, a leading musician and personal friend of Béla Bartók's, whose work he was able to play with great gusto. Wijdeveld lived in Amsterdam in the same neighborhood as I did. Delighted, I wandered along the canal to my lessons, with my piano books for beginners under my arm. I never got the impression that my inadequacies in classical music were evaluated negatively. On the contrary, I always received a warm welcome and great patience, shrouded as it were in his ability and knowledge, set off against a greater perspective. For me, that greater perspective was especially his humanity and goodness. In one of his lessons, he proposed to me that a composer had to possess two things: perfect pitch and an absolute ability to imagine, also known as "an ability to render." This ability allows someone to imagine a piece of music he has heard in his mind in the same way as we call up letters, words and sentences that someone has spoken to us.

These two musicians confirmed that a composer has to possess considerable mental ability, and it is not coincidental that mathematical- and musical-aptitude broadly overlap. The merging of them was fleshed out by Aldous Huxley in his novella *Little Archimedes*, but it is not necessary for you to read this short story to be able to imagine that the forms in which melodies, chords and rhythms can link together are well-nigh infinite. In music, it helps to have an aptitude for mathematics to oversee this labyrinth, and the mathematical insight of a composer oversees this grid of possibilities and subsequently traces a musical line, the meaning of which is recognized by his generation or in the generations that follow.

It is not an exaggeration to claim that a composer such as Mozart employed *every* possibility of the theories of harmony of his time and linked them with *every* melody that could be formed from them. His music is based on a perfect balance of *mathematical* possibilities and *melodic* performance. That is the reason why it transmits such calmness and is therefore often referred to as "heavenly." The perfect balance achieved here, as that of a crystal mechanism of which the cogs turn gently above us, seems to no longer belong to this Earth. Hardly a second passes without Mozart's music being played somewhere on Earth, giving people a positive feeling, or soothing them and supporting them in difficult moments.

Based on these examples, Gurdjieff's words "mathematical insight" or "mathematical formula" are at least as applicable for classical, in his eyes "subjective," music as any other "objective music."

About "Mathematical"

"Mathematical" as intended by Gurdjieff is a scientific insight that cannot be related to the mathematical abilities of composers. This scientific insight originates from *consciousness*, an entity that apparently does not exist in the development of Western music. A conclusion such as this is logical and unavoidable after investigating the possible meanings of words used by Gurdjieff, even if it touches on the absurd. But the consideration does not stop there. As equally unknown as this "consciousness" are the possibilities it offers. The composition (if a certain mathematical formula was known, to return to the question that was put to Gurdjieff and to which he answered positively) of a piece of music that equals a piano sonata by Schubert is of course out of the question. Common sense will tell you so. But even if such an unlikely composition were possible, the question itself is trite in comparison to a question of the continued existance of the physical body after death. This after-death existance is a possibility that this "being" also has, according to Gurdjieff.

It is not my intention to criticize Gurdjieff's statements. If there is anyone who has a right to say something about this, it is only Gurdjieff himself. His virtuosity in three entirely different artistic disciplines is incomprehensible to a normal human being. This exercise to find Ariadne's thread by analyzing the possible meanings of the words used by Gurdjieff was doomed to failure because Gurdjieff's proposition cannot be derived from the field of the arts, just as the "Major Laws" cannot be distilled from the fields of mathematics or physics. These terms can only gain meaning once the boundaries of the domains "sol" and "la" of human development have been exceeded. In this area, a different mathematics applies: that of "cosmic mathematics." It is this area that Novalis meant in the epigraph at the beginning of this chapter, and undoubtedly Gurdjieff too when he spoke of a "mathematical formula." In this field, his ideas regarding "objective art" and his "Major Laws" can be experienced, and it is likely that these terms are closely connected, because the numbers upon which Gurdjieff's Laws are founded can be observed throughout his artistic creations, and their use is too ingenious to have been unconsciously included. They are also too artistic, surprising and natural to have originated from a ruse. How exactly the creative stimulus has merged with a dynamic of experience—of which a few numbers and geometric figures are just the outward characteristics—is difficult for me to imagine.

~

We stand at the threshold of an art form that has been formed on a different level. Kandinsky emphasized in his theoretical works that art can only be made from an inner necessity.[2] The next step has been taken here. In this art, the inner "being" is a precondition. This "being" does not just have to do with "thinking"; it has stored a substance in the emotions and in the body. According to Gurdjieff, an experience is only reality if it has found a place in the body and emotions. If a person knows this process, it is possible to stimulate the forming of these substances in others, and Gurdjieff's Movements are an excellent example of this.

---

2 W. Kandinsky, *Über das Geistige in der Kunst*, Piper & Co, Munich, 1912.

PART II

GURDJIEFF'S MOVEMENTS

13

WHAT ARE MOVEMENTS?

One can know about the details, but only understand the whole.

–J.G. Bennett

Solange Claustres (1920-2015) assisted Gurdjieff for seven years, from 1942 until his death, and throughout this period took part in the groups he led and in his Movements classes. In an interview dating from 1997, she described the Movements, but as an introduction she related meeting Gurdjieff for the first time.[1]

I met Gurdjieff in 1942 and that was the beginning of a period of seven years during which I was under his instruction. In direct contact, day after day, until his death. His teaching method was simple and exact, free of ceremony, and his instructions were absolutely logical.

We received weekly Movements classes from Gurdjieff in the "Salle Pleyel" in Paris. To provide an indication of the number of Movements that he gave our class at the time you should understand that every week, and this for seven years, he taught us at least one new Movement. He never explained too much. His presence was so strong—every corner of the room was filled—that you could absorb the new Movement or dance directly and that further explanation was unnecessary.

---

1 Published in *Bres* 186, October/November 1997, pages 9-15. Quoted with the kind permission of *Bres Magazine*.

Following Gurdjieff's death, when Ms. Jeanne de Salzmann continued his work, I taught groups and Movements classes at the Institut Gurdjieff in Paris, London and Amsterdam. When I speak about Gurdjieff's teaching or about his Movements, I do this from my direct and personal experience and from what I have processed in the last fifty-six years and that is not something to be considered as light-hearted or free of obligation.

She then described his Movements as follows:

All true Masters have a practical approach and in the Movements G.I. Gurdjieff's inner work of awakening is put into practice. The laws of evolution and human consciousness are encapsulated in these Movements and dances.[2] *They indicate how and in what direction the progression will have to take place and as such they are a "school" in the true sense of the word.*

Now I have used the word "law," I must add that in literature people often refer to Gurdjieff's "psychological" and "cosmological" laws. These words are not precise enough for me. The word "psychological" is too restrictive, too limited and the word "cosmological" too vague. It would be best if the latter word was avoided altogether.

We know different kinds of Movements: ritual Movements, prayers, dervish dances, Movements according to mathematical patterns, "tableaux" Movements in which the dancers arrange themselves in certain configurations and Movements especially for women. But the objective of all these Movements is a constant: all Gurdjieff's Movements are prayers. During a private conversation with Gurdjieff, I told him how deeply I was moved each time by his Movements. He only answered: "Yes . . . they are medicine . . ."

---

2 This sentence was written in different format, as per Ms. Claustres' instruction, as she wanted to emphasize the importance of this definition.

These dances have nothing to do with the search for ecstasy or illumination. They demand precision and dedication. In brief, a discipline. They have this in common with authentic Eastern martial arts. The physical stances must be adopted exactly. Even the slightest deviation, a slightly bowed head or the careless angle of an arm changes the effect of a position and not just the appearance. Something more important changes: the perception of ourselves that is evoked through the physical stance. Each position corresponds with an inner quality.

I recently studied Egyptian and early Christian poses and gestures with a group of students. It became clear to us that each variation, for example the left in place of the right hand or the distance between the hand and the chest, created a very different resonance and released a different feeling within us. This same principle applies but to a stronger degree to the Movements. Above all, the positions have to be adopted without unnecessary tensioning of the muscles, as this does not just cause a loss of energy, but also blocks free circulation of fluids within the body. In the first place, to be able to perform these dances we must be completely honest, accept a perception of ourselves that is not influenced by emotion or sentimentality.

We must develop an exceptional type of attention to prevent confusion as a result of the complex and asymmetric movements. We must focus our thoughts consciously on the chronology, the development of the dance and be able to voice words that belong with the dance or allow them to resound within us. This way, the body itself experiences them in its own way. The difference between theory and practice becomes clear when it concerns contact with the body. Everyone thinks that they can dispose of this at their discretion. This is not so and all theoretical knowledge will remain powerless until the moment that the body becomes active.

We are then moved by a new vision of ourselves, the music and the group as a whole. In this vision we realize that we are a component of an unfathomable objective construction, but one of great beauty. We have become part of an objective art form. In other words, we find ourselves in situations in which the laws of consciousness, because I must emphasize that this concerns laws, can be experienced by us. In a moment we are released from our habits, the ballast of our culture and social conditioning. A pure perception has become possible in which we can comprehend the evolutionary laws and this entire process demonstrates what I mean with becoming aware of ourselves. The following words summarize this: practical-knowledge-awakening and finally a new and more complete openness to further research.

Gurdjieff's dances are often referred to as "sacred dances," but the word "sacred" can evoke incorrect associations. Which is why I use the word "research" in the sense of internal research.[3]

If I compare these dances with those of modern classical ballet, by Béjart for example, I do not have the impression that they are easier to perform from a technical perspective: on the contrary the asymmetry is more difficult. With which I do not want to contest that this modern ballet does not require hard and constructive work. I have often observed in traditional Eastern dances that the inner presence of the performers does not correspond with what their body is expressing. From their facial expressions it appears that deep sobriety, so characteristic for the Movements, is absent.

That was the part of the interview in which Ms. Claustres clearly explained what the Movements involve. It is important to me that the answer to the question of what Movements are was given by one of Gurdjieff's pupils who received years of instruction in his classes and

---

3 The French word that was used by Ms. Claustres is *recherche*, which can be interpreted as meaning "investigation" as well as "aspire to," "yearning."

subsequently devoted her life, alongside her psychoanalytical practice, to the teaching of Movements. She was a talented interpreter, which is clear from the fact that Gurdjieff, when he was absent due to travelling, entrusted his class to her many times and from her place in the front row of Gurdjieff's class during performances or film recordings after his death. At the moment that she came into contact with Movements she was well prepared: not only had she attained a "Premier Prix piano" at a college of music, but she also had a black belt and seventh Dan in judo.

Ms. Claustres has written a book about her experiences with Gurdjieff, but the interview here is from before this time.[4] The advantage of an interview is that questions must receive an immediate answer, which gives them a certain spontaneity. Ms. Claustres agreed to my proposal at the time to hold an interview. It was the very first she had given. It has only been published once before, in Dutch, and I am very pleased that I have been able to publish parts of her text here with the permission of the copyright holders. This text deserves this, not just because she, in 1997, was one of the few of Gurdjieff's only surviving pupils, but also because on this occasion she spoke openly about Movements, something that then, just as today, seldom happened. At the time, I translated the Dutch text into French for her prior to publication and she authorized it.

In 1996 and 1997, I had frequent contact with Ms. Claustres because she had encouraged me to hold performances of Gurdjieff's music, especially as she mediated on my behalf for the first recital completely devoted to Gurdjieff's music in a concert hall of international significance, the Large Hall of the Amsterdam Concertgebouw, in which Alain Kremski and I each shared half of the program. She also

---

4 The interview was held on the 22nd and 23rd of March 1997. Ms. Claustres' book: *La Prise de Conscience et G.I. Gurdjieff* appeared in 2003 and the English translation in 2005, both published by Eureka Editions, Utrecht, The Netherlands.

generously wrote an introduction to Gurdjieff's music for the publication of a CD of my first interpretation of his work.[5]

I can still remember very clearly the days of the interview, which took place in March 1997 in her old house in the heart of the Latin Quarter in Paris. The conversations went on deep into the night. I learned more about the Movements than in any other conversation, or perhaps better said, I saw more than can be represented in the written word. As though her words, stemming from her direct experiences, lent the veil that hides the Movements a momentary transparency. What I saw appeared to be a battle between the light of truth and the great importance of the Movements, flowing immediately from the "being" of the spiritual teacher, and the darkness of the subjective interpretation of them by others, such as myself, similar to the darkness that the part of the metropolis I was residing in at that moment was cloaked in.

---

5 This text was later republished in *The Harmonic Development*, G.J. Blom, Basta Audio-Visuals, 2004, The Netherlands.

14

MY FIRST EXPERIENCES WITH MOVEMENTS

Whatever was not of the body leaves no memory
– Yehuda Amichai

Normally, if I go back into my memories, I see images fixed in time. I move from image to image, from period to period, but my memory of my first encounter with Movements resides somewhere else, where time plays no role. It has lost nothing of its strength, because this was a new experience without any connection with what my life had presented me before.

I still attempt to comprehend why I then thought that I had perceived a penetrating light, evoked through the combination of movements that my body performed to an unfamiliar kind of music, and why I believed that I had made contact with a source that emitted a force so intense that the place from which I perceived myself no longer appeared to be within myself, but far above, and why this force encompassed not only myself but the entire room and all the other people. I cannot explain the force of these impressions, except to say that a part of my brain was activated that had never been used before. This part must have always been there, but led a closed existence. This could also explain why such an experience remains an island in my memory. It would appear that there are more kinds of memories, which have no mutual contact, arranged in groups by the various circumstances in which we have experienced something.

This first experience felt like I had participated in a ritual. The circumstances at work in this ritual can easily be listed. In the first place, the Movements teacher, in this case Ms. Claustres, who fulfilled the task of leading the ritual in such a way that direct and physical contact with the energetic source of Gurdjieff's teaching could be brought about, made possible for her through her lengthy contact with Gurdjieff and her knowledge of the Movements. As a second element, a group of participants oriented in the same spiritual direction, and who together executed complex movements fitting for the ritual. The final attribute of this ritual was the music, at that moment played by a participant in this Movements class. In this particular case, it was music composed by Gurdjieff himself, something that is somewhat of an exception in Movements classes. I have wondered if my experience may have been different if the music by another composer had been played. I am almost certain that this would have been the case, which confirms for me how pure the ingredients in this alchemy must be, and how expertly, accurately and conscientiously these ingredients must be dosed to achieve a good result.

A striking difference with other religious or spiritual rituals was the absence of ecstasy. That a group of people can quickly recharge their batteries through engaging in something together is clear. You only need to have attended a football match to establish this fact. It is also easy enough to convey a group of well-willing souls to a state in which they lose their self-control and go into trance: the exchange of one level of consciousness for another. However gripping the view of another reality was in this experience of Movements, it was not at the cost of normal functions.

Movements are so constructed that these normal functions must remain continuously active. For exactly this reason, the new impression does not overturn the existing order; but, different perceptions occur simultaneously—a tangible component of Gurdjieff's discipline: the simultaneous contact with thoughts, emotions and the physical body, for example, or the experiencing of our inner world without us losing contact with the world around us.

Movements are a ritual created by Gurdjieff, and it is this ritual that Ms. Claustres calls the "practical approach" in the previous chapter. Gurdjieff's teaching is experienced directly through the body and not as a theory. It must be emphasized that both Ms. Claustres and myself describe Movements from the perspective of a practitioner, from participation in the process and not from observing them. Watching a Movements class can leave a lasting impression, but this is less effective. Watching a film also leaves an impression, but this bears little relation to practicing Movements yourself.

Something remarkable happened at the conclusion of my first class. Ms. Claustres told us to sit down at the place we had occupied during the class and asked us to relax our bodies. After this, she walked the rows, checking the tension in our shoulders through moving them gently to and fro. An older, powerfully-built man was apparently very tense, because after attempting to induce movement in his shoulders, she called out despairingly: "This man is more rigid than a rock from the Alps. How on earth can one work on Movements like this?" The man in question appeared so wretched and helpless that a brave young woman in our class stuck up for him. "But Madame," she exclaimed as she got to her feet outraged, "You are talking to our teacher!" Ms. Claustres did not condescend to respond, walked back to her place in front of the class, spun around and said with complete conviction and as solemnly as a sentencing judge: "*He may talk about ideas as much as he wishes, but his body is not in the Work!*"

This is the first sentence of three key sentences that I have heard in the Gurdjieff Work about the role of the physical center and I can honestly admit that hardly a day goes by in my life that those three sentences do not cross my thoughts.

"The body must be in the Work . . . the body must be in the Work" . . . it rang in my ears as I cycled home after the class, as though my head had transformed into a Buddhist prayer-wheel. It struck me how nimbly my body maneuvered my old bicycle through the chaotic

Amsterdam traffic; quicker than any thought I had could be processed, I had taken and carried out all the right decisions. As an unexpected result of the lesson, I felt my body from inside out and how the tension and relaxation of my leg muscles alternated, depending on the position of the pedals. "What would you be without your legs?" a voice within me seemed to say. A new wave of thoughts washed over me. "It is not just legs that have been cut off in my attempts to understand life, but I have forgotten my entire body." I then thought it a good idea to get off my bicycle and to sit next to the canal, so that I could think quietly about the matter of how it was possible that I had my entire life denied the reality of my body through chasing after all manner of nutty ideas. I thought more deeply. Could it be that our culture of the duality of body and soul could be wrong, or at the very least incomplete? I returned to my bicycle and, without especially thinking about it, I was struck by the great difference between the many office and bank employees who were walking towards the station, with their neat suits and black brief cases, and a group of manual workers who were busy with concrete pipes in a large pit. The first ones looked like lost souls in an underworld, the second group of men were lively and their bodies exuded pride and strength. That this was also expressed in the shouting of obscenities to young female passers-by, who were addressed in broad Amsterdam slang as "crumpet," did not bother me. They could let themselves go, because through their physical work and the society in which they lived they had been degraded to the lowest rung. The cold shadows of the "neat suits," on the other hand, stood higher up the ladder and were also far better paid. Was there perhaps a relationship between denial of the body and a higher social status? Was this not also the case in the so-called higher regions of philosophy and religion? Was it not that thinking with infinite speculation, comparable to a rat that ceaselessly attempts to escape from a maze through running this way and that, is considered as higher because physicality is suppressed?

Later, I heard a story that was related by Gurdjieff. "Imagine a stray dog, the likes of which so many run around here in Paris: skinny, smelly and with a poor coat. What kind of life do they have? Fearful as he is, jumping at the smallest noise, and if you try to approach him, he immediately runs away. He drifts around. He has to eat and sniff every pile of rubbish. But now and again, lost in the maze of alleyways and streets, he can remember that he once, long ago, had a master. Suddenly, he stands still as a statue and pricks up his ears. Was that perhaps the voice of his master there in the distance? No . . . disheartened he struggles along. The dog is our body!"

15

THE OUTWARD APPEARANCE OF MOVEMENTS AND THE SOUL OF A DOLL

A puppet has no, or infinite awareness . . .
even the best dancer cannot compare . . .

– Heinrich von Kleist

I was once told of a journalist who, after observing a Movements rehearsal, addressed Gurdjieff as follows: "Mr. Gurdjieff, this has nothing to do with dancing; they appear to be puppets." "Certainly," answered Gurdjieff, "you're right about that. From the outside they appear to be puppets, but inside they are free!"

This is true. Time after time, I have seen how people entered a Movements class, behaving in a way that was normal for them. During instruction, they were asked to practice exact, geometric body positions that appeared unnatural for everyone. What was so wonderful was that, after the class had ended, the participants made a stronger impression on me; they were far more themselves.

On another occasion, Gurdjieff was asked: "Why don't you opt for the graceful gestures of Isadora Duncan, Mr. Gurdjieff, and do the Movements have to be so wooden and stiff?" In broken English, Gurdjieff replied, "This more honest."

The outward appearance of Movements is determined by the geometric positions of the limbs, the torso and the head. The comparison with a wooden puppet or a Javanese shadow-theatre puppet is very accurate. At all the positions that a person has moveable joints, so too do these puppets. Each individual part of the limbs of the puppet—for example, the upper arm, forearm and hand, as well as the torso and the head—can be moved by the puppeteer with strings, independently of the other parts. The building blocks from which a Movement is composed are the same, not dependent on strings of course, but from the conscious movement of the independent parts—which are exactly the same in a person as they are in a marionette—to bring them into a predetermined geometric position. The word "dancing" is an incorrect label for Movements. The Movements that were especially created for women could be called such, but none of the others.

AN EXERCISE

Let us now turn our words into deeds.

Stand up and correct your posture; put your feet together and try to stand up straight, as though a line runs from the middle of your skull to the ground. Avoid any unnecessary muscle tension to remain standing, and try to find a position in which your frame keeps itself in balance. Try to make contact with the body. To use Gurdjieff's image as described at the end of the previous chapter, try to win the trust of the stray dog through opening yourself to the organic life of your body.

Stretch out your right arm horizontally in front of you, with your hand extended in line with your arm, palm facing downwards. In doing so, you have already adopted one of the basic Movement positions.

Without moving your upper arm, moving only the muscles in your elbow joint, now raise your forearm with extended hand into a ninety-degree angle, until it is vertical, your palm is now facing forward. This is a second position.

Do not move anything else, but retain contact with your entire body, so that your attention is not just focused on the part of your body that is moving. Then, move only the muscles in your shoulder joint and move your entire arm to the side of your body, the palm is now facing right. Position three.

You can now stretch your entire arm to the right, once again through only moving the elbow joint, so that it is completely horizontal. Position four.

This is accompanied by music, or at least by a rhythm. You can perform the gestures in time to the beats, which will make it four/four time.

The new position is adopted, after which there is a brief rest. It is important that you do not move any part of your body during this short elapse of time. Thus, you can experience the effect this position has on your body, as though you can capture a picture of your inner self in the situation in which you are now to be found.

You make each gesture in four parts. This gives four beats to move from position one to position two. Then, to achieve position three, the quarter of the circle that your arm travels through must be divided precisely into four, in time to the rhythm.

The reason the mind has little time for thought is that you are "multitasking," that is, repeating a counting sequence—sometimes simply 1,2,3,4, but often in a cyclical way (1,2,3,4, –2,3,4,1, –3,4,1,2, and –4,1,2,3), which requires a type of concentration or attention, thereby undermining other thoughts. In some cases, instead of counting one uses letters, or another name, for example: a,b,c,d, –b,c,d,e, –c,d,e,f, etc. These numbers or names lend the thoughts little opportunity during the movements to make associations or to drift briefly into dreaming, which do not just influence thoughts but also the body, and drag emotions along behind them.[1]

The legs can also respond to the rhythm, for example, by making a small rhythmic bend with both knees at each beat, through which the

---

1 One can count both aloud or to oneself without sound. Gurdjieff once said that the numbers should seem as if they were projected on a screen in front of your eyes. Interesting advice, because it reduces any body participation normally evoked by counting either aloud or inwardly.

torso makes an upright movement—downwards and back upwards again. The left arm can make other movements, independently of the right arm, following the same rhythm, creating the asymmetry that Ms. Claustres mentioned in her description.

However simple these movements may appear, the possibilities for variation are infinite. Let us take a small variation. Instead of an outstretched hand with the palm facing downwards in the first position, we can begin with the hand in "profile," which means the little finger is now downwards and the hand assumes the shape of a cutting knife. This amendment, albeit only of the hand, does affect all three other positions, although these are initiated only from the shoulder joint. And, once again, independent leg and head positions can be added.

The exercise described above provides an impression of the positions and their sequence from which a Movement could be created. Movements are an organic whole, and so varied that a single example is certainly insufficient.

POSITIONS, EMOTIONS AND EFFORTS

Geometric positions occur a lot less often in the early phase of Gurdjieff's Movements, in which we encounter more ethnological influences, and the Movements sometimes relate a story, sometimes with dramatic, theatrical gestures. The precision of the geometric positions strikes everyone who sees or practices Movements for the first time, as does the absence of any form of free expression. This can give the impression that they are only mechanical patterns, with little in common with human sensitivity. This is true with regard to the emotions that comprise our normal daily lives; there is no room for their expression in Movements. But another process is initiated. The body and the thoughts of the dancer are no longer in the grip of habits and, in the space that is created, a new energy flows in with each change of position. A silence occurs in the dancer's inner self, dissociated not only from habitual physical and thought patterns, but also from the normal wave of emotions. While the thoughts and the body fulfill their tasks in their own areas, the emotions can orientate themselves in a new direction. Each moment is lent a certain timelessness, and even the walls of the hall in which the work is taking place appear to dissolve into a space without boundaries—a space in which the past and future no longer exclude each other. This could be called "the soul of the doll."

Different kinds of emotions are evoked through this practice: for instance, the desire and the courage to witness and experience the unknown in us. Our entire existence is usually just a successive course of habits: physically, instinctively and in our thoughts. It is not just that this circle of habits makes it very difficult to gain new experiences, it also saps our energy, just like parasites do with the vitality of their host. But, at the same time, this armor of habits protects our self-image. The practicing of a Movement destroys this armor, even if it is only for a brief time. The inner self becomes vulnerable and visible too, and it is this visibility that is the reason why observing a Movements class can leave such a deep impression. The entire process appears to be like the famous Freudian dream in which the dreamer finds himself in a crowded square and to his alarm discovers that he is completely naked.

Apart from the desire and courage to meet the unknown with eyes wide open, Movements also call upon other emotions: patience, perseverance and dedication. They demand one-hundred-percent effort, any less will just not do. This was a surprising discovery for me. In all the other things I had learned in life, this had never been the case. On the contrary, more often than not, I suddenly saw that a half-baked effort had become a set pattern in my life, and that this was sufficient for me to "make the grade." Where the absolute requirements concerned exams or compliance with social or traffic rules and the like, this was not such a bad thing, but the pattern had crept into the efforts that my own decisions, based on my own conscience, demanded. This had imperceptibly led to a split response to demands from the outside world, which were met with minimum effort, and also to the demands that came from me. Movements taught me, in a flash of insight, that a complete concentration of effort is required for taking a new step, of whatever nature it may be.

THE SOUL OF THE DOLL

The "soul of the doll" was movingly described at the turn of the last century by a dancer who never knew or performed a Movement, but whose vision was remarkable: Oskar Schlemmer (1888-1943). Schlemmer worked at the Bauhaus Academy in Dessau, Germany, from 1925 until 1929. As a theatre specialist, he was a colleague of famous avant-garde artists, including Kandinsky, and he acquired international fame with his *Triadic Ballet* for which Hindemith wrote the music. Schlemmer based his vision on an essay by Heinrich von Kleist (1777-1811) "About the Marionettes Theatre."

In a nutshell, Schlemmer's theory is that humanity, as a consequence of the "original sin," is only able to make completely subjective physical gestures, and likewise in adopting positions. Only through the purely geometric expressions of the body can we approach the Divine and reacquire the innocence we once had.[2] Schlemmer's idea does tally with the insights of the German romantic poet Novalis, who was quoted in the first part of this book. According to him, words have no meaning, because they will always suggest something else from what we wish to convey. Because geometrically- and mathematically-determined positions cannot, by definition, exist in our empirically observed world—after all, lines or planes have no thickness, angles

2 As described by: E. Roters, *Maler am Bauhaus*, Rembrandt Verlag, Berlin, 1965.

and projections, and are all of an abstract accuracy (i.e., they have no substance)—they do not fall prey to this confusion, but are part of (and bear witness to) the spirit world.

I have never heard or read a better description than that of Schlemmer's, which puts into words the matter from which "the soul of the doll" is made. That he wrote this text at the moment that Gurdjieff was developing his Movements demonstrates the existence of mysterious forces through which, at a certain period in time, the same experiments are performed independently of each other by different people in different geographic locations.[3]

The idea of employing the image of a doll to describe Movements may seem far-fetched, but the doll that comes to life is not just a familiar image in legends and children's stories, like *Pinocchio*, it was employed freely at the turn of the last century in painting—in German Expressionism, for example, or in the paintings by the Italian painter De Chirico, whose curious dolls populate tranquil dream landscapes. It was also used by Gurdjieff himself. In his second book, *Meetings With Remarkable Men*, one can read how in a remote monastery he learned of temple-dancing that had been passed on through the generations. This dancing employed constructions of adult-human size, in which human joints had been simulated—also a kind of doll. These special ritual objects had a ball in each joint on which numbers were engraved, in such a way that a certain number corresponded with each position of a limb. A complex body position could be exactly replicated on the basis of a series of numbers originating from all the joints. This is an exceptionally ingenious invention, but of course no longer possible to ascertain if it was based

3 An indirect bond does exist between Schlemmer and Gurdjieff. For a time, Schlemmer worked with the dancers Albert Burger and Elsa Hötzel, who were both pupils of Dalcroze. I will come back to the similarities between the methods employed by Dalcroze and Gurdjieff later.

on fact or fiction.[4] It is also very possible that Gurdjieff, during the time that he worked in his "universal workshop," was offered dolls for repair in addition to the most impossible objects.[5] The porcelain toy dolls from the end of the nineteenth century also had joints in which a ball facilitated the movement of the limbs. It is neither here nor there to me whether Gurdjieff's story is based on truth or not. In the case that he thought up the idea, I would actually be more impressed by the creativity with which he had illustrated the movement principle of the Movements.

4 This tale can be found in *Meetings with Remarkable Men*, London, 1963, Routledge & Kegan Paul, pages 161 to 163. Gurdjieff's description of the monastery and its geographic position are discounted as pure invention by an expert on these areas and cultures, the author Martin Brauen. In his book *Dreamworld Tibet, Western Illusions*, 2004 (Orchid Press) he provides multiple reasons for this; amongst others, the impossibility that in such areas a monastery could have existed where men and women lived together.

5 For a fascinating description of this "universal workshop" in Gurdjieff's own words, see the last chapter of his book *Meetings With Remarkable Men*, called "The Material Question."

16

AN ONGOING JOURNEY OF DISCOVERY

Finding "The Great Prayer" and the Choreographies

After my first Movements lesson, I joined the Dutch branch of the French Institut Gurdjieff and participated in group meetings, where experiences with psychological exercises were exchanged and Movements classes were given by Ms. Claustres. From the very beginning, I was put behind the piano. There was no other pianist, and I accompanied the classes, sometimes through playing the music as on the sheet, but mostly through improvisations. Between times, when I was not playing the piano, I regularly joined the class, as Ms. Claustres believed that you could not accompany a Movement if you had not mastered it yourself.

Playing for these classes was new for me. It was quite different from the jazz music I was used to. It was not about playing "beautifully" or to move the audience with emotional or rhythmic outbursts. The intention was to support the class in focusing their concentration, which was required to be able to perform the complex Movements to a particular rhythm. I quickly learned that this was linked to my own concentration, because if my thoughts wandered, however briefly, I lost contact with the class and everything went off the rails. This is how I learned about the connection between awareness, by this I mean being present all the time in everything you do, and the quality of the music. A major effort was required to mobilize my attention for the duration of a Movement. Usually, they did not last longer than a couple of minutes, but they feel infinite if you do not allow yourself to slip away into dreamlike associations. This exhausted me to such an extent that I often fell asleep behind the piano during the break, as one class left and another assembled.

Besides concentration, other demands were made of my music, and these were really brought home to me. The search for the appropriate tempo was a recurring torment; it was not exceptional for it to take ten attempts before Ms. Claustres gave her approval. This was not the end of the ordeal, however, because any weakening in the strict regularity of the tempo would be indicated in a way that my ego could not always swallow. After my teacher had once called out, during one of these exercises, "Can't you play *anything* decently?"

I felt my blood boiling and answered, articulating each word slowly and clearly, "Yes, I can."

"Now, what are you waiting for?" was her quick fiery answer. In my anger, I swiftly mumbled a prayer to my trusty, musical guardian angel, the blues pianist Jimmy Yancey, upon which I rapidly hammered out one of his fast boogie-woogies on the keys. I do not know if my guardian angel could have had a positive influence, because Ms. Claustres took the bull by the horns and told the stunned class, in no uncertain manner, that she was sick of their passivity and that, without wasting another second, they should perform the Movement in time with the fast rhythm of the piece of music. This resulted in a hilarious scene that I will not quickly forget, and it is the only time I believe that a Movement has been accompanied by an authentic boogie-woogie.

EARLY LESSONS, THE FIRST FIFTEEN YEARS

This boogie-woogie incident was a funny occurrence, but this is not the reason I have mentioned it here. In this teacher's classes, there was no taboo on the expression of emotions and the teacher herself was the prime example of this. However, her expression of different successive emotions was really different from the progression in emotions that were familiar to us, in which the emotion engulfs us before we properly realize what is happening and there is no way back. It was more as if she consciously experienced the beginning of each emotion, whatever that might be. I linked this to the changing rhythms that often occur within a single Movement, in which the transition from one to another must take place in a state of awareness, so that balance is maintained.

I was also struck by other things. One, that some pupils were moved from row to row, at the teacher's discretion, without any discernable reason.[1] I observed these interventions carefully and believed to have discovered a pattern, as though a row represented a certain type of person. This was an interesting way in which to be able to study different types of people. Another observation was that the teacher provided a new stimulus at precisely the moment that the attention of the class had started to drift, and boredom or resistance arose. Exactly at this point, the process was turned around. Being able to sense these moments, and then knowing which stimulus was necessary, appeared to me to bear witness to a special ability. Later, I understood that this was the search for the stimulus that had to convey the "octave" (with which the class was started) through the "interval," in order to achieve the ultimate goal: the higher octave tone. At the time, I only had theoretical knowledge of this Law. When someone used these words—"Law of Octave"—I knew what they meant, but no more than that. Here, I witnessed how this Law worked in practice.

The examples given here—the expression of emotions without losing oneself in them, the typology of the rows and the search for a new stimulus—I have never experienced in any class since. Especially in the 1990s, when I attended many classes in many different countries, it became increasingly clear to me how the instruction of Movements

---

1 Each Movements class comprises six or seven rows of people standing behind each other; the usual technical term for this is "file." People also stand next to each other; this is called a "row." These words are often mixed up, which is also the case in my text. With "row" I mean "file" here, a word I could not use in the text because the reader may not have been familiar with it.

was identified with a predictable pattern that had nothing in common with the way I had been taught—in which everything focused on awareness and complete concentration in order to preserve that; all else was secondary. In those early years I had learned that, providing there was awareness, the body could perform the Movement with its own intelligence. What I now usually see is *exactly the opposite*: through repetition, a pattern of Movements is introduced to the body, and it is hoped or expected that a change will occur in the state the dancer is in.

I participated in these Movements classes for fifteen years. When Ms. Claustres had to interrupt her instruction in the Netherlands, the moment had arrived for me to bid farewell to this organization—a difficult decision for me, but one I have never regretted.

A CHALLENGING TRANSITION

After the conclusion of my time within the organization, I felt lonely. The participation in the groups, the classes and other activities had, bit by bit, laid waste to all my social contacts. There had been simply no time left for anything else. Worse still was that my relationship with my former wife appeared to have suffered as a result of my constant absence, one of the factors that led to our divorce.

I remained faithful to the world of Gurdjieff's ideas through reading his books and especially through studying his music. I re-contacted my piano teacher, which really helped me through this difficult period, and this contact was maintained until he died. From time to time I had to go to Paris for my work, and I used the opportunity to visit Ms. Claustres. The relationship with her was as good as it had been in the past, and was unaffected by my decision to turn my back on the groups. This was in stark contrast to the attitude of the former members of the groups who had considered themselves my "friends."

In 1994, I decided to end my work as a manager: the travelling, the loneliness of hotel rooms and the sacrificing of my time for the money-juggernaut had become too much for me. I withdrew with my partner and our newly born daughter to a small North Sea island where the nights were illuminated by shafts of light from the lighthouses, and time was determined by the slow turning of the tides. We concentrated solely on renovating our home. Our money was rapidly depleted, however, and I started to consider my social possibilities. They were few. I was fifty plus, and finding new employment at such an age was not possible. In addition, I no longer wished to return to the treadmill of work in commerce. The more I thought about it, the more hopeless my situation appeared and, on top of this, I now carried heavy responsibilities for a child who could barely walk. But, precisely in times like this, when the future looked like a black hole, music had always provided a solution for me—the only arena in which I felt I could make a positive contribution.

A QUIET SOURCE OF WISDOM

I determined that I wanted to organize courses in listening to and playing the music of Gurdjieff and de Hartmann. With this ambition, I travelled to Amsterdam, almost a day's journey, to advertise my course at the esoteric bookshops and spiritual centers. But, my ideas met with apathy and were sometimes even laughed at by the population of the spiritual centers in the city.

Sadly, without a single result, I had visited all the centers and bookshops and by twilight I fell into a depressed state. It was impossible to travel back the same day, so I entered a small café and, as I sat down at the bar, a whirlpool of somber emotions and thoughts took hold of me. Suddenly, I felt a "flash" inside myself. I "saw" a large meeting room with lots of people around a table who were all shouting at the same time that I should drop my insane plan! They had all sorts of other suggestions about how I should spend the evening. Some ideas met with cheering approval from all.

Amidst the clatter, only one of the people at the table in my vision remained quiet and seemed to address me directly, although not with words that I believed I heard. A different type of communication reached me, yet structured in the same logical way as a spoken or written sentence. I instantly believed that this person who could remain calm amidst the turmoil of the others had something to do with the quiet form of attention that I, somewhat surprisingly, had acquired from years of practicing Movements. The suggestion, made to me through this personalized attention, was to *make one final effort* and present my idea to the first person who would lend me an ear.

I immediately left the pub and walked around the corner, arriving at a canal filled with what looked like black ink. I knew this part of town like the back of my hand, but suddenly there stood before me a large building, brightly lit, that I had never seen before. It appeared to be a new spiritual center called "Oibibio." I wanted to approach the reception desk, but that was easier said than done, because the entry room was jam-packed with fashionably-dressed people who all appeared to know exactly why they were there. Clumsily, I bumped into a man who noticed my confusion, because he asked me what my business was. I quickly explained my idea about studying the Gurdjieff/deHartmann music.

"That is strange," he commented, "I have been looking for someone for months to give a dozen or so courses about this. Come to my office and we can fix the dates straight away."

It is this coincidence, devoid of any logic, that was to immediately change my life forever.

DISCOVERING CHOREOGRAPHIES

The Sunday afternoons during which I gave courses in this center, or held recitals of Gurdjieff's music, brought me into contact with many people who were interested in this music, and who assisted me by organizing other performances. In just a short time, I gained international contacts and held recitals in many other countries. It pleased me tremendously to be able to serve Gurdjieff's music this way, and it quickly became clear that almost all the people I met were even more interested in Movements than in music.

Previously, I had been involved in these practices through a sense of idealism, but beyond our small group there had been no interest. Now, things had changed. I was continually asked about my experiences and what I knew about this area, and people showed me the Movements they knew. Incidentally, with many people I could seldom recognize *what* they were actually doing. Others appeared, at least, to know some of the forms of Movements. And, for the first time in my life, I saw to my amazement the notation of Movements on paper: choreographies. I had no idea that such a thing existed. Apparently, there were entire collections of such choreographies, which were given to me in confidence. The magnitude of these collections varied from a few dozen to more than a hundred choreographies.

In the time that I had practiced the Movements, I was asked in advance not to write anything down. I not only complied with this condition, I felt no desire to take notes. The moment in which I learned a Movement was intense, and writing it down would have transformed the vitality of that moment into a mental construction that would have undermined the first experience. So, it was with mixed feelings that I determined to carefully examine the increasingly growing stack of choreographies.

In taking this decision, without realizing at the time, I crossed a line. After practicing Movements as a religious ritual for twenty years, I suddenly saw the results before me from people who had been involved on an entirely different level. It seemed that their objective had been to collect and record as much as possible of the *outward appearance*. This form was dependent on the maker of the choreographies who was not named. Each appeared to have a style of their own: one described a Movement in words, the other drew schematic dolls to depict the positions.

I certainly did not approach the studying of all this material, which had quickly grown to the size of an archive, as a novice. I knew the titles of the Movements that I had to accompany with existing sheet music, and I could remember a reasonable number of Movements, but this number was smaller than the quantity from which I could now study the noted form. Even so, sections of almost all the choreographies were familiar to me. It was a real shock for me when I realized why: I had only learned Movements of short duration, and only uncomplicated ones had I learned in their entirety. But of the others, the vast majority, I had only been taught fragments, *without ever being told that they were only sections of a larger piece.* On top of this, the fragments that I had learned during a certain lesson never connected with the fragments from a following lesson.

I understood that, if I indeed wanted to learn the Movements in their entirety, I had to collect as much information as I could from people who knew them themselves, or who had access to historically accurate information. This was no easy task, but to this day I have continued to work on this with great devotion. Sometimes, to acquire a single choreography I had to undertake a lengthy journey only to discover afterwards that the choreography in question was as good as worthless. On the other hand, sometimes a contact that did not appear to be very promising provided access to important new information.

THE GREAT PRAYER

One invaluable contact was made after playing a recital in Amsterdam. I was introduced to a young man who invited me, in a polite sounding English accent, to visit the group he participated in to be able to see for myself their versions of a number of Movements. I must be honest that I did not have high expectations at all, but because a number of members from the School for Philosophy, with whom I got on well, were also going, I agreed. Once we had arrived in England, we drove to a location where the Movements were to be displayed, a dingy gymnasium. A group of about twenty people, including many elderly, had gathered and positioned themselves calmly in the classical formation for a Movements class. Their faces expressed deep seriousness.

Accompanied on the piano by the young man I had met in Amsterdam, they showed us one Movement after another. Most of which I knew, but I saw many unfamiliar variations. The highlight was the performance of "The Great Prayer," a remarkably long Movement comprising 140 different body positions. I knew parts of it, but the stylized and geometric positions as I knew them were transformed on this occasion to far more lively gestures, some more graceful, others more solemn. The gestures left the deepest impression on me that expressed doubt and despair, and in such a way, powerfully and moving, that I had never seen before, either in Movements, or elsewhere. These expressions of despair were the opening of the dramatic scene in this Movement in which an individual's struggle (or better, "humankind's,") with death is portrayed.

Occasionally, life provides us with such a powerful intuitive experience that there is no place for doubt. Witnessing this version of "The Great Prayer" was such an experience. I was absolutely convinced that this had to be the correct historical form and not the one I had been taught. This affected me so deeply that I had to go outside, into the drizzle that the English countryside seems to have a patent for, where the positions of "The Great Prayer" replayed in my imagination as I had just seen them, as though it was a roll of film. In a sudden moment of clarity, I understood that I had made contact with a Movements tradition that was independent of the tradition within which I had studied. That this was the explanation for the differences in the form of the Movements that I had just seen for myself moments before. It would take several days before I was able to comprehend all this.

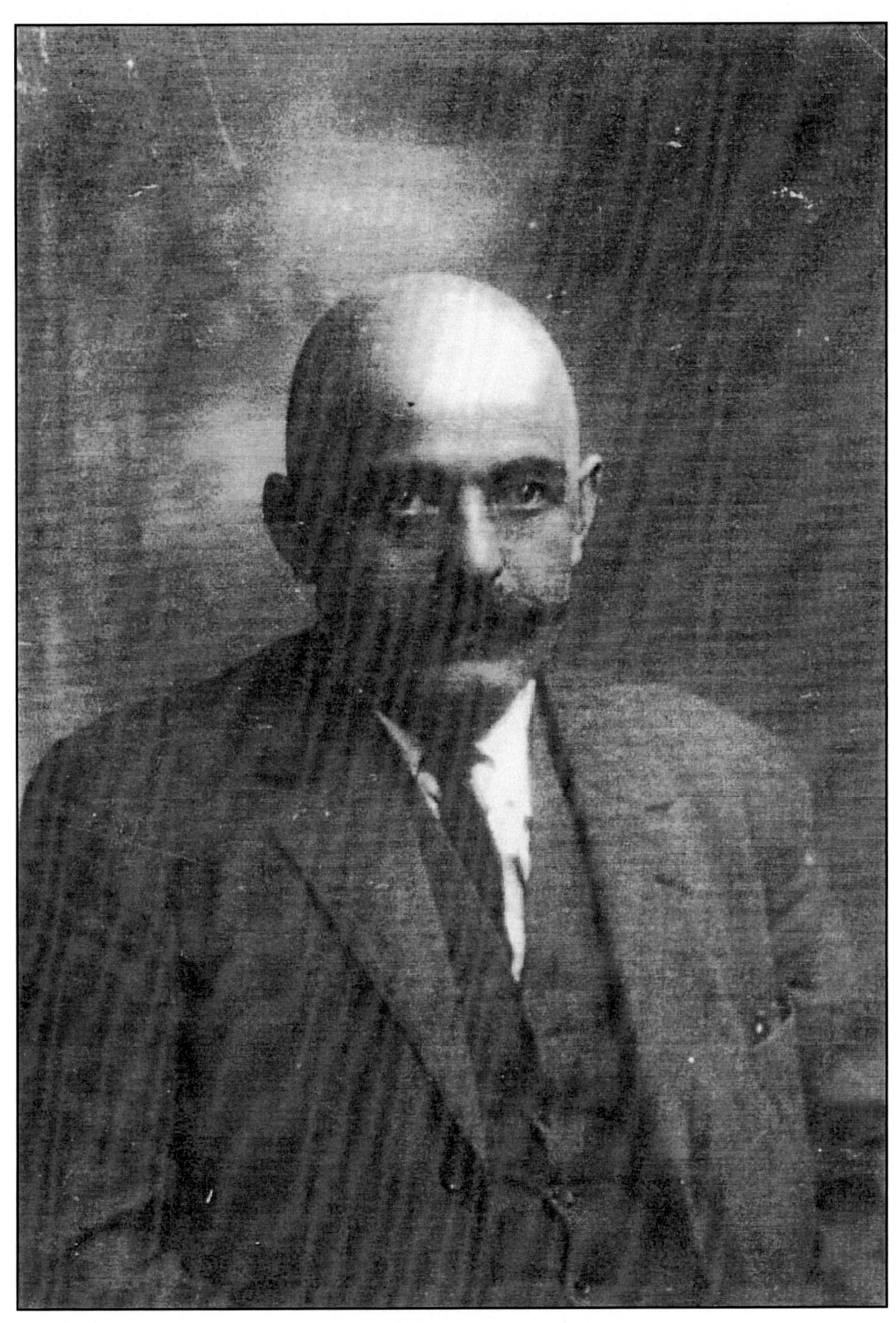

G.I. Gurdjieff, around 1920.

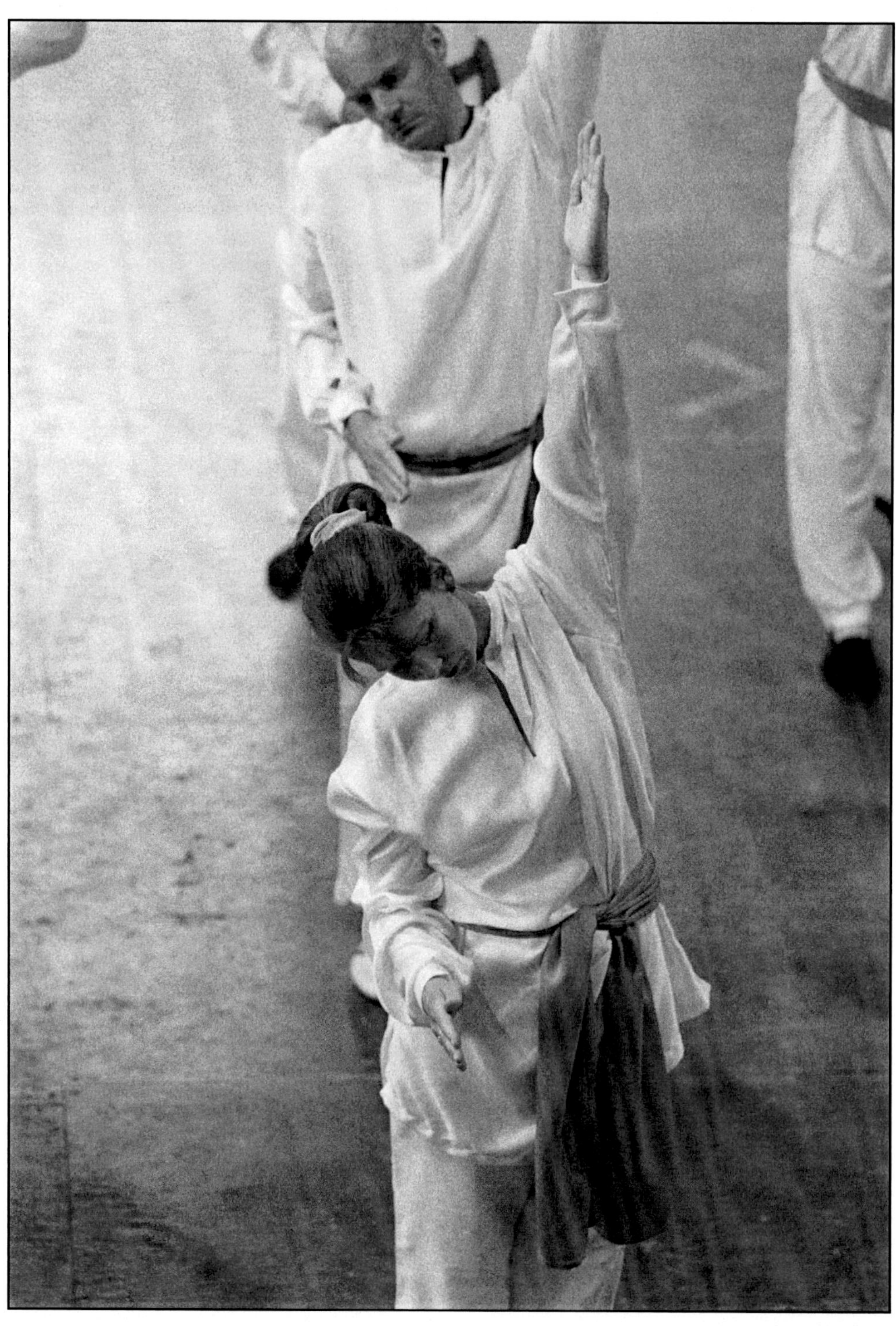

A position from the Movement "Big Seven," dating from a performance in Amsterdam, 1999. Copyright Marco Borggreve, Netherlands. Used with permission.

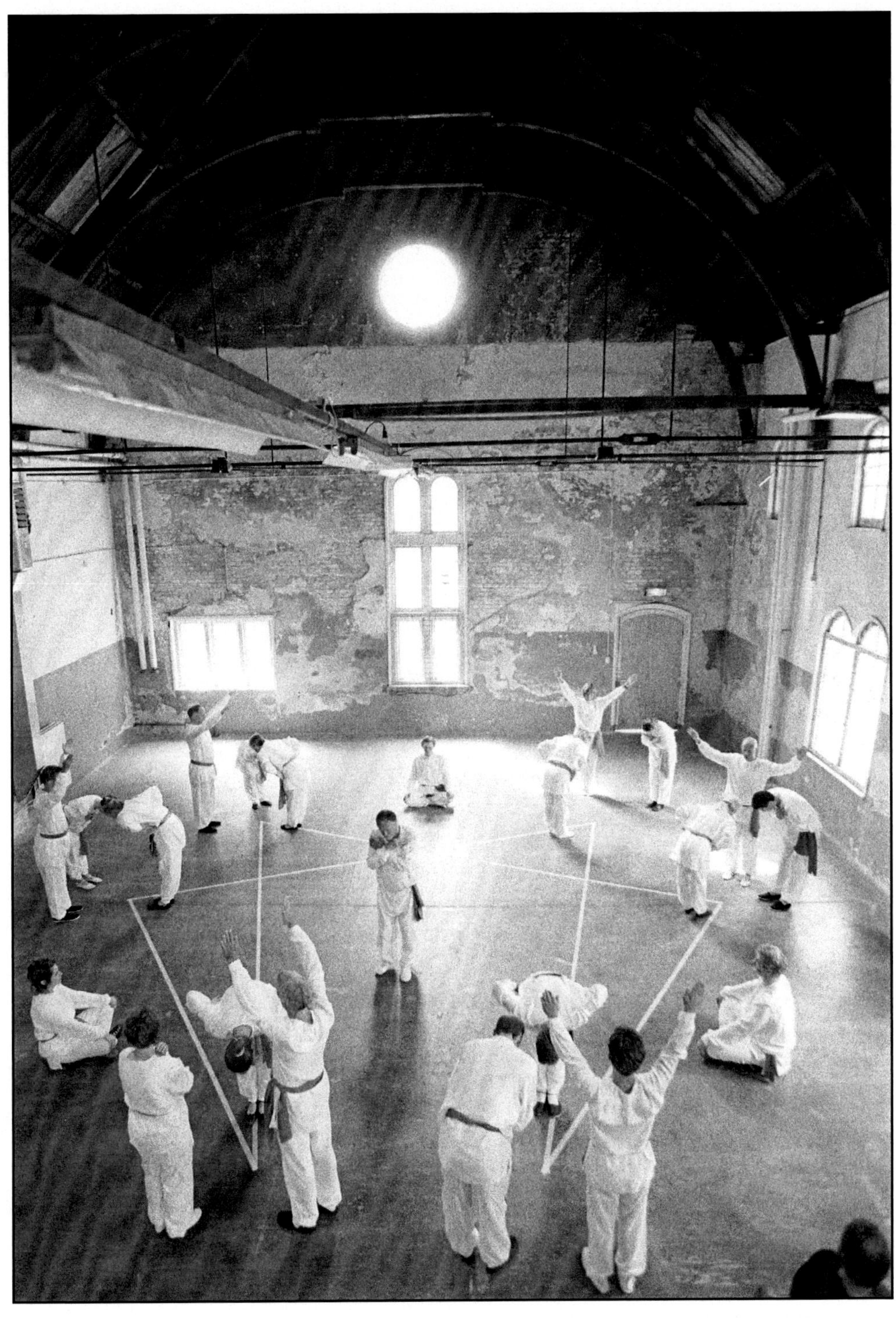

An Enneagram Movement with multiple roles, dating from a performance in Amsterdam, 1999.

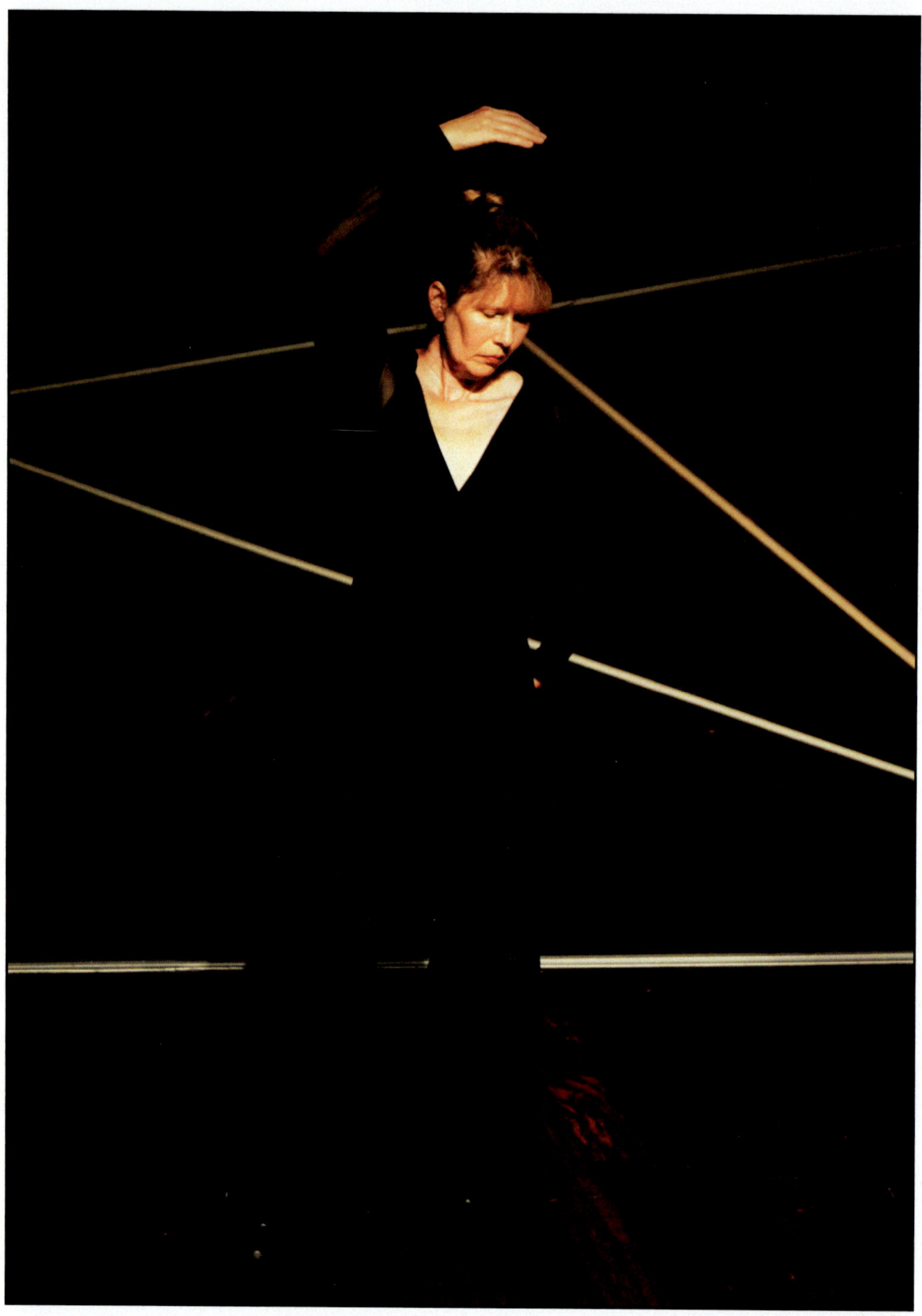

A position from the Movement "Female Prayer of Friday 21 October." Photo by Salih Tiryaki during a performance in Konya 2013. Copyright: The Committee of the Mystic Music Festival Konya, Turkey. Used with permission.

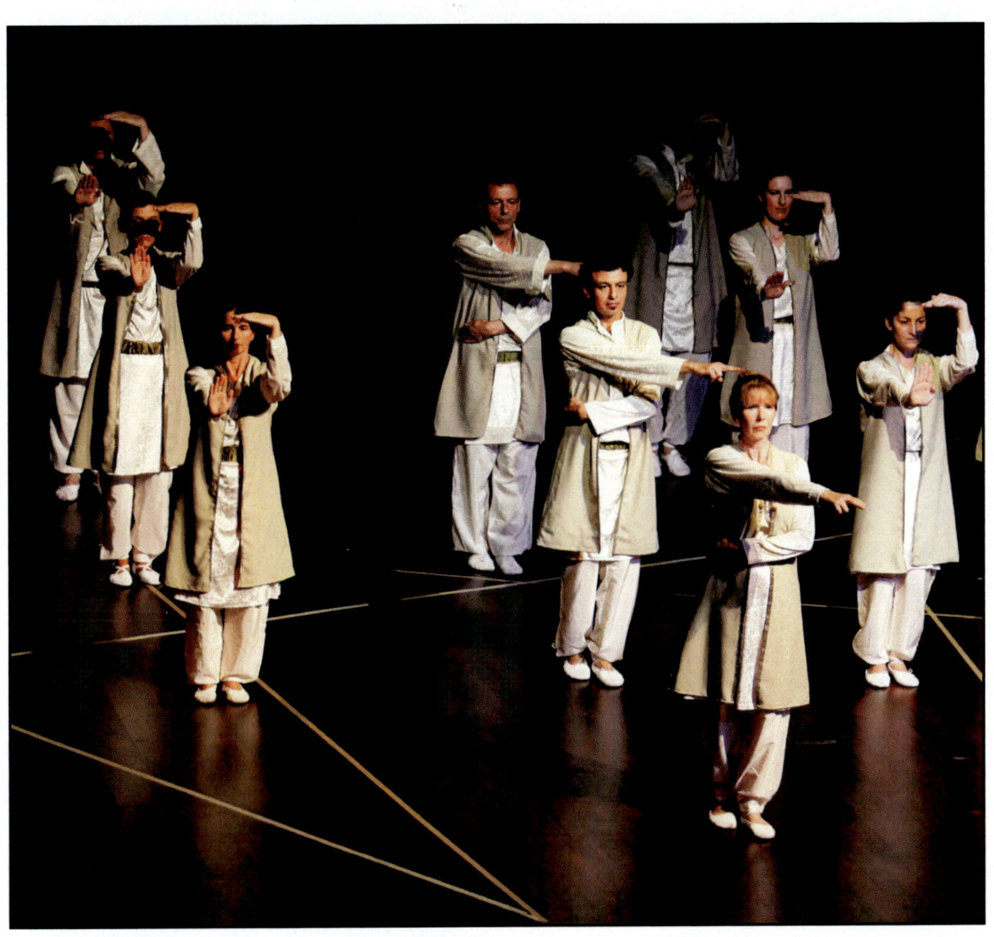

A position of the Movement called “Enneagram 12” (also called “La Croix” or “Multiplication 10”). Photo by Salih Tiryaki during a performance in Konya 2013. Copyright: The Committee of the Mystic Music Festival Konya, Turkey. Used with permission.

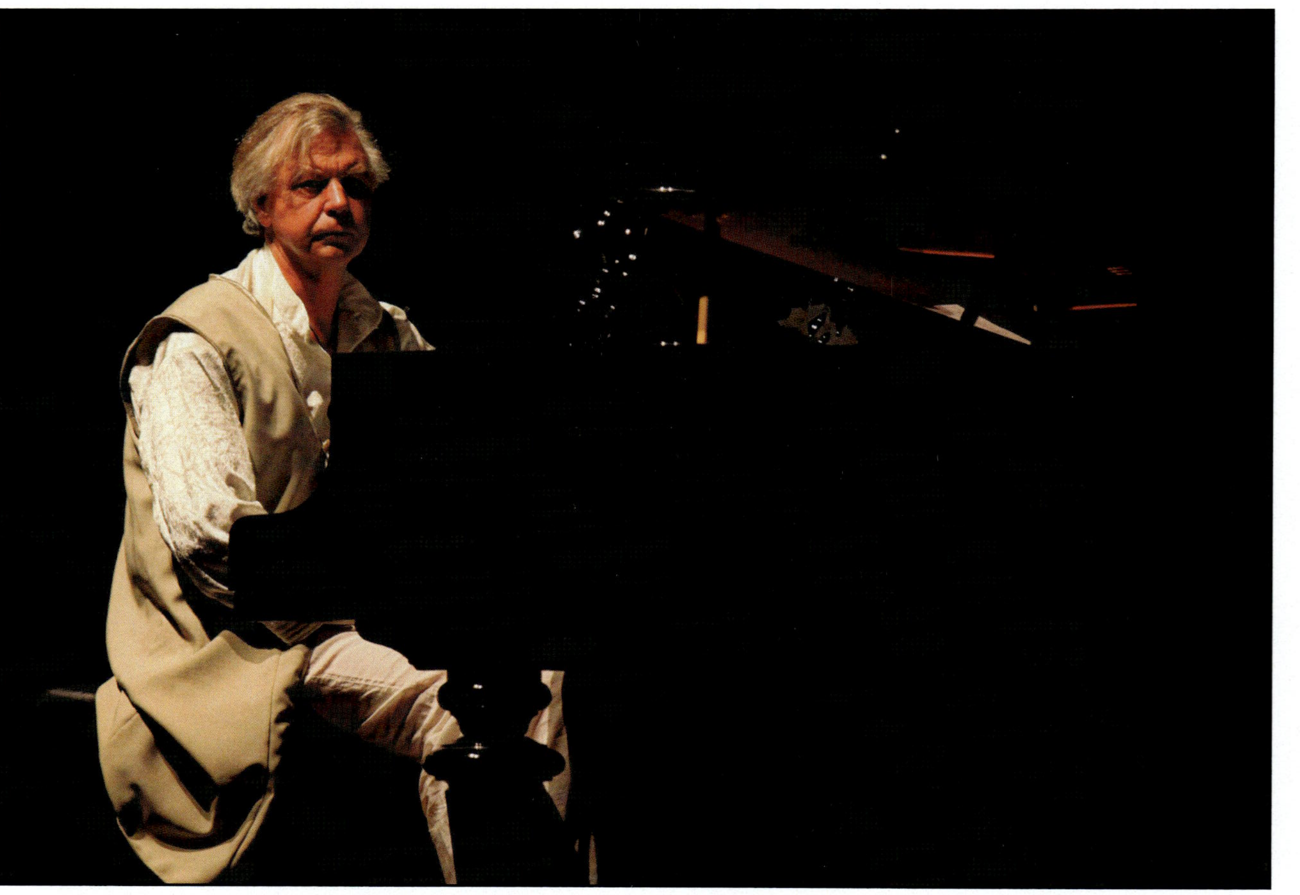

Author, Wim van Dullemen accompanying Movements. Photo by Salih Tiryaki during the Mystic Music Festival performance in Konya in 2013.

After the performance, it became apparent to me from the conversations with the people from this group, who received me with great hospitality, that they represented the organization that Ouspensky had established in England at the time, which was called the "Study Society" or the "Society for the Study of Normal Psychology." Ouspensky's large organization of yesteryear had thinned out considerably, but their dedication to and knowledge of the Movements was exceptional. This amazed me, because until then I had understood that Ouspensky was not interested in them. It appears to be all due to his wife that they eventually made their way into his organization. This had perhaps not been consciously hidden from the outside world, but even so it had remained more or less unknown to us.

THE SEARCH CONTINUES

Ouspensky's groups in England were instructed in Movements by Jessmin Howarth (1892-1984) from 1936 until 1939. The transmission of Movements to younger generations after Gurdjieff's death was chiefly the work of two people, as will be discussed later in this book: Jessmin Howarth and Jeanne de Salzmann.

Ms. Howarth was a musical prodigy and was later mentored as a dancer by Émile Jaques-Dalcroze. When she met Gurdjieff in 1922, she was a choreographer for the Paris Opera. She participated in Gurdjieff's theatre performances in 1923 and 1924, established herself in the United States, and instructed Movements until her death in 1984. The Movements as she remembered them from her time at the Prieuré, and from the performances in Paris and the United States, were taught with great passion and with attention for even the smallest detail. After her stay in England, she returned to the United States. Ms. Howarth's instruction in England was never written down, but instead passed on using an ingenious method that limited changes in the Movements, which inevitably occur in such a process, to a minimum.

As already mentioned, it took several days before I had processed these impressions. I had now come to the realization that Gurdjieff's Movements had been passed on through channels quite independent of each other, but how many there had been I did not know. The morning after I arrived home from my trip to England, I had the idea that, at the root of each "channel," a single pupil must have stood—one who passed on what he or she had understood from the Movements. In other words, they reach us, the second generation, only after they have absorbed a personal color, determined by the degree of understanding of the first-generation pupil. This idea gave me the direction for where I should continue to search. The different versions had to be found and compared, so that a single historically-reliable version could be constructed.

We know that three different stories can come about if someone tells three people the same story and they then relate it to others. With regard to the Movements, Gurdjieff did not just tell a single story to multiple pupils, he also told different pupils different stories at different periods of time. To acquire a comprehensive and historically reliable picture of the Movements, it is necessary to place the stories, which were each passed on separately by a single pupil, side by side.

"How could it be possible that I had missed something as simple as this, hiding in plain sight?" I asked myself. This gave me an uneasy feeling, because here a subconscious mechanism could have been playing a role, a blockade that had not just disguised this fact, but very possibly was still doing this with other "simple" facts. I arrived at the conclusion that this did not concern a particular small detail that only played a role for me, but that this subconscious mechanism was the main problem—and still is—from which all the ignorance and confusion about Gurdjieff's Movements has originated. The analysis of this problem is essential to be able to comprehend the apparent disinterest of Gurdjieff's pupils in historical data, or the secrecy that is so characteristic for this part of his teaching.

FORM AND CONTENT: A NECESSARY BALANCE IS NEEDED

The problem is that the content and the outward appearance of Gurdjieff's work are seen as two contradictory elements. For Gurdjieff's immediate pupils, his teaching, Movements and music were linked to his personal presence. In this blinding light, they were experienced as revelations, and facts regarding the outward appearance were not considered relevant. Examination of these facts would even detract from the strength of the revelation itself. In the case of the Movements, but also in the case of all of Gurdjieff's other works, this has led to such a great suppression of facts that, for someone who was not part of a ring of immediate pupils, it is impossible to acquire a reliable picture of historical reality, despite the thousands of books, articles and websites concerning this topic. Everyone who attempts to practice Gurdjieff's work is dependent on the information that consciously or unconsciously has been censored or manipulated. It is difficult to imagine the degree to which the mechanism described above has shrouded Gurdjieff's Movements in a mist of secrecy in which even the simplest of historical data—like the titles and data about how certain Movements were taught—have in chief been lost, let alone the reliable quantification or analysis of their development.

It would not be fair to throw this suppression of facts entirely at the feet of Gurdjieff's pupils—after all, he had always forbidden the making of choreographies—but their attitude certainly only served to create the current situation. The mixed feelings with which I started to study the choreographies were, in fact, introduced to me through the attitudes of those who had instructed me. I was now able to release myself from this and to step over the barrier that had separated the form and content of the Movements for me, a step into a new world. I have never regretted that my life followed the course in which I was first involved with the content of the Movements and that only later could I start on the "form." *Thorough knowledge of both is a precondition for experiencing the greatness of the creation of the Movements.*

The polarity with regard to Movements is increasingly extreme. The Institut Gurdjieff and its international branches appear to withdraw into what they experience as the "content," and the later generations appear to be especially fascinated by the "outward appearance." In this hopeless situation, the opposites will eventually be destroyed or changed unrecognizably. Form and content *have to be* brought into balance through a new stimulus before a positive development is possible.

THE DILEMMA OF A SINGLE SOURCE

Another conclusion I was able to draw after my trip to England is that *the historical truth about Movements could never be found in a single place, nor could it ever originate from a single individual.* By "historical truth" I do not mean an accurate form of a single Movement, but a historically-reliable picture of the whole: chronology, development, classification and cataloging. It was not difficult for me to accept this conclusion, because I stood alone following my departure from the Institut Gurdjieff and no longer cherished the illusion that those who had instructed me held the lease on the only version of the truth, with other versions fading to heresy. The entire Movements comprised, as was also the case for Gurdjieff's teaching, multiple parts defined by periods of time, and pupils who had played a role in them. My independent position allowed me to see this for what it was, without an emotional response, in which I fully realized that my knowledge was insufficient to acquire the complete overview of Movements that I sought, spurred on by an inner drive. I had no other choice than to continue categorizing the stack of choreographies, in the hope that eventually a historic reality would reveal itself to me. Then, I unexpectedly received support from two people who would expand my knowledge of Movements and lift it to a level that I had never attained before.

Christiane Macketanz

A psychoanalyst had invited me to provide Movements instruction in Berlin, where I met Christiane Macketanz (1959 –), the first of the two people who offered the support I needed. She, too, had learned Movements from one of Gurdjieff's pupils, but in a different organization from the one I had been a part of. Since then, she has been my help and stay in researching Movements and, once we got to know each other better, during the course of things she became my partner in life and the mother of our son, Sascha. Christiane has extraordinary body control. Her precision in the positions and actions of Movements is greater than any I have ever seen, but even more importantly, with regard to technique, she can indicate exactly what someone is doing wrong and how this can be remedied. This was new for me, because in the years that I had practiced Movements I had never witnessed individual corrections being given, all that was requested was complete dedication. Through her instructions, I was handed a tool that facilitated, without sacrificing concentration, achieving greater precision.

Dushka Howarth

The second person who became a source of support rang me out of the blue, during the same period, late in the evening from the United States. She introduced herself as Dushka Howarth and apologized for disturbing me so late.[2] I had heard of her, and knew vaguely that she

2 Dushka Howarth (1924-2010) was the daughter of Gurdjieff and Jessmin Howarth. Following a theatre production that Gurdjieff gave in France and the United States, Jessmin Howarth, then heavily pregnant, did not return to France, but remained in the United States. After the war, Dushka had a lot of contact with her father, and stayed with him in Paris from Dec. 1948 to Sept. 1949. She acquired her knowledge of Movements from both her father and her long collaboration with her mother, who was active as a Movements teacher until her death. Dushka taught Movements for many years, in South America and the United States.

was Gurdjieff's daughter, but that was all. She declared that she had contacted me because she had seen a catalog about Movements music that I had compiled and she wanted to draw my attention to several errors and correct them. She did not delay, and a stream of information followed.

I was surprised that Gurdjieff's daughter had taken the time to call me, but it was not about me. It was a characteristic way of working for her to correct errors regarding her father's legacy, no matter who had made them. She had a melodic voice and calm, well-considered timing of words and it took no effort at all to listen to her. Once the errors in my catalog had been cleared up, our dialogue took a different direction, towards Movements in general, to her experiences in the time that she had taken part in her father's classes and the years that she herself had taught in South America. The conversation lasted all in all for more than three hours and was the first of many telephone conversations, certainly more than ten, that I would have with her in the following months. These calls took up just as many evenings, because each conversation lasted at least as long as the first.

The free and associative stream of her recollections, thoughts and opinions that these conversations initiated, continued to flow without obstruction and was only occasionally interrupted by a question from me. Nothing was too much effort for her in providing as comprehensive as possible an answer. She had a great need to express herself, and I suspect that she was lonely—she was not visited very often at the time. In any case, she had little opportunity for sharing with others the unique quantity of factual information she possessed. She had made a start, however, with writing down her recollections.[3]

Dushka Howarth had a direct way of expressing herself and her

3 Jessmin and Dushka Howarth, *It's Up To Ourselves: A Mother, A Daughter, and Gurdjieff*, Copyright 1998, published by the Gurdjieff Heritage Society in 2009.

sense of humor was infectious. The conversations were regularly interrupted, because she had to go to her archive to look for a particular file that contained information about the topic. This was sometimes a photograph or choreography, but very often also personal letters that she read out in full. After each conversation, I attempted to record a summary of all that I had heard, but I was usually so fatigued and so bowled over by everything I had heard that the summaries are scant.

Dushka Howarth and her mother, Jessmin Howarth, had been very close, not just in family terms, but especially also with regard to the Movements. Her mother's authority in this area was patently clear and it was Dushka's most important criterion and frame of reference. She had also inherited the large archive from her mother. When I visited her later on, together with Christiane, we saw how this archive covered the walls of her living room. That was not all. Everywhere you looked, there were still more files, tattered cardboard boxes with "IMPORTANT" or "PRIVATE" written on them in large letters, and large yellowed envelopes. Even the space under her bed was completely filled.

Dushka always helped me with information I requested. Sometimes, with data about how Movements were instructed, choreographies of special or partly lost Movements that she permitted me to copy, or about the way in which this material was passed on through the various channels of transfer. Through this contact, I attained a new and more comprehensive picture that I will attempt to sketch in the following chapters, which is certainly in part thanks to her. This does not mean that the conclusions I have arrived at in some cases also originated from her, but the facts did come from her, or at the very least were confirmed by her.

17

THE CHRONOLOGICAL TRIPTYCH

Gurdjieff gave Movements over two periods of time. The first (Period I) began in Russia in 1916 and ended in 1924, after his accident. The second period began in 1937 and was concluded upon his death in 1949. There are clear differences between the function of the Movements in these two periods and the Movements themselves are different too. These differences are significant, but were not at the cost of the role that they both had in his teaching. This role was and remained central.

The distinction between what people could call the "old" and "new" Movements will be confirmed by anyone with clear insight into this material. I propose to divide the second period, the so-called "new Movements," into two parts, now referred to here as Period II and Period III. This intervention is of my own doing and, as far as I am aware, has never been done before. The reason for this triptych is that there are three distinct phases, in time, during which the situation influenced the Movements' development process.

PERIOD I: 1916-1924

In this first period, from 1919 onwards, a repertoire was studied with the objective of performing it in theatre productions. These performances, which took place in 1923 and 1924, were the first major manifestations of Gurdjieff as a spiritual teacher. Open to the public at large, they ensured that his Institute in Fontainebleau gained international fame. The Movements for the performances had been studied by a select group in the preceding years for five to six hours a day. That much time and attention was never devoted to the Movements in the later periods.[1] This means that the Movements from this first period have reached us in more detail than those from the second and third periods. Another characteristic of the Movements from the first period is that they were accompanied by Gurdjieff's own music. All the music for Movements from the second and third period was composed after Gurdjieff's death. He never even heard, never mind approved it.

Another aspect of the Movements from this initial time is that they are partly based on authentic folk dancing and religious ceremonies, like the ones Gurdjieff studied during his travels. These influences, also known as "ethnological," are also present here and there in the later periods, but never to the same degree. Gurdjieff's creativity was immense, and so here too, as is also the case with Gurdjieff's music, the question arises about which Movements, or which parts of them, fall under the banner of "traditional" and where Gurdjieff's own influence manifested itself. In the next chapter, I will try to answer this question.

The performances of the Movements of this first period can be divided into categories or types of Movements. The programs made for the performances were arranged as such, likely by Gurdjieff himself, and if not, at least with his approval *(see Addendum 1)*. There are so-called "obligatories," mandatory exercises that each participant in a class had to first master, "Dervish dancing," female dancing, "work" Movements, in which it was demonstrated how an Eastern community performed traditional manual work, and several ritual folk dances, such as a harvest dance. Following this, two "mystery" pieces were performed, as well as an ancient ceremony in which a female medium could predict the future while under hypnosis. Also, the ritual manner

[1] This was related by Jessmin Howarth during the instruction of her classes, which was recorded on tape and transcribed later.

in which pilgrims moved, and a funeral ceremony, were included in a program lasting several hours.

All these Movements were explained in the program, and their origins were also explained. Each Movement was given a title. This is also often true for the second and third period, but most of the titles, to the extent that they existed, were given after Gurdjieff's death.

Certain categories—"obligatories," "work" dances and ritual folk dances—do not recur later on, nor do the ceremony with the medium, and the pilgrims and funeral rites. With regard to the "mysteries," we will see in the next chapter that they were created by Gurdjieff and, as such, have much in common with the Movements from his later periods. It is striking that in this initial period the "female dances" are so well represented; later they become sporadic. In two of these dances, animal movements are imitated, the oldest form of dance known to humanity. In the case of "Dervish dances," there are two examples of warrior dances—variations of Eastern sword dances, which are no longer found in this pure form in later phases.

The difference between male and female energies is great in this period, while later this is hardly noticeable or completely absent. This contrast, too, gives these "old" Movements a character of their own. Within the group of "Dervish dances" and in the "female dances" too, unique Movements can be found that tell a story, position by position, sometimes in a remarkable way, with each note of the melody evoking a new body position. This exceptional principle was also never repeated.

Of the twenty-five or twenty-six Movements (depending on the performance) that were shown during the demonstrations, twenty-one have survived. Unfortunately, the two important "mystery" pieces that lasted longer than all the others are among the lost. How this could have happened is also discussed in the next chapter. During this period, Movements were taught that were eventually not included in the performances, such as several solos for which music was composed, or the intriguing Movement in which dancers had to move as automatons. In the months following the performances, up until his accident, Gurdjieff created another dozen or so Movements that, barring an exceptional few, have remained intact.

PERIOD II: FROM 1937 TO THE END 1947 / BEGINNING 1948

For the thirteen years following his accident, Gurdjieff did not concern himself with Movements. Important activities for him at the time were composing music, writing his books and the maintenance of contact with Orage and his American pupils, whom he visited on several occasions.

At the end of the 1930s, Jeanne de Salzmann had assembled a new group of pupils in Paris, who were later transferred to Gurdjieff. It is more than likely that she started to instruct this new group of French pupils in Movements around 1937, and showed Gurdjieff the results to stimulate him to resume Movements.[2] The result of this "transfer" was comparable to the action of igniting the fuse on a keg of gunpowder because, in the decade that followed, a creative explosion of hundreds of new Movements occurred. Jeanne de Salzmann believed that of all the Movements taught by Gurdjieff no more than a quarter have survived.[3] This statement relates chiefly to this period. The recollections, from those present at the time, about the number of new Movements that Gurdjieff provided in each class differ widely, from at least one, to four, and even five. Gurdjieff commonly held one class each week, which lasted two hours. The schedule was often expanded to two classes, and once or twice three classes, in a week.

To understand these years properly, realize that during this period the development and instruction of new Movements had Gurdjieff's

2 This date is also based on the source mentioned above.

3 Jeanne de Salzmann related this to a Dutch group I was part of when we visited her in Paris (1971).

priority. Gurdjieff's creativity was described by participants of his classes as an empirical experiment of great intensity that lasted for years. It was no longer about studying Movements for a performance, but he did his level best to assist his pupils through developing exercises that improved attention, concentration and willpower. I have been told that after each new creation Gurdjieff would carefully study the results and, if necessary, provide a new Movement to correct the inner state of the pupils so as to be able to provide another stimulus in the right direction.

In the Movements from this second period, we encounter only two categories from the first period, the Dervish dances and the female dances; but conversely, new categories have occurred. In comparison with former Movements, the religious and ethnological components have been reduced; they made way for abstract positions that have to be performed in mathematical transpositions. It is as though, during the interval of more than a decade, Gurdjieff had processed his experiences with Movements, and now had returned with a more personal, unique style in which mathematical and geometrical crystallizations dominated. The drama of human existence, captured in such a gripping manner in some "old" Movements, had opened the door for a more abstract construction that truly gave the classes an immediate opportunity to "work," in the sense that Gurdjieff attributed to the word. A great many of these Movements are difficult to execute and require great effort with regard to precision, speed, discipline and attention.

Another new element that must not be omitted in the description of Gurdjieff's later phase are the "inner-self exercises" that accompany some Movements. These also occur in the "old" Movements, but less explicitly. "Inner self" refers to special, properly described activities that must take place *within* the dancer, simultaneously with the execution of the Movement. This is certainly not the case for all the Movements, but when they do occur they create a link between the psychological exercises of this discipline, which are beyond the scope of this book, and the practice of the Movements. I do not feel comfortable with describing examples of these inner-self exercises, as I believe that this can only take place in direct contact. But the fact remains that, if one does not know the inner-self exercises, the Movement can only be studied for its appearance—an empty house where nobody resides.

Why a Third Division?

The descriptions above apply to all "new" Movements, but why should the time from 1937 until Gurdjieff's death be divided into two?

The first reason regards the dates on which the Movements are given. This historically important information has been lost for many Movements, but fortunately not for all of them. Of forty or so, the dates are known to me—a series commencing March 1944 and ending September 1949. From this series it appears that a change took place between the end of 1947 and the beginning of 1948, when Gurdjieff started what is called the "39 series."

There is almost no overlap between the Movements from before the first months of 1948, which are all indicated with a name or title, and the Movements from the "39 series" following this, indicated by a number and sometimes also a title. This suggests that, from this time onwards, the last series was worked on almost exclusively. In the meantime, and after 1937, more than a decade had passed in which Gurdjieff had instructed his classes in literally hundreds of new Movements before he started on what was to be his last series.

The second reason concerns the type of Movements that were given in this period. Following Gurdjieff's death, and probably even before, people attempted to catalog the Movements and distinguish the different types from each other through giving them a name. The following categories came about:

- "Enneagram Movements"
- "Prayers"

- "Dances"—female dances are meant here
- "Dervish Movements"
- "Tibetan Movements"
- "Morse Code Movements"
- "Multiplications"
- and "Pythagorean Movements."

Each Movement was then numbered, employing an old categorization system, for example: "Enneagram 6," "Tibetan 2," "Dance 4" or "Multiplication 15." I do not know how long this classification was employed, but the categories are clear and the subsequent titles—category and number—are still used for many Movements.

Four of these categories are completely missing in the third period; they only occur in the second period. This is about half, but in itself this is not so important. In the later third period, other categories occur—such as "Tableaux Movements" and Movements that have to be performed in a circle or semi-circle—and a degree of fluctuation of types of Movements within an already developed area of the "new" Movements is to be expected.

It is striking that the "Enneagram Movements" are missing in the third period, that of the "39 series." These Movements, performed on the symbol of what was crucial for Gurdjieff in his teaching, were performed in Russia from 1916 until the end of his life. Even so, they are absent from the performances in 1923 and 1924 as well in the last period, which I refer to as the "Third." Could the reason be that he played his cards close to his chest in public and remained rather reserved? I suspected so, and this was confirmed for me by pupils who were with him during the war years and who experienced the contact with him as far more intimate than in the period from 1948, when a new stream of visitors started.

The "Enneagram" and the "Morse Code Movements" are unique parts of Gurdjieff's Movements and only occurred in the second period. This period saw an exceptional number of Movements, much greater than the sum of the first and last period together.

Finally, it cannot be excluded that, in the third period, which is described below, a change in the instruction of Movements had an influence: different instructors gave lessons in these final years, in the United States and in England. A speculative explanation for the absence of "Enneagram" and "Morse Movements" in the third period could be that their performance was only permitted with Gurdjieff present.

PERIOD III: FROM END 1947 / BEGINNING 1948 UNTIL GURDJIEFF'S DEATH

No longer hampered by the restrictions of the war years, a new stream of visitors could now see Gurdjieff. This included Ouspensky's pupils who, since his death, had sought contact with him; or John Bennett, who renewed his contact together with a group of his pupils; and many more besides. In the final phase, Gurdjieff's teaching blossomed once again, and the many international visitors offered him a new perspective. This had consequences for the function of his Movements.

During the wars years and immediately afterwards, the Movements were given exclusively to a local group of young French pupils, but from this third period on they would have a wider range, and Gurdjieff devoted himself to creating an entirely new series that could also be practiced in other countries under the instruction of teachers he selected, such as Alfred Etievant, one of the most important male dancers, who was to instruct the "39 series" in the United States.

Dushka Howarth, who attended Gurdjieff's classes for many months in 1949 related to me every aspect of how this new series came about.[4]

---

[4] From telephone conversations with Dushka Howarth (1997-2000). This text differs from the text in the book she later wrote, but is a literal representation of what she told me during telephone conversations.

The familiar routine with which classes are now commonly opened, such as simple exercises or sitting in silence, did not exist at the time. We met at the agreed time in the Salle Pleyel, and without speaking we took the places we had been allocated in the class. Everyone who had arrived in their place prepared, in what seemed to be the best way for what was to come, being the practicing of one of the Movements that had been given in the previous lesson. Once Gurdjieff had entered, he took up his place next to the piano, behind which a pianist was already seated, and he demonstrated one position after another of a new Movement. If he was fatigued or did not feel well, he supported himself with one arm on the piano to demonstrate the Movement with the other arm, which the class was expected to immediately copy. After this, he tapped a rhythm out on the top of the piano and told the pianist, usually Jeanne de Salzmann: "Now just do it." Obviously, there was no music for these new Movements, it had to be improvised. Once the Movement had been worked through, he carefully absorbed the atmosphere and psychological state of the class and was often dissatisfied. He sometimes left the class briefly and returned to make several, usually small, adjustments. For example, an arm that had been horizontal had now to adopt a diagonal position, or a wrist that was first outstretched now had to be bent at the hand and, in doing so, create a certain angle. But sometimes these changes were not enough for him and in such cases he gave a strict order: "No, stop what you are doing and forget it. Do not practice this ever again." This sometimes met with protest from the class of pupils who had been moved emotionally by the exercise, but he casually dismissed this. If a Movement produced the results he had intended, he said: "That's it, this one is ready for use . . . what number are we at now?" By this he meant the incremental number that this series under construction, the "39 series," was given.

CREATIVE IMPULSE OR CAREFUL PREPARATION?

The question arises, did Gurdjieff's new Movements come about as a result of spontaneous creativity, or were they carefully prepared in advance?

The answers I have received to this question are inconclusive. My intuitive impression, based in part on eyewitness accounts, is that they were often created in the moment. It is certainly true that in a subsequent class he could return to a previously given Movement and make a change or add a new element to it. It also occurred that two different Movements would be combined to form a single larger one. This confirms that he could not only remember the Movements in detail, but that in the interim, even though it was only in his mind, he continued to work on the improvement and refinement of them.

When Dushka Howarth told me all this, I was left with the impression that only the Movements from the "39 series" had been recorded with Gurdjieff's whole-hearted permission, and this covered all the Movements from the entire period from 1937 until Gurdjieff's death. In other words: that all the others that were not included here did not have his approval and, as Dushka Howarth said to me, were "open to question."

I have come to the conclusion that her account is the complete truth, but that this only covers the period from the end of 1947, being the period in which she herself was present some of the time. I cannot conceive that Gurdjieff's disapproval also applied to the hundreds of Movements that he had given a decade before—certainly not because "Enneagram" and "Morse Code" Movements were included, and there were many of them in ever changing configurations. I suspect that Dushka Howarth probably had projected her own experiences of this last period on the previous decades, for which she had no direct experience.

The "39 series" is also known as the "French series," in contrast to the "American series" that is comprised of the same Movements, with the addition of another seven Movements that Gurdjieff instructed in the United States. The order of the numbers runs differently in the American series, and it is unclear why this is the case. Dushka Howarth, who attended them in the United States during this period, did not know the reason for this. Most likely, the order that Alfred Etievant had employed in instructing this series in the United States was maintained.

A HIERARCHY OF MOVEMENTS?

The importance of the Movements from the period that I have designated as the second period is confirmed by the Movements that Jeanne de Salzmann selected for her Movements films. In this project, lasting more than twenty-five years, which can be considered as her life's work, one-hundred-fifty Movements were recorded on film. One hundred of them are from this second period, and only fifty from the first and last period (third) together. Even the "39 series" is not shown in its entirety.

Her selection confirms that she attached special interest to the Movements from the second period. This raises the question of whether or not there is a hierarchy of Movements; in other words, are Movements from a certain period more important than Movements from another. Jeanne de Salzmann has answered this question with her selection for the film recordings. Dushka Howarth agreed with her mother (Jessmin Howarth) that the "old" Movements ranked the highest, because they are accompanied by Gurdjieff's own music and above all have remained better intact. Other commentators have a higher opinion of the "39 series." This is not surprising, because the accompanying music for this series was written by Thomas de Hartmann, admittedly after Gurdjieff's death, but no other musician who wrote music for Movements had such unique experience of Gurdjieff, or such compositional skills. Besides, these were the last Movements that Gurdjieff gave during his life, and the impression existed that he wanted to create his final magnum opus. This impression was reinforced by the teachers who, following Gurdjieff's death, started to teach Movements in other countries, in England, the United States and South America, and almost only taught Movements from the "39 series." As a result, the Movements from the second period have largely remained unknown. Incidentally, this still applies to the most important Movements from this second period.

This is a good moment to recount a historic fact that has also been forgotten: the "39 series" was divided into two independent series from the very start—an "esoteric" series and an "ordinary" series of Movements.[5] These had different numbers, and only later on were they bundled together in a new series. From the current numbers it cannot be deduced from which original series the Movements originated, in other words which ones are the "esoteric" and which are not. This fact also explains the peculiar mixture of the "39 series," which comprises elaborate rituals and compact, more physical exercises. The first date known to me of a Movement from this series is the 19th of February 1948, for number 10. I am inclined to believe that, at the beginning of this series, Gurdjieff reverted to a number of older Movements that he had given years before. I once saw a choreography, made in 1944 by a French pupil, which clearly described elements from what is now known as "Movement number 4" from this series. This fact could again explain why important rituals are to be found especially at the beginning of this series.

---

5 According to Gurdjieff, *practical* knowledge, in contrast to pure theoretical knowledge, is only to be given to the "inner circle" of his pupils. The Movements according to those qualified to know also often have elaborate "inner-self" exercises.

The differences in the opinions listed above—about which period was the most important—appear to be formed on the basis of the Movements that people are most familiar with, or those for which they received instruction from Gurdjieff himself. In my view, it is not possible to give a preference to a particular period. They are, to return to the example given in the previous chapter, "three stories told" to different people in different periods of time. A thorough knowledge of the Movements from all of the periods is required in order to acquire a relevant picture of Gurdjieff's creation in its totality. The triptych fleshed out in this chapter is a useful model, because it facilitates a better understanding of the development of the Movements.

18

CROSSING THE LINE BETWEEN TRADITIONAL DANCES AND GURDJIEFF'S OWN CREATIONS

The "old" Movements from the first period were based chiefly on traditional material studied by Gurdjieff during his travels, but his own creativity clearly shone through in a number of Movements. For our purposes here, a the dividing line can be drawn between the two "mystery" Movements (referred to as the "two mystery pieces" in the previous chapter—these are the Movements "The Initiation of a Sacrificial Priestess,"[1] referred to as a "mystery" in the program of the time, and "The Big Group") and all the others. Both had a central role in the performances, also due to their length. It is now widely accepted that these Movements have been lost. So how can we possibly say anything about them, and on what basis can we draw a dividing line?

WHY THESE MOVEMENTS WERE LOST

The answers to these questions raised above rest in consideration of why these Movements were lost. Despite their loss, historically

---

1 In the literature the word "sacrificial" in the title of this Movement has been omitted later on. This probably has a reason: the idea that a priestess is going to be sacrificed (in what way is unclear, it does not have to mean put to death, but could refer also to a life in a different form, a life completely dedicated to her mediumistic role with privileges and/or restrictions to mix with the community, like a nun in our recent history) is for us simply "too much." We don't know, but the omission of this word remains an example of how our attitude towards things we do not (want to) understand gradually distorts authentic information.

important notes have survived for both Movements. Around 1954, Jeanne de Salzmann undertook a journey to the United States to meet with Olgivanna Lloyd Wright, as well as with Jessmin Howarth. The reason for this extraordinary visit was that these three ladies, who played a key role in the passing on of Gurdjieff's Movements, wanted to undertake a joint attempt to reconstruct the "mystery" piece, "The Initiation of a Sacrificial Priestess."

Unfortunately for them, and for all the generations to follow, they failed in their attempt. Jessmin Howarth knew her own role in this piece, and had recorded this in a choreography, and most likely the others both knew their roles, or parts of them, but the reconstruction petered out because too many roles remained that could no longer be ascertained, as the original performers had died or were no longer available. "The Initiation of a Sacrificial Priestess" was a Movement in which individual dancers each performed their own Movement, different from the others, which however formed a harmonious but complex whole. This is apparent from the photographs that were taken. This was also the case for "The Big Group," and is why both these Movements had such an exceptional position in the program at the time. Only two other Movements, "The Great Prayer" and the "First Dervish Prayer," included several different roles that had to be performed simultaneously; but these two did not contain anything like the complexity of the two "mysteries," which also had a different kind of accompanying music from the other "old" Movements.

Breaking away from the uniformity of a Movement through multiple individual roles is more characteristic of Gurdjieff's later Movements than of old Eastern rituals, and points clearly in the direction of his own creativity. In addition, there is the most significant clue: the "Initiation of a Sacrificial Priestess" and "The Big Group" are the only Movements in the performance of which the origin is not stated in the explanatory program. However, in the case of "The Initiation of a Sacrificial Priestess," the program does say that it contains a fragment of a mystery called "The Seekers of Truth." This is exactly the name that Gurdjieff, in his second book, gave to a group of researchers of which he was a member.

MORE ABOUT "THE BIG GROUP"

"The Big Group" too has a fine legacy. Several years ago, a choreography made in 1923 surfaced for this lost Movement.[2] This authentic document is a primitive but exact representation of the length of the melody-notes of the music for this Movement. Comparison with the sheet music, published by Schott III, 32, excludes any doubt. The Schott publication does not provide a title, nor does it provide information that this piece was composed as accompanying music for a Movement. It is only in the footnotes that a reference is made to the existence of an orchestration.

Analysis of this old choreography makes it plausible that this was prepared so that the different lengths of the melody-notes could be learnt by heart. A few positions are described, but so scantily that Movements cannot be reconstructed from them. Even so, it is an important document because it appears that, just like in "The Great Prayer," the physical gestures were evoked by the notes of the melody. It is also important that the document can be held alongside the sheet music, through which it becomes clear which are melody-notes and which are only "passage" or "linking" notes. Once this problem could be solved in this manner, the true character of the music was revealed and, indirectly, the true character of the Movement: a revelation from another world, that of cosmic mathematics.

"The Big Group" Movement and the accompanying music offer us the most Hermetic formula of the numbers three and seven that I

2 With thanks to Gert Jan Blom, who gave me the opportunity to study this document.

have ever come across in a piece of music. On top of this, the formula results in a piece of music that evokes a strong emotional response, independent of whether or not the listener is aware of the formula.[3] Add to this the geometry of Gurdjieff's Movements, which are demonstrated simultaneously in many different roles, and it is easy to understand that we are dealing with a work of art of revolutionary power.

It could again seem as though Gurdjieff's creations originated from an obsession with numbers, which is why I repeat that this numerical symbology refers to that which Gurdjieff called the "Great Laws," the Three and the Seven, which he experienced in his inner self, and which essentially colored all he created. Should this not suffice to absolve Gurdjieff from following a pointless dogma, I permit myself to digress and to relate a story that was told to me personally about an event at which the storyteller, John Bennett, was present.

The incident occurred during one of the last dinners that Gurdjieff gave in his Parisian apartment. At this particular dinner, it was clear that he did not feel well and was sick or completely exhausted. After the meal had ended, one of the party, unrequested, started to tell Gurdjieff about the existence of the "twelve tone" series in the new musical developments, everyone else present considered this not just the wrong information at the wrong time, but also expected a small disaster, because most discussions about art were usually annihilated by Gurdjieff without the slightest consideration. To everyone's amazement, Gurdjieff was suddenly very interested and wanted to know exactly how the series was composed, and how the exact relationship between the tones was organized. He asked several questions, and it took a while before these principles from the new classical music

3 The music from the "Big Group" comprises four parts, each comprising seven bars of seven notes, with the exception of the third that comprises seven bars of nine notes. The formula of the melody notes is 3x7x7, the pauses in which the dancers may not change their position, but in which the notes of the melody play on, is 3x3x7.

gradually became clear to him. He remained quiet for a time afterwards, as though he was reprocessing all the information, and then indicated with an approving ". . . er . . . aha . . ." that he had understood the system. If someone like him, in the last phase of his life, could show such interest in the development of a type of music that was alien to him—that is, to modern classical music—he can hardly be accused of dogmatism.

BLENDING TRADITIONAL/RITUAL AND ORIGINAL CREATIONS

In the dozen or so Movements that Gurdjieff taught shortly after the performances in 1923 and 1924, and before his car accident, the characteristics of his own beliefs become clearer in the stricter geometry, as well as in the simultaneous practicing of different rhythms and positions. For example, this can be found in "The Fall of the Priestess," which is just the beginning of a long Movement that he had planned to make, but never finished. In the "Men's Enneagram," the dancers were given the numbers of the enneagram for the first time, another sign of Gurdjieff's own creativity moving into the foreground.

The miscomprehension that all his Movements had existed for a long time and originated from a secret tradition still abounds, which is why I have advanced Solange Claustres' vision in this book. As she stated in an interview, "A number of the Movements originate from different mid- and Far-Eastern places, where Gurdjieff was able to study them in special group or religious communities while travelling. But, a large proportion of them are of his own creation, made by him."[4]

In Chapter 17, I attempted to indicate a dividing line between these two parts (traditional vs. his own creations), but this must not

[4] Interview with S. Claustres, see footnote 5, chapter 13.

be considered as too black and white. Gurdjieff's later Movements also have elements of the traditional, for example the central role of a priestess, who stands behind the class with her hands raised to the heavens, is a familiar image from Persian and Azerbaijan folk dances. An exceptional example of the way in which Gurdjieff employs traditional material in a stylized form is the Movement "Sharsche Varsche" from the "39 series"—one of the most powerful and dynamic from the entire range—in which the feet move to a different rhythm from the torso and arms. The torso is bent backwards and forwards alternately in time to a hefty rhythm, while one arm with a waving gesture from high above the body is brought to the chest, which is contacted with force by the fist. No one has ever been able to tell me what the words "Sharsche Varsche" stood for, until we recently discovered that this Movement originated from a ritual procession to honor the Holy Hussein, who fell at the battle of Kerbala, one of the twelve Imams.[5] I shall provide a detailed description of this procession, because in this eye-witness report the intensity of these types of rituals, which so interested Gurdjieff, still glows through.

> *In the distance, the muffled beat of a large drum could be heard, threatening as a warning from the Invisible. The dusty street glowed in the sun that shone directly above Schimran (the city in Persia where the author was located). The drumbeat edged slowly closer and incessantly the cries "Sha-ssé . . . Wah-ssé" rang out: Shah Husein . . . Wee Hussein. The procession became visible and above the mass of people three large flags flapped. On one of the flags Ali's name was written in large golden letters against a black velvet background. On the second, a large left hand could be seen, the hand of the Prophet's daughter, Fatima, both blessing and threatening. On the third, so large that it*

[5] With thanks to Christiane Macketanz, who found this description in the book: *Ali & Nino* by Kurban Said, 1937, Leela Ehrenfels, Vienna, Leipzig.

> *almost obscured the view of the heavens above, just "Hussein," the grandson of the Prophet. The crowd proceeded slowly through the street with the penitents leading, dressed in black mourning attire but with bare backs and holding heavy chains in their hands that were whipped across their bleeding shoulders to the beat of the drum. Behind them walked a large semi-circle of broad-shouldered men, who took two rhythmic steps forward and one back. At each step, their chant "Sha-ssé . . . Wah-ssé" rose up and they hit their balled-up fists against their bare hairy chests. They were followed by—in white robes, like those of the dead, with deeply bowed heads—martyrs, with shaven heads and long daggers in their hands, their faces closed off and dark as though they were looking into another world. "Sha-ssé . . .Wah-ssé." At each cry, the daggers flashed in the sunlight and fell across their shaven skulls, blood running over their white robes. One of them fell to the ground and was quickly transported away by the crowd. I saw a beatific smile on his face.*

Both the name of the Movement—"Sharsche Varsche"—that, just like in this procession, has to be called out time after time, as well as the similarities of the ritual movements of the second group, who pound their chests with their fists, is linked to this ritual. Gurdjieff has added another element to the basic movement of the torso and the punch. The other arm reaches high above the body, and with the hand it traces, to the rhythm bent in four directions, a cyclical geometric pattern. Is it not likely that this is Gurdjieff's interpretation of the flag with Fatima's hand imprinted on it that flapped to and fro above the crowd?

Finally, Gurdjieff added another new element. At the front, surrounded by male dancers, a female couple, entwined in a classical Western-European dance position, perform a calm dance, a tranquil scene amidst the vortex of energy that is evoked by the male dancers. This element can have many meanings, but it remains as unfathomable as the creator of the Movement himself. I do not imagine it will be easy to find an equally vivid example of the approach with which Gurdjieff, within a single Movement, incorporated and combined traditional influences with his own creative ability.

In conclusion, we can assume that a large proportion of the "old" Movements have marked traditional influences, but that the two large Movements from the theatre program that have been lost were Gurdjieff's own creations. Here and there, in other Movements from this group, elements occur that play a greater role in his later periods. These are geometric transpositions often combined with a form that is called "canon."

TITLES OF MOVEMENTS

It is impossible to describe Movements in words. It is only possible to gain an impression if you can watch them, accompanied by music. For this reason, Amir Kaufmann, an Isreali independent filmmaker, Christiane Macketanz and myself collaborated to produce a film titled, "A Body Towards An Aim," in which many Movements are shown, to serve as a vital adjunct to the purpose of this book. This film can be downloaded from Hohm Press (*www.hohmpress.com/video*). Details on this download, and more about the film will be found in Addenda III, "About the Film," at the conclusion of this book.

Not words, or choreographies, or a series of photographs can even approach the vitality of a Movement. They are comprised of both complex and simple gestures, and the transitions from one position to another, together with the rhythm and atmosphere of the accompanying music, can only be represented dynamically. Even then, watching a film can never replace the impression of performing them for yourself. Nevertheless, in this chapter I attempt to provide a preliminary quantification, and this can only be tackled through describing in categories. We will see that these categories have gradually developed, and this provides a historic perspective.

First, I must discuss the titles of the Movements that will subsequently be dealt with in the examples. With the exception of the titles from the initial period, they are not descriptive. Many titles describe nothing, but comprise only the date on which they were given, usually without a year, for example: "10 May," "10 December" or "26 June." Then, there are other titles that only indicate the time: "First Movement Since Return from the United States," "Last Movement of This Year." Then there are titles that do describe something of the Movement, but in very vague terms such as: "Opposite Each Other," or "Knee Bends." Words that are to be spoken during a Movement can also function as a title: "I Wish to Have Being," "Father, Mother, Brother, Sister." Then there are titles in which the number of positions are stated, like: "Six Positions." These are confusing, because there are commonly more Movements with the same title. Finally, in this summary, which is far from exhaustive, there are titles in which the type of Movement is indicated, but this time with a date as well: "Canon of 15 November," "Multiplication of 24 September."

If I may propose a few rules of thumb for navigating this title chaos, they would be the following:

- The titles from the first period, *see Addendum 1*, are generally used, even if sometimes translated into another language, and provide a guide as to whether or not it concerns an "old" Movement or a later one.
- Titles that are composed solely of a number—6, 34 or 39—are always from the "39 series." However, the numbers can be confusing, because they can also concern the American variant of this series, which has a different sequential order, *see Addendum 2*.
- Where this later group of Movements occurs in the rest of this book, I will place a # tag and then the French number, followed by the American number, for example: #6, 28.

- All other titles concern Movements from the second period.
- These rules only apply for titles that have originated from authentic lines of transmission, not for titles that have been made up retrospectively by whomever.

THE USUAL FORM OF A MOVEMENTS CLASS

The usual form, or configuration, of a Movements class is a square, comprising six or seven rows of participants who stand precisely adjacent to and behind each other. The people standing behind each other are called a "file" (a "fil" in French, thread), those standing next to each other form a "row." Depending on the number of people in the class, there can be two, three, four or five rows, but the number of files has been prescribed exactly for the Movements, usually 6 or 7 but sometimes also 4, 5 or 8. We have an old photograph in our archive, presumably dating from the end of the nineteenth century, which shows a group of girls in St. Petersburg receiving gymnastic education. These girls are organized in exactly the same formation, and it seems likely that Gurdjieff joined this tradition, even though the number of files is symbolic for him. This introduces a cosmic element to this ordinary arrangement—a gymnastics class now represents a miniature universe in which the effects of Gurdjieff's cosmic Laws become visible.

This gymnastics class can perform a Movement in which all the participants stand on their spot and perform the same Movement, and this forms the simplest configuration. The next variation is when the files make different Movements from each other, or when each row differs from the other. There are many possibilities for breaking up the class, as it were, into a new configuration, of which the aforementioned geometric displacements and the "canon" were historically the first precursors.

In the "old" Movements, the transpositions are still minimal: the dancers exchange their place with the person next to them, or there are a few steps forward and backward, and the "canon" also only occurs twice. The term "canon" is common in music, where it means that a melody is started by one or more musicians and, while this melody is being played, others play the same melody, but they start one interval later. The melodies are heard together, but are so constructed that a harmonic order occurs.

In Movements, the term "canon" refers to the simultaneous performance of a series of gestures or steps, commonly six or seven. As file after file starts the series of gestures one after another, each at an interval, until all the files have been addressed, all the gestures can be seen simultaneously at any given moment. This principle would later become one of the most fundamental elements in the Movements. The same applies for the displacements (also a variety of transpositions), which we will consider next.

DISPLACEMENTS AND TRANSPOSITIONS

In certain Movements, the dancers perform their head, arms, legs and body positions while staying in one place. In the majority of Movements, however, they have to leave their place to make a series of steps, eventually to return back to their starting position. These "displacements," taken by one file after the other, or by the whole class simultaneously, are never random. On the contrary, they are strictly described in the sense of the number of steps, quarter turns, sidesteps and the exact arrival place, as if the dancers have to travel forth and back on the imaginary lines of a geometrical symbol drawn on the floor below them.

In another frequent type of Movements, the dancers do not travel forward and backward on their own little labyrinths, but have to take the place of another dancer who has left his or her place, in turn, to go to somebody else's place. This type I call "transpositions."

These displacements and transpositions introduce the element of continuous motion into a class. The world as depicted by the class changes second after second, measure after measure, in a perpetual process. It is striking that in a Movements class this process of change is perceived as harmonious.

Not only do the displacements or transpositions fit precisely together, as little wheels in a bigger clockwork, but the attention in each dancer, generated by his or her mental, emotional and physical tasks, creates an impression of the presence of a consciousness that is not influenced by the ongoing changes.

Often I have been, in my position as teacher in front of the class, moved to tears seeing this spectacle. The dignity of the dancers and their awareness prove to me that obeying a Law can generate a type of consciousness of a new and stronger quality. Due to the emotions and associations that take hold of me in these moments, I don't know any longer if I am looking at a class, or if I see planets in the infinite universe following their paths and obeying their Laws. Other images come to me: could it be that I am looking at humankind as it was supposed to be, conscious of its task and destiny, or is it the state that humanity can reach after it has understood that consciousness and creation are more productive than forgetting and destruction?

To describe all the variations in displacements and transpositions in Movements would require another book, and possibly even more than one. I have to limit myself to two characteristic transpositions: Enneagram Movements and Multiplications. Describing and analyzing them I cannot avoid entering the fundamental numerological system on which they are based.

ENNEAGRAM MOVEMENTS AND MULTIPLICATIONS

My experience in teaching Movements has taught me that, whenever I try to explain the system of numbers used in Movements, invariably the faces of a substantial part of the class immediately start to express one of the following reactions: "I hate numbers," "I have never understood mathematics and never will," or "Numbers are so boring that I prefer to wait until this is all over and finally something interesting will start." I always try to reassure these class members by telling them that the basic system is so simple that there is nothing to be afraid of, but I doubt if I ever fully succeed in overcoming this resistance.

I will give my explanation another try right now, because understanding these two often used transpositions (Enneagram Movements and Multiplications) is only possible after having grasped the simple numerological system on which these are based.

Although what are called "Multiplications" are a historically later variation of "Enneagram Movements," I have to start with them for clarity's sake. I remember clearly when I had to do this transposition for the first time in my life in a class guided by Ms. Claustres. The only indication given was: "First the two files on the right go left and then back to their place. Then the first file right goes left and back. Then the mirror of these two displacements starting from the left, then the three files right change places with the three on the left."

After these scant instructions, a fairly quick rhythm was given and the Movement was immediately started . . . Of course chaos reigned all over the place, participants collided, others were so confused that they stood as if petrified with eyes wide open, some were dragged on by others, who at least seemed to understand something, to their new places. In Ms. Claustres classes, passivity was the worst option you could take, so we all struggled along and learned the traffic rules quickly: those "displacing" to the right go in front of those going left; if you have to travel a larger distance take bigger steps than if you displace only the distance of one or two files; keep in line with the others in your block; constantly be aware of what your neighbors are doing, and so on.

The steps had to be executed with *precise* arm and body positions. "Not anyhow," was Ms. Claustres motto, to which she added: "*You* are responsible for the precision of your body, not Mr. Jones in the street."

For a long time, the only thing I knew about Multiplications was the short formula quoted above. I had not the slightest idea that it was based on a numerological system, and I doubt if I would have been interested in it, because there was more than enough work to concentrate upon in ever-changing configurations, positions and feeling atmospheres. The most reliable element to focus upon, however, never changed: attention and presence in the very moment.

Without us knowing or realizing it, our class at that time demonstrated the working of Gurdjieff's Law of Seven in actual practice.

How?

By showing how a small part becomes a bigger one, a whole or a unity, in a dynamic process of several steps or stages towards its development.

. . . And the Law of Seven

This whole or unity is symbolized by the number 1, the Law of Seven by the number 7.

The number 1 is divided by 7. Mathematically, this $1/7^{th}$ part is 0.142857. To this first smaller part we now add a second $1/7^{th}$ part, and then another, until the number 1, the whole or unity, is reached. This whole process generates the following number sequence, whereby now the 0 and decimal point have been left out:

142857
285714
428571
571428
714285
857142
1

There is something remarkable to be seen in the above numbers. In each stage of the addition, always the same 6 numbers are seen, albeit in a changed order, dependent on the stage! The same numbers as listed above are obtained if we multiply the first 1/7th part with 2, then with 3, with 4, with 5, with 6, and with 7. Hence, the rather confusing word "Multiplication" for this type of transposition.

I advise the reader to prepare 6 small squares of paper on which one of each of the numbers 1-4-2-8-5-7 are written; that is, one number of the sequence per square. Place the papers side by side in front of you, on a table, establishing the first sequence. Now, shift the pieces of paper accordingly to obtain the order of these six numbers for each separate addition, until 857142 is reached.

Each piece of paper represents a file in a Movements class, and moving them on the table in front of you, you will see the basic pattern Gurdjieff wanted the class to represent. We should not forget, however, that the task for the dancers in remembering these patterns was strictly meant for the brain, the "thinking center" as Gurdjieff called it. Additionally, the physical tasks—that of moving to another place in the class—would be considerable, especially considering that the independent arm and body positions would have to be executed at the same time.

In Chapter 10, two variations of the Law of Seven were given: the one "outside time" encompassing all seven elements at the same time, and the one "inside time", a chronological process of one after the other. Clearly, the Multiplication discussed above falls in this last variation of this Law. One could argue that the Enneagram Movements, the next transpositions to be described here, symbolize the seven elements as active at the same time, and therefore "outside time."

Enneagram Movements and the Law of Three

The enneagram is a geometric symbol created by dividing the circumference of a circle into nine equal sections. From the points that are created, the top one is labeled number 9 and the others in a clockwise direction are 1 to 8. The points 9-3-6 are connected with straight lines, creating an equilateral triangle that symbolizes the Law of Three.

The remaining numbers—1, 2, 4, 5, 7, 8—are the same numbers on which the Multiplications are based.

In the enneagram, six numbers are connected with straight lines in the sequence that these numbers have above: 1 with 4, 4 with 2, 2 with 8, 8 with 5, 5 with 7, 7 with 1. The collective image of circle, triangle and the geometric shape that occurs through connecting the figures is called an "enneagram," after the Greek word for the number 9.

In many of Gurdjieff's Enneagram Movements, the dancers move along the connecting lines from one point to another. They pass through one of the above cycles of the six numbers, and each connecting line between two numbers represents a phase in a process. When six dancers simultaneously start their "journey" from each different point, the six stages are passed through simultaneously, and if one was to view the enneagram from above, one would see the entire process taking place.

Gurdjieff gave a great many different Enneagram Movements, of which at least twenty have survived. As far as their outward appearances are concerned, there are two types in this category. In the first type, the dancers move forward along the lines of the enneagram drawn on the dance floor, just like worshippers did in the Middle Ages, following the labyrinth hewn out of the stone cathedral floor. These Movements are usually danced by twelve people, six that move along the lines (this often takes place in a rotational movement and this is why these Movements have a lively tempo), and at each of the six points stands a dancer outside the circle who performs a separate Movement that corresponds with each respective Enneagram Movement. However, sometimes there are two people stationed at each point, each with his or her own role, and occasionally the "journey from point to point" is undertaken by multiple people who move forward in a special configuration.

The points of the triangle are usually not incorporated in the Movement itself. The points of the triangle are symbolized by three figures, standing or sitting, who in general do not move or participate physically in any way to the Movement. Sometimes they speak, one after the other, the words, "Affirming" "Denying" "Reconciling," embodying and emphasizing in this way the eternal and lawful existence of these three independent forces that, by blending, create life in whatever form imaginable.

However, in some Enneagram Movements these three figures are not stationary, but they change places by moving on the three lines representing the sides of the triangle. By doing so, they demonstrate the characteristic of the Law of Three—that the forces change: what was affirmative becomes negative, what was negative becomes reconciling, and so forth. The three forces are in motion, as if the triangle starts to roll like a wheel. This triangle-in-motion is in these cases completely separate from the Movements taking place, at the same time, on the lines of the Enneagram—that is, on the connecting lines between the numbers 1, 4, 2, 8, 5 and 7.

Although an Enneagram with a moving inner triangle is more in concordance with the characteristics of the Law of Three, a possible, practical explanation for its rarity could be that it is very difficult, if not almost impossible, to perform without collisions or other interruptions in the flow of the transpositions. I have only witnessed women dancing along the inner lines of the enneagram, and never seen men dancing along these lines in authentic Enneagram Movements. Even in the films that were made in France and the United States, women exclusively danced along the inner lines. In our classes in the past, and those we presently hold, this task was and is also given to men. The impressions I have gained through the years are so intensive that I believe this must, however, be a role specifically for women, such as in the legends, in which only women were permitted to perform holy dances in ancient temples.

In the second type of Enneagram Movements, the enneagram is not visible; these have the ordinary configuration of a Movements class. Enneagram Movements of the second type (for example the numbers 8 and 12 from the series) are always slow. They are exceptional, because ancient Christian symbols are displayed, in the hand and arm gestures, and must be experienced in the inner exercises. Gurdjieff called his teachings "esoteric Christianity" and it is apparent from these special Enneagram Movements that these were not just empty words.

Despite the great differences among the Enneagram Movements in movement, tempo, rhythm and atmosphere, they each give the participants a wonderful, quiet insight into the universe of which every part is in movement, but of which the entirety appears to be oblivious of time.

All of Gurdjieff's Movements are significant, without exception. Each and every one is a prayer, as Solange Claustres indicated in the already mentioned interview, but there is no doubt that the Enneagram Movements form a central part of his teachings, in the same way that the heart does for the human body.

Jeanne de Salzmann saved the Enneagram Movements for future generations, but a long time passed before she did this. It was fifteen years after Gurdjieff's death when she finally showed one from this series in her films, in 1964; one later in 1968, and four in 1971.

Differences and Difficulties

The Multiplications have the same mathematical basis as the Enneagram Movements, but have been cast in a more abstract and difficult-to-understand form. The series of numbers cited above, in which the base 142857 is multiplied—which explains the misleading name "multiplications"– is now performed by groups or "blocks" of dancers that simultaneously change places. Each dancer within a block represents a number from the series and must travel to the other new place from the next series. At this new place, almost without exception, a Movement is added that has to be performed before the dancer can again leave for another position. This inserted Movement is indicated with the technical term from the Movements terminology "*sur place*," "on the spot."

Enneagram Movements also have this "*entremède*" or "insertion." Gurdjieff must have considered the Multiplications a fruitful form, because there are a lot of them. From the second period, there are at least thirty that have survived. And also, in his last creative phase, in which the "39 series" saw the light of day, there are two examples to be found.

It is unfeasible to describe the many variations of this Multiplications' formula in Gurdjieff's Movements. Here too, the tempo, expression, atmosphere and dynamic alternate as markedly as in the Enneagram Movements. The transition of Enneagram Movements to Multiplications was a gradual development. The very first "Multiplication 1," a spectacular Movement based on seven different rhythms, clearly shows this. Firstly, the transpositions are performed individually, as in the Enneagram Movements, only then do the dancers start the collective transpositions characteristic for the Multiplications.

Initially, during Gurdjieff's life, and also afterwards, some participants of his classes hypothesized that, if a class had *six* files, the files *always represented* the six enneagram numbers, which means that a "canon" in such a class looked very like a hidden enneagram. This is probably not the case, but it serves as a warning for us. We should be wary of perceiving the different categories too dogmatically and allowing our picture of the organic whole of the Movements from distorting it through subdividing it into strict and dead "blocks" or "groups."

THE MORSE CODE MOVEMENTS

Gurdjieff was fascinated by the Morse code, a now historical system for electronic communication in which letters were transposed into two signals, a long and a short: "dash" and "dot." The succession of these two signals was rapid; all that could be heard was a successive series of "taa-ta-ta-taa-taa-taa-ta-ta" and only a trained ear, such as that of a ship's marconist, could distil words and sentences from this. Why did this code so appeal to him that he based an important part of his Movements on it? No certain answers can be given on this matter, but it appears to tie in with his affinity for not formulating directly or logically, but in hidden ways. An attractive explanation could be that the dancer in such a Movement has to live in two worlds simultaneously: the "long" world and the "short" world, which continuously alternate in an unexpected pattern.[6] This is what makes practicing a Morse Code Movement such a difficult task. The living simultaneously in "two worlds" is analogous to a state of consciousness in which an individual observes themselves and the outside world, without losing sight of either.

The Morse system was familiar to pupils from the first generation who had attended the Prieuré. A number of them had to learn long lists, up to 400 words in length, in Morse, because this code was to be used in the section of the theatre performance in which extraordinary phenomena were demonstrated, in the same style as "magic shows" still do that today. For example, the pianist in the performance would play a fragment from a piece of music that none of his listeners could know—a piece suggested secretly to him by someone from the audience. But, at a certain place in the music, the pianist "played" the name of the piece and the composer in Morse code, so that someone who knew the code could then shout out the title and name of the

6 As explained by Christiane Macketanz during one of her classes.

composer. In another example, at the back of the hall, a member of the audience whispered the name of an animal in the ear of a pupil who subsequently transposed the name of the animal into Morse code through a rapid succession of two small physical gestures, hardly discernable for others, but which could be read from the stage. Then, to everyone's amazement, the name could be disclosed, although it would have been impossible to hear at such a distance. Learning this code was not a goal in itself, but a means to acquire stamina through practicing almost impossible exercises—whether these concerned 400 types of animals in Morse code, or learning hundreds of Tibetan words that people were expected to recite to themselves while performing taxing physical labor.

A striking characteristic of the Morse Movements is that this code, which is normally associated with a mechanical electronic system, is linked to deep primary or religious feelings. The names of these Movements speak a clear language, for example "Amin," "The Soul," or "Father and Mother." Sometimes, there is an inner exercise connected to this in which an emotional image must be pictured, while simultaneously certain Movements must be performed in the Morse rhythm, such as in "*Dur-Rud.*" Here, the first part of this name, the French word "*dur*" expresses a feeling—"heavy, almost unbearable"; and the second part, "*rud,*" is simply the mirror image of the first word. This unusual combination of elements is accompanied by the sensitive music of Thomas de Hartmann. This task is impossible to execute with our ordinary approach, and can only take place from the position of being open to new impressions that normally cannot reach us, obstructed as they are by the armor of our ego. But, it is these impressions that admit us to a new, crystal-clear view of the world, a world of harmony, filled with deep meaning, such as in the Movement "Adam and Eve."

I have often had to accompany this type of Movement and in some cases prepare compositions for them. Each time, I experienced that this unpredictable succession—of "long" and "short"—releases the music from personal association and culturally infused ideas about melody and rhythm, and as such makes them more valuable. As far as I am aware, there are certainly another twenty or so Morse Movements.

The elements described above are rarely isolated; within a single Movement, several are usually applied. For example, in "Multiplication 18," multiplications are alternated with a section in Morse code, while at the same time another transposition is performed. Above all, the multiplications are accompanied by a circular movement of the arm that, rhythm after rhythm, points to the continuously changing numbers of the enneagram.

TWO ADDITIONAL CATEGORIES

Two other categories of Movements from the second period are worth mentioning. These are the Five Pythagoras Movements (also called "Exercises from the School of Pythagoras") and the Tibetan Movements. The first category is so heterogeneous that the only thing these Movements appear to have in common is that they initially had to be accompanied by counting in Greek. The second group is characterized by unusual movements and positions. One of the female dances from this group, "Tibetan Number Two," is an exception that proves the rule that, in the later periods, few female dances measure up to those from the first period.

CHARACTERISTIC FORM-COMPONENTS OF THE MOVEMENTS

An extensive list could be provided of other elements that characterize the Movements, but only a few of them are common. Some are only present in a handful of Movements, and sometimes these occur just once. I have limited myself, in the list of variants that follows, to the most characteristic form-components:

1. The already discussed "inner exercises." These are very different from each other and can vary from a single task, for example concentrating on a certain emotion or image, to the exceptionally complex sum of instructions that, one after another and sometimes to each beat of the music, have to be followed through the course of the Movement.
2. The recital of words or short sentences/phrases characteristic for Gurdjieff, in time with the music.
3. Changes of rhythm.
4. The singing of a melody or scale. "Do Mi Sol," "The Scale," and exercises #5, 2-#12,13-#13,12-#15, 29 are the only ones I am aware of for Movements.
5. A gesture and/or series of steps that are repeated in reverse—"Back and Forth"—such as in "The Eleven," #12, 13-#13,12-#28, 36.
6. Vibrations of hands and arms or of the entire body. The first mentioned are common, of the latter I only know in three Movements, "The Great Prayer," the "Pilgrimage" and "Men's Enneagram."
7. The "Stop," an independent exercise from the early years, was implemented later in some Movements: the Fourth Obligatory—#19,1 and #12, 13. In the last case, the Stop lasts long and creates the space for an elaborate set of inner exercises.
8. Whirling. Jeanne de Salzmann ended her films several times with whirling Dervishes, such as in the famous Mevlevi *sema*. However, this is relatively uncommon in Movements, except in the case of the Enneagram Movements, where it is common. The turning direction in Gurdjieff's Movements is always the opposite from the Dervish ritual of the Mevlevi.
9. Relaxing or tensioning of limbs or parts of the face.
10. Special eye movements.

HOW MANY MOVEMENTS STILL EXIST?

With regard to the compilation of a catalog of Movements, something that I had originally planned to do in this book, I have now come to the conclusion that an extremely long summary of Movements' titles would be of little purpose. It is, of course, important to know how many Movements still exist at the moment, but even Dushka Howarth or Solange Claustres could not estimate this, because it is still questionable which Movements can be considered correct in the historical form. My cautious and preliminary estimate is based on 30 Movements from the first period, about 175 from the second and 46 from the third. This comes to a historical total of 250 Movements. Although Dushka Howarth first estimated the figure to be much higher, she eventually, when we discussed this topic, was of the opinion that this number was not far from the truth. The number of pieces of music that were composed for Movements, also 250, corresponds with this. In this case, I have not included the many exercises given by Jeanne de Salzmann after Gurdjieff's death. It is not an unnecessary luxury to mention this, because these exercises are today viewed as authentic Gurdjieff Movements, although they differ substantially.[7]

7 Countless exercises have been given by Gurdjieff pupils. Many of the exercises given by Jeanne de Salzmann were passed on erroneously as Movements by Gurdjieff, including: Blue-Red-Black-Yellow; I wish- I am- Everywhere; Finger Tip Dervish; I wish to be- I can work; I am-I wish-I can work; The two rhythms; I am- I wish- I can; and "Father I."

19

THE MUSIC FOR THE MOVEMENTS

Gurdjieff once related the following story: During one of the voyages from his youth, he had set up camp in a remote mountainous area as the evening fell. He was not able to get much sleep because, from a valley in the distance, he heard music that was obviously being danced to. Due to the darkness, he could not see the dancing. But, in the night and the day that followed, he tried to imagine what the dance must have looked like, based on the music he had remembered. The next evening, celebrations and dancing continued in the valley, but now he had made sure he was nearby so that he could see the dancers properly. The movements of the dancers were exactly as he had imagined them in his reconstruction.

AN ANCIENT SOURCE?

Anyone interested in dancing should consider the meaning of this story. It is an example of the bond that movements of the body and music—two art forms that do not leave any trace in the material world—made with each other in the beginning of time. It does not just confirm the close ties between music and dance, but suggests that they are so inextricably linked that with every rhythm only one movement "belongs," and with each melody a series of gestures, and that each chord evokes a single emotion in the entire body. This appears to contradict the multitude of forms that human creativity has produced, but raises an interesting question. Could there be ancient, archaic forms in existence that serve as the basis of this multiplicity, and in which the cohesion between movements and music has been recorded?

At the end of the nineteenth century, many musicologists were obsessed with the idea that music had originated from a single primal form. Spurred on by the leading Berlin School of the time, they went in unanimous search of the "sources of music," and attempted to reconstruct the primal sounds from old musical instruments, like a stone xylophone or Egyptian flute, as well as from musical recordings of isolated tribes from which all other music was believed to have originated. (That their research is now seen as nothing more than a historical curiosity is partly their own fault—several researchers did not shy away from faking their proof—but this is still a pity.) The sound recordings from the beginning of the last century made by the Japanese researchers Masu and Kurpsawa are one sterling example. Here, the singing of a Takasago tribe from Formosa can be heard. This tribe had never had contact with the outside world, and the registration counts as one of the most important music registrations ever made. The harmonic singing of these headhunters comprises canons and fugues, and displays correlations with Georgian songs. An explanation for this incomprehensible, yes really impossible, similarity could be that both have their roots in the same, even more ancient, form.

Gurdjieff's Movements can be seen as not just research into a repertoire of physical expressions/gestures that can exercise a comparable central function, but likewise into the music connected with them.

GURDJIEFF'S COMPOSITIONS FOR MOVEMENTS

Gurdjieff himself composed the music for the Movements for the theatre performances in 1923 and 1924. Originally, it was not permitted to write down this music, which is why Thomas de Hartmann learned it by heart. Only once, for the rehearsals, when it became unavoidable that multiple classes practiced at the same time, did Gurdjieff give permission to write down the music. Another pianist was allowed to play the music at the same time for another class.[1] This music that was first noted for piano was subsequently—in an incredibly short period of time—arranged for a large orchestra by Thomas de Hartmann. This was the only music composed by Gurdjieff himself for his Movements; all other music for Movements was created after his death. There is one historical exception to this, but more about that later.

One element in all the music composed for the Movements later on *did* come directly from Gurdjieff: the rhythm. This was always recorded clearly by Gurdjieff. How quickly this rhythm was to be played is another question, which is usually difficult to answer.

Gurdjieff's own compositions display such a unity in melody, rhythm and arrangements of chords that accompany the Movements in such an organic way that his work cannot be equaled by any other composer for Movements. He had a preference for orchestra music for his performances. The compositions made by others are for piano solo. It would be incorrect to conclude that piano is the ideal instrument for accompanying Movements. That other instruments were not utilized was because the necessary musicians were not at hand. A piano has the advantage that rhythm, harmony and melody can be played simultaneously on it, and with other instruments you require a small ensemble for this.

This theme arose many times in my telephone conversations with Dushka Howarth. She believed that other instruments, such as a violin or flute, evoke other resonances in the body that sometimes serve a certain Movement better than the sound of a piano, with its somewhat limited hammered sounds. Here we are faced with the same practical mechanism that has also "frozen" the original, oriental attire for Movements into a costume consisting of plain white clothing that

---

1 From personal letters from the late Thomas C. Daly, at that moment the administrator of Thomas de Hartmann's estate, dating from January and February 2001, written to Gert Jan Blom and the author of this book.

is somewhat lacking in character; this has also been the case in the change from the traditional Eastern headdress into a headband that, although it might sparkle, does not come near the splendor of the headgear common in Eastern society.

Gurdjieff's compositions comprise thirty or so pieces for piano and more than forty scores for a large orchestra. These overlap each other, but only to an extent. The Movements that were given in the months following a performance were no longer reworked for an orchestra, and in the orchestral scores, several traditional Eastern dances were included, of which the piano notes are unknown, at least to me.

All this music was never officially published. With the exception of a few compositions that were included in the Schott albums, such as the "Initiation of a Sacrificial Priestess" and "The Big Group." In the course of the years, various private publications appeared with the music publisher Janus, but these publications were exclusively intended for the Institut Gurdjieff and its international branches.[2] None of these publications are complete; among others one of Gurdjieff's most beautiful compositions is missing, made for the Movement "The Lost Loves."

Gurdjieff's music for his Movements suits the dances so well that it could serve as an example for his story with which this chapter began. As previously indicated, the compositions for the "Initiation of a Sacrificial Priestess" and "The Big Group" are in a class of their own. The same applies to the music for "The Great Prayer." The piano version of this one is an experiment in which a melody with an oriental, extraordinary scale is consistently harmonized for four voices, only using the notes that occur in the scale. This creates the tension,

2 First publication by Janus, Paris, no date. Subsequently published by Triangle Editions, Inc. No date or place.

strange chords and unusual atmosphere for this piece. The melody comprises nine notes, arranged in a different order each time, irradiated with three chords. The wave movements of these notes appear to be a ten-minute long enlargement of the vibrations that can be heard in oriental music, sometimes even within a single note.

Rosemary Nott, a pianist who was present in the Prieuré, and consequently knew Gurdjieff's music for the "old" Movements, replayed all these pieces shortly before her death. She did this so that her son could record them on tape. This recording, over three hours long, is a historic source for the interpretations of tempo and dynamics.

Let us consider the three most important form-elements in music—melody, chords and rhythm—to determine what is striking in Gurdjieff's compositions for Movements.

MELODY

Even if Gurdjieff had done nothing else in his entire life but written these melodies, he would have deserved our admiration. There are no musical formulas or artificial insertions, and each melody is concluded, completely authentic, convincing and of natural simplicity and beauty. These characteristics culminate in his music for the female dances.

CHORDS

Gurdjieff's stamp was clearly on the melody and the rhythm. He left the harmonization in multiple voices to de Hartmann. This form-element has a lot in common with the many piano compositions that were written between 1925 and 1927, composed by Gurdjieff and notated by de Hartmann in this period. The harmonization of de Hartmann was influenced by Chopin, especially where Chopin represented folk music such as in his Mazurkas. In order to support the Eastern melodies, the dominant chord is often omitted in minor and replaced with a chord comprising the fundamental and the increased fifth, a method also developed by Bartók (pieces in major are uncommon). Another striking chord is the stacking of two fifths, as previously done by Chopin. That these musical interventions were also utilized by other composers does not diminish de Hartmann's artistic achievement. As always, his work is effective, modest and sensitive. The two musical interventions described were later to play a major role in all music for Movements made after Gurdjieff's death, and give the harmonies of many of these compositions their predictable, quasi-oriental character.

RHYTHM

The rhythm in Gurdjieff's compositions is simpler than one might expect. The complex multi-rhythms from Eastern countries hardly occur at all. On the contrary, the rhythmic structure of Gurdjieff's Movements is extremely simple. To understand this, however, we must not perceive the rhythm as a static entity, but consider it from an Eastern perspective as something to which you can always add something, in the way that a child stacks building blocks.

The following rhythms are applicable to the majority of the Movements:

- 2/4 To be counted as "one-two and," in which the second basic pulse is divided in two (Dervish Movements).

For the following variation a third count or basic pulse is added:

- 3/4 To be counted as "one-two and-three" (a large number of Movements from the second period). Once again a count is added to arrive at the third variation:
- 4/4 To be counted as "one-two and-three-four (the slowest, solemn Movements).

This outline fails to do justice to the many variations in rhythm of the Movements, but it is irrefutably true with regard to the extent of *the structure* of the rhythms in the Movements. This means that the rhythmic structure of the Movements is constructed through adding a count or beat, twice, to the previous rhythm, and can therefore be represented by the series of numbers 1, 2 and 3. It may no longer surprise anyone reading this book, but this rhythmic structure is yet another example of the virtuosity with which the large and complex construction of Gurdjieff's Movements is built from a basic principle that is difficult to observe at first. I remember that this series of numbers—1, 2, 3—could be read in the first sentence in the very first version of *Beelzebub's Tales to His Grandson* as the year in which the story opens. In the second version, edited by Gurdjieff, this was changed to 223. This does not mean that everything is simple in the music for Movements. The rhythmic complexities are on a different level. The rhythm must not be accelerated or decelerated—an arduous task for Europeans, not so for musicians from Africa or the Near East. More than one rhythm can take place in a single Movement; the transitions from one rhythm to another require a high degree of presence and musical empathy.

THREE IMPORTANT COMPOSERS

The most important composers who have written music for Movements following Gurdjieff's death are Thomas de Hartmann, Helen Adie and Edward Michael. Together, they have made more than two hundred compositions for the accompaniment of Movements, all piano solos. In summarizing, one can say that de Hartmann's music stems from his experience as "court composer" for Gurdjieff, that of Helen Adie from her sincere devotion to Gurdjieff, and the music by Edward Michael was especially composed by him for the accompaniment of the Movements on Jeanne de Salzmann's Movements films, to be discussed in the next chapter.

Thomas de Hartmann (1866-1956)

The relationship between Gurdjieff and Thomas de Hartmann came to an end in 1929, following a cooperation of twelve years, and they were never to meet again. Despite this, de Hartmann remained loyal to Gurdjieff and his teaching. Shortly before Gurdjieff's death, he wrote a letter to de Hartmann and asked him to compose music for his new Movements.[3] Immediately after Gurdjieff's death, de Hartmann started work on this, but first he had to see these Movements, because they were unknown to him. Solange Claustres recollects this as follows:

> *De Hartmann wanted to do Gurdjieff a favor by writing music for the later Movements, especially for the "39 series." To assist him, I demonstrated all the Movements that he did not know, a few times with the assistance of Josée de Salzmann or Marthe de Gaigneron. In fact, he only saw a single dancer and never an entire class, which must have made matters difficult for him. He made a lot of new pieces of music, but I have problems with a number of them and they do not appear to be as good as they could be. I think it very likely that the reason for this was that he could only observe a single performer.*[4]

De Hartmann also received written instruction for a dozen or so other Movements from Jessmin Howarth.

Considering all these circumstances, it is all the more remarkable that his compositions are of such a high level. By July 1950, he had reached such a stage in his work that he was able to accompany the

---

3 From the previously mentioned telephone conversation with Dushka Howarth.

4 As quoted, with permission from Solange Claustres, in the booklet accompanying the CDs "Music for Gurdjieff's 39 Series," Channel Classics, 2001.

majority of the Movements, shown in a major performance in memory of Gurdjieff, with his new music. So, composition of this music cannot have taken him much more than six months.

In these works, his characteristic style reappears; they are as inspired as those he made a quarter of a century before with Gurdjieff. But it is possible that there was more than just inspiration at work in the compilation of this music. Solange Claustres believed that Gurdjieff himself was the composer of many of these new compositions, especially the music for all the "Prayer Movements" from this collection. In her opinion, de Hartmann based these pieces largely on his memories or reconstructions from his earlier notes. Her views must be considered most seriously, as she was in close contact with de Hartmann precisely during the period in which he composed these pieces.[5] The possibility that de Hartmann used older material cannot truly be excluded. In fact, there is a single piece that is immediately identifiable as an earlier composition by Gurdjieff—the one written for #4, 27, also known as the "Essentuki Prayer"—to which only the rhythmic pattern in the bass was added. There are also indications that de Hartmann's composition for the Movement "I Am Father, Son" is nothing more than a composition that Gurdjieff previously wrote as a musical accompaniment for the chapter "Ashiata Shiemash" from his first book.

It is best to consider the question of whether or not de Hartmann used Gurdjieff's music in a broader perspective, through learning what he said about it himself. He declared that, in all the time he was separated from Gurdjieff, he still felt connected through a "magnetic

---

5 Solange Claustres, private conversation, November 1996, Amsterdam. This conversation took place during a dinner party at the house of Mrs. D. van Oyen. Also present were her daughter Dorine and the author. Given the historical importance of Solange Claustres' opinion, that casts doubt on the right attribution of the music for the "39-series," I emphasize here that Dorine van Oyen has verified the quotations and confirmed their authenticity.

bond."[6] It appears as though he summarized his musical collaboration with his teacher in these works for the last time. The bond that he mentioned belongs to a more magical world than our own, but resulted in beautiful music. The sheet music from this collection was never officially published and may not be performed without the permission of the copyright holders.[7]

Helen Adie (1909-1996)

Helen Adie was a classically trained pianist who played a not unimportant role in the world of recent English classical music, especially through her interpretations of work by the composer John Ireland, whom she knew personally. She met Gurdjieff in Paris in 1948 and attended his Movements classes regularly until his death. She claims that it was Gurdjieff himself who asked her to compose music for Movements. In the early 1950s, she moved to Australia with her husband George Adie, where they established an Australian branch of the Institut Gurdjieff. While I have heard much about her, I never met her personally, but know her through her musical works. All her compositions for Movements, including all the handwritten manuscripts, were made available to me for study, a task that I am still devoted to.

Helen Adie created approximately fifty complete compositions for Movements. She scored a number of them for two pianos, and even some for song and cello. She was not attached to her work, so she did not collect it; as such, her work can still be found from many different sources. From the handwritten manuscripts, it is also clear that she was not quickly satisfied. For some Movements, she made multiple

---

6 See Footnote 1, above.

7 Janus and later Triangle Editions, Inc. No date or place.

compositions, and for others she continued to write new openings, with different melodies and chords.[8]

Helen Adie was an original composer, she always remained true to herself and expressed her feelings in the style of the music that had formed her, never lapsing into a quasi-oriental form. Her music can be of great rhythmic strength, but the core, hidden behind the sounds like a bride behind her veil, is an intense desire to become one with her ideal, a dedication without a single reservation for the greater good in creation. CDs of her interpretations of Gurdjieff's works have been published, but I do not believe that these are representative. She is only truly done justice in the recordings of her own work, in which she plays deep from within her heart, which must have been great as it still radiates to us through her music.

Edward (Edouard) Salim Michael (1921-2006)

The eventful life of this extraordinary man has been described by his widow, Michele Michael, in her book *The Price of a Remarkable Destiny*.[9] His life, from his early youth in the Near East on, was always marked by poverty, extreme hardships, illnesses and failing recognition for his musical gifts. Yet these gifts were phenomenal. Only two years after he received his first musical lesson, his composition "The Dionysis for Orchestra" was performed by the London Philharmonic Orchestra, in 1942. Michael was a musical prodigy and belongs to the same brilliant line as his contemporaries Clara Haskil, the Romanian

---

8 "34 Compositions for Movements" by Helen Adie were published as a private publication in Australia, no publisher stated, nor place nor date, a publication that does not include all the compositions for Movements by Helen Adie. Unfortunately, upon comparison with original manuscripts it appears that this beautiful publication contains a good number of errors.

9 Originally published in French by Guy Tredaniel, Editor, under the title *Le Prix d'un Destin Remarquable*, 2012. English translation dates from 2015.

classical pianist, and Charlie Parker, the American jazz saxophonist. He was a composer and a violinist. His excellent technical abilities as a pianist are therefore all the more astonishing. In the period between 1951 and 1967, Michael wrote fifty orchestral compositions, among others a very beautiful and moving Mass for the Catholic liturgy. He was neither a Catholic nor a "Gurdjieffian," but incorporated many different influences in a spiritual quest that was, above all, of a very personal nature.

In the same period, as requested by the Institut Gurdjieff, he wrote some eighty compositions for piano solo to accompany the Movements that were to be recorded on the films made by Jeanne de Salzmann.[10] That means that, for over half of the Movements preserved on these films, the music was composed and also performed on the piano by him.

In the mid 1970s, Michael decided to stop his musical activities to devote himself entirely to his inner quest towards an all-compassing Divine reality and unity. Shortly afterwards, Peter Brooks asked him to write the musical scores for the film *Meetings with Remarkable Men*, but neither a huge honorarium nor repeated requests could change Michael's mind. What a pity!

Michael's compositions for Movements are not listed in the overview of his musical works as it appears in the above-mentioned biography. This omission was explained by his widow: "From what I know, my husband considered that this music could not be separated

---

[10] Edward Michael's compositions for Movements were published by Editions Janus, Paris, no date. This publication contains sixteen compositions. Six LPs with his own interpretations were also published privately, most of them, but not all, being part of the music played on the sound tracks of the Movements' films by Jeanne de Salzmann. These LPs were always very rare and have become virtually unobtainable. Also privately published: *Musique Pour Les Mouvements des Films 1964, 1968,1971,1974.* No publisher, time or place stated. This last publication contains the sheet music for forty-four compositions by Michael, not included in the first album.

from the private films made by the Institut Gurdjieff on which the Movements were preserved. As such, this music was not intended to be publicly performed and belonged only to those involved in the Gurdjieff Work. I suppose this was arranged with Madame de Salzmann."[11]

Despite the good intentions of Jeanne de Salzmann and Edward Michael, however, fate wanted it otherwise. His compositions for Movements have now spread to such an extent that everybody, without exception, involved in teaching or practicing Movements, uses them, often without even knowing the composer's name.

As a first impression, Michael's creations for the Movements seem to be based on a limited and even predictable harmonic and tonal structure, something one would not expect from a musician of his capacity and imagination. In my opinion, he remained in this harmonic and tonal frame, not out of his own musical choice, but because this frame was advised or instructed to him as being a representative harmonic structure for the musical accompaniment of Movements. Despite this limitation, his work is musically inventive and provides great clarity for the performers of the Movements. Obviously, Michael understood perfectly that, more than anything, structure and simplicity of form is imperative in the accompaniment of Movements. This can be illustrated by the favorite musical exercise of Thomas de Hartmann: to hit a single note on the piano and then to ask his pupils to concentrate on that sound, to follow it consciously until the sound had completely vanished. So too in the case of Movements: the supporting force of a single note can be greater than that of an entire series.

Edward Salim Michael must be regarded as the ideal Movements accompanier. This is due to his great gift for rhythm that enabled him

---

[11] Letter from Michele Michael to the author, dated Sept. 2017.

to keep a tempo without the slightest deviation, but even more so to his rare power of "representation." This means that, for the duration of an entire Movement, he could continually preserve his overview. He never loses himself in the notes he actually plays at any moment, but keeps, in this overview, at all times contact with their function in relation to all those he played before and those that he will play after. This facility gives both his compositions and his own piano performances an extra quality that is more of a spiritual than of a strictly musical nature.

These qualities of Michael have, in my opinion, greatly contributed to the performances on the Movements films of Jeanne de Salzmann. He did not only provide "music": his gift for attention and a constant awareness of the simultaneous process of Movement and music enabled him to radiate presence and quietness in each moment of his playing. This, in its turn, created a response in the group of dancers that, even in a film-registration, I could clearly feel. The Movements-films of the Institute owe a great deal to the services of this prodigious musician and honest searcher for the Truth.

AN OLDER VERSION FOR THE ACCOMPANIMENT OF THE "39 SERIES"

Helen Adie followed Gurdjieff's Movements classes in Paris. In her hotel room in the evening, she noted down the music that had been played during the classes. At the time, as previously mentioned, this concerned only the "39 series." She wrote down twelve accompaniments for these Movements very precisely, just as they were played at the time, in all probability by Jeanne de Salzmann. *These documents contain the only music we currently know of that was played during Gurdjieff's classes and was played with his approval.* They are also of exceptional value, because the form of the Movements can be derived from the music. This music was especially intended, and this is different from the pieces by de Hartmann, to support the Movements.

THE ACTUAL FUNCTION OF MUSIC FOR MOVEMENTS

Solange Claustres has captured splendidly what the actual function of music for the Movements was:

> *When Gurdjieff travelled to the United States and asked me to take over his classes, there was still no music written for a number of the Movements and he instructed me to improvize the music during the lessons. This was far from easy, but it taught me a lot about the function of the music. It is absolutely not an "accompaniment" but a living component of the inner work that takes place in the class. The sound determines everything; it has to compliment the inner process that the Movement has evoked.*[12]

Clearly, a symbiosis must exist between the class and the accompanying musician. The cohesion between the vibrations of the music and the movements of the Gurdjieff Movements form the basis of what she means by "inner work." This is such an essential factor in the practicing of Movements that we need to stop a moment to consider this.

During a Movement, the body is first released from its habits and the thoughts have no time for digression. They are involved in the task, such as the structure of the Movement or counting the beat of the music, in the way that a dog is consumed with a bone for a while. Through this, the sensitivity can be open to new impressions, not colored by body or mental associations. The emotional life appears to go back in time, to the moments from our childhood when we felt life intensely. A silence of a new nature can fall in the class—a creative silence, not a compulsive silence out of fear or dogma. A more intense form of self-awareness always opens a new creativity,

---

[12] See Chapter 13, Footnote 5.

which can be experienced in the moment. In these moments, even the most simple of musical notes can acquire a deeper meaning. *The body of the dancer resonates* and the accompanying musician is no longer a guide, but has become part of the resonations that directly influence his or her music.

The practice of the Movements to music from mechanical media, such as a CD, excludes such moments, and has the added danger that the physical component gains the upper hand and the balance among the three centers—head, emotion and body—is disturbed.

In concluding this chapter, I have to get off my chest that, while writing about this music, I have had a bitter taste in my mouth as, regrettably, it is in most cases inaccessible for people who might be interested in it. This often-beautiful music does not deserve the shadow that has been cast over it, and the responsibility for this fact belongs with those that have resolved to be secretive. This responsibility entails a heavy burden and engenders the serious question, who is able to determine that music originating from a spiritual goal may be passed on to one and not another?

20

HISTORIC PERFORMANCES AND FILM REGISTRATIONS

Public performances of Movements are rare. Even so, through the course of the years, various ones have taken place, organized by Gurdjieff's pupils and performed by the members of their groups, such as the performances by Rina Hands in England in the 1970s and, twenty years later, by Dushka Howarth in South America. Lots of Movements were shown in these events, and the film registrations of these were not unimportant. Even so, these performances do not comply with the criterion "historic," by which I mean those performances and film recordings that were decisive for the history of the Movements after Gurdjieff's death. Except, of course, for the performances by Gurdjieff himself in 1923 and 1924, there are two other performances that comply with this criterion without reservation. They took place in 1939 and 1950, in the same hall, Colet's House in West London.

1939 PERFORMANCE

The performance in London in 1939 was given by Jessmin Howarth, and performed by the pupils she had instructed in the three preceding years in Lyne's Place, Ouspensky's study center in Surrey, about an hour's drive from London. This performance was the conclusion of her lesson program and also her parting gift, because she would leave England shortly after this and return to the United States. Twenty-six Movements were shown to a select public, twenty-two of which were Movements that had also been presented in the performance by Gurdjieff, and four Movements given by Gurdjieff shortly afterwards.

Jessmin Howarth's knowledge of these Movements was tremendous, and I doubt if her authority in this area was ever equaled. She had participated in Gurdjieff's performances. Afterwards, she instructed these Movements herself in the United States, without interruption, even in the many years when no one worked on them in Gurdjieff's immediate environment. Jeanne de Salzmann recognized Jessmin Howarth's authority and had the habit of referring questioners on to her, when she herself was faced with inquiries about the "old" Movements.[1]

The "mystery pieces" were missing from the 1939 program, as were a few other forgotten Movements, such as the "Pythia" and the "Pilgrimage," for the previously mentioned reasons. Not all the Movements for women were performed: the "Prayer Number 1," also known as the "Chords," was missing, as well as the "Women of Essentuki," also called "Essentuki March," and the "Oriental Dance" too, an exceptionally impressive women's dance. It is likely that Jessmin Howarth did not manage to get around to instructing these dances due to her relatively short stay in England. Her program was already large enough, but it does mean that these dances could not be included in the tradition of the Study Society, and they are still absent today. They were passed on by her in the United States.

Despite the absence of several Movements, this performance was a repeat of Gurdjieff's own performance in which the majority of his "old" Movements were performed in an authentic manner. No film recordings were made, but 122 photographs were taken, all large format, in which many details are visible that have been forgotten since then, such as the wearing of a blindfold during "The Great Prayer."

1 Telephone conversations with Dushka Howarth, as previously mentioned.

1950 PERFORMANCE

The performance in London in 1950 took place under the auspices of Jeanne de Salzmann. Two performances took place, in the second half of the month of July and, in the meantime, film recordings were made. Thomas de Hartmann himself provided the musical accompaniment. In many ways, it was an unparalleled *tour de force*. Not quite a year had passed since Gurdjieff's death, and the intention was to show a large proportion of his new Movements, to a—once again——preselected audience. Understandably, tremendous uncertainty existed among the performers about this endeavor. Could these Movements be performed with the same conviction and inspiration without Gurdjieff being present?

Such an extensive program was offered that it was hardly conceivable that it could be performed by a single group of dancers. It opened with the six "Obligatories" and was followed by the "old" Movements—the "Trembling Dervish," the "First Dervish Prayer," the "Canon of 7," the "Ho Ya" and "The Great Prayer," as well as the performance of several female dances. This was followed up with no fewer than seventeen Movements, one after another from the new "39 series," plus another five more recent Movements.[2]

The group performing was a combination of French and English dancers. The most gifted performers came from France—Solange Claustres, Marthe de Gaigneron, Lise Tracol, Alfred Etievant and Josée de Salzmann, all pupils who had been instructed by Gurdjieff. The performance left a deep impression on the invited guests and confirmed how closely Gurdjieff's teaching was connected with his Movements and, although he was no longer present, the extent to which his inspiration and strength lived on through these Movements.

---

[2] With thanks to Kate and Tinky Brass, who gave me access to the original program.

This experiment is of historical importance because Jeanne de Salzmann came up with the idea of recording the Movements on film and, as such, preserving them in a historically responsible form. This was a decisive moment in the history of the Movements. It led to the series of film recordings, under the direction of Jeanne de Salzmann, seeing the light of day in subsequent decades.

FILMS OF THE MOVEMENTS BY JEANNE DE SALZMANN

The Movement-films project was Jeanne de Salzmann's magnum opus and covers a period of thirty years. As far as I am aware, ten films were made in all. These included films made in 1951, a repeat of the 1950 recording, and then in 1955, 1957, 1959, 1960, 1964, 1967, 1971 and 1974. The series was concluded with a film, most probably from 1978, showing, in addition to the performances by a younger group, a number of lessons by Jeanne de Salzmann. This film had an instructional goal and was not part of the previous series.

In total, one-hundred-fifty Movements were recorded in these films. Only the first film contains a substantial share of the "old" Movements and of the "39 series." The majority of the Movements in the other films originate from the second period. Of these films, I have seen a few, and some I have even been able to study in detail, but half of them I have never seen. Nevertheless, I know which Movements they contain, because I have been able to study all the sound tracks.[3]

These films are the property of the Institut Gurdjieff, which plays them from time to time for its members. As a document that shows how Movements should be performed, they are invaluable, especially

[3] With thanks to Dushka Howarth, who was so kind as to provide me with the opportunity, while visiting her in 2000, to study these audio recordings. She considered it important for my interpretation of Movements that were to be published on CD.

because the first row comprised almost only Gurdjieff's direct pupils. It is worth noting that watching these films can evoke strong emotions, but that a detailed study is necessary in order to really learn from them.

How authentic are the versions of the Movements in these films? This is literally what I asked Solange Claustres. In her opinion, they are correct representations for the most part, with the exception of a number of Movements about which she did not share Jeanne de Salzmann's opinion. But, the overall picture is a reliable representation of the Movements as given by Gurdjieff. Her opinion is important: at the moment we talked about it, she was one of the very few witnesses still alive from the period in which the majority of the Movements were created.

Dushka Howarth, to whom I put the same question, pointed out that what she called Jeanne de Salzmann's "creativity," made "many Movements more beautiful than they actually are." With this, she did not so much mean a change in the Movements themselves, but the way in which they had been worked to make them more convincing on film. They were often shortened, placed in different configurations, and in a number of cases several Movements were compiled as a whole. It is sometimes clear that the camera work took precedence over the historical configuration, such as in the Movement #12,13 that was filmed in a semi-circle, while it is supposed to be performed in closed circles. Another objection is that, with the exception of the first film, the Movements were performed to music that had been recorded in advance. These comments do not detract in any way from the historical importance of these films.

THE FILMS FROM JESSMIN HOWARTH'S CLASSES

The work of Jessmin Howarth has also been recorded in films. However, they are of an entirely different character. They are spontaneous amateur recordings of her classes and the performance of Movements studied over a lengthy work period. I do not know how many of these films were made, but the five that I have been able to study made a deep impression on me. The presence of Jessmin Howarth, the informal atmosphere and her sometimes extensive explanations to her pupils, some of whom were very talented, make these films complementary to those of Jeanne de Salzmann, and historically they are no less important.

~

Once again, the question posed at the end of the previous chapter—about who gets to decide who is privileged to view this sacred material—becomes more poignant than ever to consider. All this material is inaccessible for many people who are interested in it. It is kept secret by the organizations that dispose of it. They only show it to their members, and then so sporadically that the viewers cannot actually learn anything from it. Is it not likely that the many who yearn for the spiritual strength of the Movements are exactly those for whom Gurdjieff developed his Movements? Is the restriction of only showing these films to members of an exclusive organization, in other words those who wear the "club tie," a wise decision? In the final chapter of this book I will try to examine this question from several angles.

21

THE TRANSMISSION OF MOVEMENTS AFTER GURDJIEFF'S DEATH

The point of human love is nothing more than the rescuing of actual individuality through sacrificing egoism.

– Vladimir Solovyov

After Gurdjieff's death, two pupils did everything within their power to pass on the Movements and to preserve his legacy. What qualifications does a person need to be up to such a task? He or she must have a natural talent for physical movements and this must have been developed since childhood in an environment in which dance was taught by experienced educators. It also requires a natural affinity with music and rhythm. This was and still is the basis for being able to teach this extremely demanding discipline, and from the outset this must be linked to a spiritual study of Gurdjieff's philosophy of life. Movements demand lengthy study, on average for at least ten years for a first elementary stage. The real, in depth study of the Movements knows no end.

These criteria are still applicable, but were also valid when the two pupils mentioned took the reins after Gurdjieff's death, and their decisions and authority were accepted by everyone. They were Jeanne de Salzmann and Jessmin Howarth. These women had much in common: both of them had been on his side from the beginning, and both of them bore him a child. Both of them had been trained in the world of dance that at the time was influenced by Dalcroze's innovations; they were professionally active; and, to top it all, they were trained musicians. They both lived very long lives.

Let us reflect for a moment on the training that both of these ladies enjoyed before they met Gurdjieff, and illuminate a characteristic of the time in which their education took place.

THE PIONEERS OF NEW DANCE

Émile Jacques Dalcroze (1865-1950) was an exponent of the development that classical dance underwent at the beginning of the twentieth century. His approach focused on the development of human possibilities through musical and rhythmic-gymnastic study. His predecessor had been François Delsarte, the undisputed father of the new dance.

In order to comprehend the development in dance, it is important to consider its psychology, but this was different from what we now associate with this word. These pioneers believed that what a person *felt and thought* should not be considered, but that what their body communicated, what was outwardly visible, should be looked at . . . and only this. This bodily observation was a more objective yardstick for what was going on within a person than the endless analysis of their feelings and thoughts. Delsarte had already compiled an encyclopedia of all human movements: for example, so the arm, with upper arm and forearm and hand, is able to adopt no fewer than 278 different positions.

The possibilities for human development, in the search for the "new man," were transferred to physical expressions, such that the body in its singularity can connect with the mathematical-rational and the mystic-religious. The most important designer in this field would be rhythm, the connecting link between the macro- and micro-cosmos, the pulsing force that is shared by all of creation and everything found within it.

Apart from Europe, Dalcroze had an especially large following in Russia, where Prince Sergey Volkonski disseminated his ideas, and those of Delsarte, with verve. It is little known that early avant-garde film in Russia was influenced by this school, and that only directors and actors who had been trained in this system were worked with. This background information is of importance because Jeanne de Salzmann was active in Georgia, in the former Russian cultural area, as a teacher of the Dalcroze system, and Jessmin Howarth was also trained by Dalcroze himself.

The fascinating ideas of Delsarte, Dalcroze and Volkonski appear to almost describe the principle of the Movements, and the clear affinity between Movements and some studies by Dalcroze cannot be denied. The first performances by Gurdjieff in Paris led to protest demonstrations by Dalcroze followers, who congregated in front of the theatre with placards bearing slogans like "SWINDLER" and "THIEF." Things are seldom what they seem, and this was the case here too. Just as Gurdjieff had not stolen Chopin's ideas, through influence from de Hartmann, or Nietzsche's through Ouspensky, no theft had taken place here either.

GYNMASTICS INFLUENCES

Another element that seems to have ties with Movements are the gymnastic exercises that saw the light of day in the nineteenth century. It is remarkable that the speculations about the origins of the Movements, which often hint at a mysterious Himalayan monastery, completely ignore that Gurdjieff himself had written that, in his youth he had practiced mostly yoga and the gymnastics of the "Swede Mueller."[1] There are two historical figures who potentially could fit the bill for the "Swede Mueller" and it is unclear which of the two Gurdjieff meant. The first is Dr. Georg Friedrich Mueller, of German origin. In 1849,

[1] *Meetings with Remarkable Men*, page 185 of the second printing, 1963.

he founded an Institute for the Rehabilitation of Invalids in Germany, where many gymnastic exercises based on Swedish gymnastics that were gaining popularity at the time were given. Memory training was also practiced, practical activities were performed, and a lot of time was spent on music lessons. It was a sort of "Prieuré avant la lettre."

The second candidate is also not a Swede but a Dane: L.P. Müller. He was active a little later, but far more famous. Müller wrote several books containing gymnastic exercises and precisely drawn choreographies, of which Christiane and I have several in our archive. His writings bear the mark of his time: for example, there is an explanation of which gestures should be used to dry off the body as quickly and effectively as possible after bathing. This example is less ridiculous and innocent than it appears, because it was linked to other research that was all the rage at the time. This was a study by F.W. Taylor into the minimizing of loss of energy in routine movements.

The interest of the time in the intelligence of the human body did not just claim a spiritual form, in the case of Dalcroze, or artistic forms, among the Russian avant-garde, but Taylor even focused on the workers in a production process—which would later lead to a condemnation of his methods. Several decades later, the interest in the possibilities of the human body would degenerate in abject forms of physical idolization through the rise of Fascism.

~

The affinity that Movements seem to have with the interests of Delsarte in the psychological meaning of physical expressions, with the teachings of Dalcroze, with the "Swedish" gymnastics and with the research into the efficiency of physical movements, in brief the spirit of the times in which they were taught by Gurdjieff, must not mislead us. Every work that deserves to be called a "work of art" was made *within* a certain time, but that which gives it its value, its spark, *transcends* the moment in time.

Movements are an art form in itself, completely distinct from all other known and familiar forms of dance or physical disciplines. We grope around in the dark with regard to the fundamental origins from which the art form was developed further by Gurdjieff's creativity. He wrote that it was the only surviving objective art form on Earth that still exists among a small Asian group. The analogy with some of his musical works, the "Hymns from a Great Temple," which are so anachronistic and exceptional that they suggest having originated from an extremely old and isolated community, argues in favor of taking his words seriously.

DIFFERENCES NOTED – DE SALZMANN AND HOWARTH

Having summed up the *similarities* between the two Movements teachers, their training and the spirit of the times in which it took place, let us turn our attention to the *differences*, which are just as significant. Jessmin Howarth was active in the United States. She was also appointed as "Director of Movements in America" by Gurdjieff and Jeanne de Salzmann in France. There was a clear difference in the specialties of the two. Howarth's field was the "old" Movements, that of de Salzmann the "new" Movements. This resulted in the "old" Movements being forgotten in Paris, quite understandably so, considering the sheer volume of more recent Movements that were available to them. Stating this fact is most likely a kick in the shins for people who learned Movements there, but it remains indisputable.[2]

---

[2] In addition to my own experience, Dushka Howarth also showed and read me letters from teachers from the Institut Gurdjieff in which this was confirmed in so many words. I was also able to go through an archive that had records of all the Movements that were given over a period of two years in this Institute's main center, including the dates on which they were given, to which class and by whom. In this entire period only two "old" Movements were given, and then only in a fragmented form.

Both Jeanne de Salzmann and Jessmin Howarth were exclusively active within the Institut Gurdjieff and the American branch of it, with the single exception of the previously mentioned work that Howarth did for Ouspensky's Study Society. This meant that their knowledge and influence was limited to these organizations, which was undoubtedly their intention. It is true that in the years after Gurdjieff's death, Jeanne de Salzmann continued to support some of the circles independent from her, surrounding other Gurdjieff pupils, like those of Hands, Nyland and later those of Desselle too, with Movements given by her students. However, this still remained entirely within an enclosed circle outside of which no information about the Movements could be found. This situation was to change dramatically with the break between Jeanne de Salzmann and John Bennett.

JOHN BENNETT'S INFLUENCE

Originally, Bennett's organization in England received Movements support, instructed by Solange Claustres and others, but as de Salzmann and Bennett went their separate ways, this came to an end. In fact, the axe fell so quickly that, for example, they knew the choreography for the important Movement "The Great Prayer," but they had no music for it, so that they had to compose it themselves. This modern composition was later given to me at times, always in a secretive and confidential capacity, and referred to as the "ancient esoteric version of this music."

The Movements were not unfamiliar to John Bennett. He had also visited the Prieuré briefly and had participated in Gurdjieff's classes in the later years in Paris too. Not just on his own, his second wife Elisabeth was taught by Gurdjieff in Paris too, as were several of his pupils. There was a connection here with the Ouspensky line of transmission, in which a thorough understanding of the "old" Movements existed. But the sum of all these influences could not equal the years of experience, knowledge and qualities of de Salzmann or Howarth. The most interesting factor for the history of Movements concerning John Bennett is not really his knowledge or instruction of this part of Gurdjieff's teaching, but the way in which he dealt with it, typical for his character.

Bennett thought highly of the Movements and realized all too well that the break with Jeanne de Salzmann had cut him off from the most vital channel through which Movements were passed on. He certainly suffered from this and attempted to renew this contact, unfortunately without success. He was not the type of man to give up and, together with his wife and pupils, he bundled all the knowledge they possessed at that moment in a repertoire that was, although far from complete and containing many defects, *made completely available to all his pupils, without exception, and instructed in intensive study programs.* For the first time, a conscious effort was made to compile an archive, incomplete as it was, but nevertheless the first collection of choreographies that no longer fell under the control of the Institut Gurdjieff.

Bennett's view of the esoteric was different from many of Gurdjieff's other pupils, and he shared everything he knew with his pupils. It is this development that blew a hole in the defenses within which Gurdjieff's Movements until then had been so fearfully guarded. And, it is this event that caused the current dramatic situation for the Movements.

In anticipation of the final chapter of this book, I will say that this split has an equally positive and negative side; it is simultaneously a blessing and a curse. The "blessing" is that this broke the one-sided, autocratic control over a cultural legacy for humankind. The "curse" is not so much in the fact that this often-incomplete form was considered as authentic, but that from this moment it was detached from the inner process that carried through to the external form, and it is exactly this connection in which de Salzmann and Howarth so excelled.

THE WRIGHT CONNECTION

In addition to the main line of transmission, that of de Salzmann and Howarth, and the split from this, that of Bennett, a third independent line of transmission, that of Olgivanna Lloyd Wright (1898-1985), must not be overlooked. As far as I am aware, this line of transmission no longer exists. She was one of Gurdjieff's very first pupils and was high in the hierarchy of Gurdjieff's dancers from the performances in 1923 and 1924. Following these performances, she remained in the United States and married the famous architect Frank Lloyd Wright. Her contact with Gurdjieff was never broken, and he visited her and her husband many times. In Taliesin, in the so-called centers of activities run by Olgivanna and her husband in the United States, in Wisconsin and in Arizona, Movements were also practiced. Obviously, Olgivanna knew the "old" Movements well, and these were performed there in sometimes exuberant, but beautiful and original costumes. A number of "new" Movements were added to the repertoire after her daughter Iovanna had returned from Paris where she, partly upon Gurdjieff's insistence, had followed Movements classes for six months. Her unpublished diary kept during her time in Paris is the most direct and honest report of Gurdjieff's classes I have ever seen.

Iovanna wanted to become a dance choreographer and designed many dances. The problem is that, from the beginning, she intermingled Movements with her own creations. It is only possible to draw a dividing line if one is thoroughly familiar with the Movements that she has incorporated. Her choreographies came into circulation later, outside the scope of the Institut Gurdjieff, which was not at all interested in them, through the Bennett-line pupils, who mistakenly considered Iovanna's choreographies as authentic Movements.

The choreographies by Iovanna Lloyd Wright comprise a few exact representations of Movements, a good number are in part authentic Movements supplemented with her own inventions, and finally her own creations—of which there are the most. Iovanna had studied Indian dance, and in her work the hand movements from this tradition are especially striking. Three of these dances are worthy of mention: the "Babylonian," the "Assyrian Women Mourners" and the "Temple Hymn." Gurdjieff's pupils have always denied that these are authentic Movements and believe they should be considered as "inventions" by Iovanna Lloyd Wright. The question is to what extent this should be accepted. I think I am on the right side of all the speculation concerning the authenticity of these three dances in accepting that Olgivanna often assisted her daughter with her choreographies, and that the three dances mentioned here comprise, in chief, *fragments from "old" Movements by Gurdjieff that Olgivanna remembered, but had been forgotten by others.* These fragments have possibly lost their context and been somewhat randomly stuck together, but they radiate a great poetic power.

The "Babylonian" is accompanied by a piano version that cannot be found in any other line of transmission, but it is identical to the orchestral version of the "Pythia." The gestures by the dancer, who has been hypnotized, can be clearly recognized, just as the reading of the future from her folded hands, and I think that this is a fragment from the forgotten "Pythia."

The "Assyrian Women Mourners" comprises just a few gestures. They are of impressive beauty and have an affinity with those in "Oriental Dance," an authentic women's dance from Gurdjieff's fledgling years as a teacher.

In the tradition of Olgivanna Lloyd Wright, some inner exercises from her time with Gurdjieff have been preserved, which teach us how the simple actions of the Movements must be experienced within. These too are nowhere else to be found and I would not miss them for the world.

The line of transmission from Olgivanna Lloyd Wright had no further contact with the other main lines, and this was partly the result of tension and mutual distrust that even existed among Gurdjieff's pupils from the beginning, and only grew stronger after his death.

My reason for reflecting on this line of transmission has less to do with the three dances, which in the abundance of hundreds of authentic Movements do not carry that much weight, despite their beauty. Rather, that in the collective rejection of these dances by the other Gurdjieff circles, and the absence of any research into their possible historic background, a mechanism has been exposed that does great injustice to the historic truth. The dozens of exercises that Jeanne de Salzmann developed after Gurdjieff's death have been completely accepted and even integrated to such an extent that they are now considered to be Gurdjieff Movements. Even so, they are different, they are all based on simultaneous movements to alternating rhythms. They are undoubtedly of value and they bear witness to an insight into the dynamics of the body, but they look a lot like Dalcroze exercises, which also combine simple actions with a different rhythm each time.

Why is it that the three aforementioned dances from the Olgivanna Lloyd Wright line of transmission are pushed aside as "sentimental subjective" expressions, while the exercises by Jeanne de Salzmann are as good as identified as Gurdjieff's Movements? This comes from the central position that Jeanne de Salzmann took, in which she was supported by her pupils who had also studied Movements with Gurdjieff for an extended period, such as Marthe de Gaigneron and Alfred Etievant. This is a disturbing example of a distorted picture of Gurdjieff's Movements caused by sociological patterns.

In Gurdjieff's fledgling years, his Movements comprised more and different elements than just simultaneous actions that have been fleshed out in Jeanne de Salzmann's exercises. They embody deep human and religious emotion in such a penetrating manner that it is difficult to forget them, even if you have only seen them once. In my case, they have given me my deepest experiences in dance. Positioning other elements in the foreground has unjustly displaced this facet of Gurdjieff's creation.

THREE LINES OF TRANSMISSION, A COMPARISON

Let us return to the three most important historical lines of transmission: that of the Institut Gurdjieff, the Study Society and the Bennett line. The strengths and limitations of each line become clear if we examine the following criteria:

1. to whom were they taught
2. the number of Movements that were taught and the period from which they originate
3. the relationship between form and content and the question whether they were passed on in their entirety or in a fragmented form.

1. In both the Study Society and the Institut Gurdjieff and its international branches, Movements are taught exclusively to members, not to outsiders, as an integrated component of the entire teachings they practice. Even during his life, John Bennett organized courses that lasted a year, in which the entire repertoire known to him was studied intensively. The Bennett tradition has always been more open and, after he died, his pupils adopted the initiative to teach Movements to anyone who wished to learn them in shorter periods: working weeks known as "intensives," in which the practice of Movements dominated all the other activities, if such even took place.

2. The Study Society repertoire is comprised of just the twenty-seven Movements taught by Jessmin Howarth, but she had such a command of them that they were given in a historically correct manner. and given in their entirety to all the members, who mastered each and every one of these Movements from beginning to end. The Bennett line has a mixture of "old" and "new" Movements that were also passed on in their entirety, but often in a less authentic form than the Study Society does. The Institut Gurdjieff or the Gurdjieff Foundation disposes of an unequalled number of later Movements, especially from the second period, but the downside here is that many older Movements are no longer practiced, which is truer for Europe than the United States.

3. The Institut Gurdjieff is unequaled in the experience and insight of how the inner self is linked to the form of the Movements. The other side of the coin is that within this/these organization(s) a startling lack of attention prevails for the form of the Movements, because only fragments are taught, a practice that was once qualified by Dushka Howarth as "a total disrespect." This has led to the absurd fact, which I have often experienced personally, that a member who has practiced Movements there for a decade or more, in fact, does not know *one single Movement* in a complete form.

It is striking to see that these three lines of transmission each reflect a phase in which Gurdjieff taught his Movements. The precision with which each member of the Study Society knows the old Movements dates back to the lengthy training programs by Gurdjieff, sometimes years in duration, prior to the performance. The attention for the "new "Movements and how to connect the outer and inner in them flows from the last phase of Gurdjieff's teaching and the determination of Jeanne de Salzmann to preserve these exercises for the future. The openness for experimentation with newer forms of Movements transmission, by the Bennett line, came from the openness of John Bennett himself.

This overview suggests that no single line of transmission is perfect.

22

CHOREOGRAPHIES – THEIR POSSIBILITIES AND IMPOSSIBILITIES AND INNER AND OUTER REQUIREMENTS FOR PRACTICING MOVEMENTS

We have a small group of pupils to thank for the fact that no fewer than 250 Movements have been retained for future generations. Important proponents of the Movements from the first generation of pupils have been discussed in the previous chapters, and from the generation following them, Marthe de Gaigneron, Alfred Etievant, who died quite young, Solange Claustres and Josée de Salzmann can also be mentioned. One can only begin to comprehend how exceptional their efforts were with an insight into the immense variety of positions, transitions and rhythms of Movements.

How could they remember such complexities?

First of all, through the instruction from Gurdjieff himself, who taught them these Movements; subsequently, the development of the body's memory, through the visualization of the course of a Movement; and finally through the recording of a choreography.

Solange Claustres says the following about this:

We were not permitted to make choreographic notes after a Movements class. Something that I also always forbid my students to do, because our first complete impression can be distorted by this to a one-sided, mentally defined image. I have always felt privileged that my body could register and remember all the Movements.

> *This does not negate the fact that if I was waiting somewhere, or travelling, I always used the time for recalling one body position after another. The Paris metro was ideal for this. I remember very clearly that I, ostensibly passively rocked back and forth by the not unpleasant wobble of the metro carriage, committed a whole series of Movements to memory, right down to the minutest detail. I attach a lot more value to such a visualization than to a choreography. It is impossible to read a Movement you do not know from a choreography.*[1]

Because choreographies play an increasingly important role in the study and teaching of Movements, the last sentence of the quote should be emphasized. *Choreographies were made by people who knew the Movements, as an aid to remembering the many details later.* They were not made in order to reconstruct an unknown Movement. Learning an unknown Movement requires the instruction of a teacher who has mastered the outward appearance and inner quality of the Movement. Those who made choreographies during Gurdjieff's life, despite his emphatic ban on making them, realized all too well that this step reduced the creative inner experience to a mechanical reproduction, and yet this disadvantage did not weigh up against the possibility of the Movement being lost forever. The choreographies that were made are of historic importance. They serve as evidence of the Movements as they were experienced—evidence that was able to reach us, even after the passing of the makers.

---

1 Published in *Bres 186*, October/November 1997, pages 9 to 15. Quote reproduced with the kind permission of *Bres Magazine*.

CATEGORIZING THE CHOREOGRAPHIES

First of all, we will consider a rough categorization of the choreographies, based on the large volumes that have accumulated in the personal archive of Christiane and myself over the last twenty years.

The Old and the "39 Series"

The historically relevant part of our collection is relatively small, and is limited to:

- Jessmin Howarth's notes for the "old" Movements
- for the "39 series," the notes by Marthe de Gaigneron
- descriptions in a mixture of English and French by an unknown pupil, also for the "39 series"
- and the choreographies that Alfred Etievant took with him to the United States.

All these documents were prepared while Gurdjieff was still alive.

The Second Period

The choreographies for Movements from the second period were, as far as I can ascertain, made later, exclusively in French, briefly before and shortly after their filming by Jeanne de Salzmann. All these choreographies comprise text—drawings are but sporadic—and were made by pupils who were present in the class when Gurdjieff taught these Movements. Nevertheless, there are discernable differences due to the subjective observation of the pupil.

About Differences

An interesting example of differences in second period Movements is based on a historical comparison that I was able to study of two versions of one and the same Movement, by two teachers who had both learned it directly from Gurdjieff. There were already five clear differences in the execution, and this was a relatively simple Movement.

It is not difficult to imagine that every additional juncture in the passing on of Movements has its own new subjective characteristics that allows these differences to expand exponentially, or better said "explode." This does not mean that all the choreographies dating from after Gurdjieff's death are worthless. But that, as a result they never correspond. This is a major problem, especially if we consider that this concerns an "objective art form" in which everything was recorded with precision. In the search for the *possible* original form, choreographies can be of use, but they can just as easily distort a Movement completely.

With regard to differences in the outward appearance of multiple versions of the same Movement, this is caused by many factors. All our known choreographies, including those in the part mentioned above, lack an indication for the tempo; they only offer vague clues like "quick" or "quite slowly," and the music that was composed for Movements later is usually prone to subjective influences. Instructions for the rhythm are commonly unclear, sometimes even incorrect. In addition, the "atmosphere" of the Movement is never stated: is it a solemn slow Movement with an especially emotional appeal, or a neutral geometric study that the body must master in a high tempo? Which inner observations is the Movement aimed at?

The second group of uncertainties regarding differences in the execution of the same Movement is about the body positions. There are so many possible small deviations in any Movement that it makes it impossible to describe or draw a choreography. Just a few examples, from an almost infinite list:

- if the head is bowed, at what angle?
- should the neck be bent, or just the head from the ball joint?

- if the arms are to be raised, should the chest be part of this movement, through rising if only by a centimeter?

Then there are the transitions from one position to another, a special area that is impossible to describe and is different from Movement to Movement.

If Movements are not learned from people who actually know them properly, but have been "deciphered" from choreographies, it will almost certainly produce a raw, almost caricature-like depiction. *This is because in the practicing of Movements, and also in the ability to teach them, it is the invisible capacities that are especially significant.*

To illustrate this, I will give an example from piano education. In the past, the movements of a good pianist were carefully observed, and instruction was tailored to imitate the movements of his or her hand and arm. It was only in the course of the last century that it was discovered that processes take place *within* the pianist's body that are far more important, such as relaxation and coordination of joint movements from within, precisely that which was not visible and could not be outwardly imitated. It was also discovered that the mechanical practice of methods, such as the continuous playing of scales while reading a novel, only had a negative effect.

PRACTICING A MOVEMENT

The invisible skills required for practicing a Movement stem from a natural talent that unfortunately rarely occurs. Such skills can be acquired to some degree through focused and lengthy study, however, they will never achieve the level of a natural talent. A number of these "invisible" skills would include:[2]

2 With thanks to Christiane Macketanz, who designed special exercises for all these elements.

- Disposing of a representation of the body in the space, with regard to the exactness of limb positions
- a rapid frequency of alternating between muscle tension and muscle relaxation
- the development of the "small" muscles, especially those grouped around the spine
- a good balance between "large" and the aforementioned "small" muscles
- fast communication time between brain and body, between which incredibly large individual differences exist
- understanding of "momentum," which means that after a particular stimulus for a brief period, absolutely no effort is required
- the performance of a Movement with a part of the body without losing contact with the part that is stationary
- the ability to continually distribute the available energy for a simultaneous outward and inner process.

These are all purely physical abilities that have very little to do with other requirements, such as an ability to concentrate, or the acquisition of what is known as "sensation." This latter concept is of vital importance for both the Movements and for practicing Gurdjieff's teachings in general, but difficult to describe. It is perhaps best to consider "sensation" as an entirely new experience, the result of a *substance* that is slowly formed in the body through the merging of the mental and the physical centers. This substance can *only f*orm through conscious efforts in cohesion with the "radiation" of this substance from a body in which it has already been developed.

The practicing of Movements requires the construction of a new contact with the body, not only during Movements, but in everything we do. The old habits must be critically examined and new possibilities must be explored. The pattern of our movements, accumulated long ago, has resulted in a mixture of partly over-activated and partly atrophied muscles, to which associations of emotions and thoughts adhere like moss to the cobbles on an old path. As with a phoenix, a new, freer pattern of movements must arise. This demands dedicated study, just as for every other complex skill, whether this concerns the carpentry for a helical staircase, the design of an electrical circuit, the translation of a poem from Chinese pictograms or the study of Cambodian temple dancing, which has around 2000 body positions.

What comprises the inner form in practice? Every participant in a Movements class must have a basic understanding of Gurdjieff's teaching and must have made the effort to apply this teaching to themselves. In the way in which lightening discharges only in the place where a small electrical discharge from the Earth has taken place first, so is the work that a person performs on himself ignited through the revelation of a Movement. The observations evoked by the Movement act as a signpost that shows us the path we must take. The observations can be the start of the formation of well-determined substances that are then stored in the body, a stable reality in contrast to our volatile emotions and thoughts. *Movements are the esoteric part, in Gurdjieff's words "the practical part," of his teachings and as such inextricably linked.*

NO EASY WAY

The summary of requirements as described above will certainly evoke resistance in those who believe in quick (instant!?) results, and do not realize the necessity of learning a process over many years. Such learning requires a struggle, without any mercy with one's acquired habits and limitations—conditions needed for these efforts to yield a realistic image of oneself.

Also, the practical skills connected with an esoteric discipline are often taken too lightly. Perhaps it is the fact that people who open up to new spiritual paths also open themselves to new possibilities within. They free themselves from the uncompromising and often generally accepted cynicism. But the downside of this is that the border between reality and illusion often becomes blurred, certainly in the beginning of this process, and the absence of proper criticism can lead to an overestimation of one's powers, which is not an uncommon phenomenon in esotericism.

TYPOLOGY AND THE INDEPENDENT "I"

In a lecture once given by Orage to his students, a copy of which is kept in Leeds University Library, he provided a typology of people. This description moved me, and it is more than likely that he learned it directly from Gurdjieff.[3] This typology groups people according to the three centers: thoughts, emotions and body. Each of these centers then has three possible gradations, 1, 2 or 3: 1 is a high level, 2 the average and 3 the lowest level. These center-gradations are with a person from birth, but only in the form of potential. The environment in which a child grows up determines whether or not this can be realized. If, for example, the thoughts at birth have a "1," this can only be realized providing the environment is also a "1." If it is of a lower quality, the development will be stuck at a lower level. The result of these two factors, talent and environment, can never be changed.

So, there are twenty-seven different types of people who differ in possibilities from each other and who will never understand each other, because a center can never equal, anticipate or understand a center of a higher level. The result of this "Babylonian" chaos does not encourage naive optimism, but makes one think especially about the results in education. *If teaching instruction is given at a level lower than that of the capacity of the pupils, not only can they learn nothing, they also*

[3] With thanks to Robert Bows who provided me with a copy of this lecture.

get stuck at an even lower level. According to this vision, the hopeless situation in which a center cannot develop, whatever the efforts, can only be overcome in one way—through the forming of an independent "I," which is exactly the goal of Gurdjieff's teaching. Only from here can all obstacles be removed. This is the crossroads of the outward and inner form of the Movements, and I believe this is exactly what Jeanne de Salzmann meant when she said that Movements could only be performed by the "astral body."

23

RECENT DEVELOPMENTS

Sacred Scripture can, just like works of art, lead a life completely independent from the intentions of their authors or creators.

– G. Scholem

Gurdjieff gave us his Movements almost three generations ago, and tremendous efforts have been made to ensure that the stimulus given by Gurdjieff is steered in the right direction. After a period of comparative calm, this stimulus has accelerated throughout the last decade in a direction that may permanently influence Movements in the future. This is why I have described the current situation as "dramatic" in this book. To clarify, not a drama of the kind with which the newspapers are packed—wars, famine and poverty—but a drama in the classical sense of the word. The theme has great complexity, and the actions of the players, no matter the righteousness of their conviction, results in the opposite of what, with every good intention, they attempted to achieve. Others who attempt to negate this are equally caught in a negative spiral of forces that, in the end, will climax in something no one can foresee. It is not my place to presume and judge in a moralizing sense, about who is right and wrong, who is guilty or innocent. Although I *can* give my impression. If, in the short term, a new stimulus cannot be found to reconcile the diametrically opposed interests, the Movements will change unrecognizably even within the course of this generation and they will no longer be able to fulfill the purpose attributed to them by Gurdjieff.

What has caused this, perhaps unavoidable, situation? Dramas in the aforementioned classical sense—not dramas caused by illness, accident or natural disasters—occur both in individual lives and in the existence of organizations, political or religious. They are the result of earlier mistakes, from ambiguities or weaknesses originally barely noticed. But, due to external unforeseen influences, these mistakes suddenly simultaneously manifest in a situation that leaves a scar, even if escape from the situation is ultimately possible. Similarly, the development of the Movements seems to have ended up in a desperately tangled knot.

The Movements are an esoteric practice of a high order, comparable with a force of alien origin that has collided with Earth. By "alien" I do not mean flying saucers, but a stimulus that has germinated from a higher form of awareness than is accessible for us. This may seem illogical, but here lies the heart of the problem. Like a virus that digs itself into a cell, or a wandering spirit that attempts to connect with a body, so too must religious forms of culture survive within institutes and organizations that are not alien, but are earthly in creation. Ordinary human traits have also contributed to this. Not that I consider myself above them, on the contrary, but they are easier to see in others than in myself, certainly when held under the magnifying glass of spiritual ideals.

THE OSHO CONNECTION

The first occurrence that initiated the acceleration of interest in the Movements was a response to the film *Meetings with Remarkable Men*, a romanticized version of Gurdjieff's second book made at the end of the 1970s under the auspices of Jeanne de Salzmann and her institute. This film included a few fragments of Movements, and ultimately they were framed as symbolizing the objective of Gurdjieff's search, like a secret in a hidden monastery. This made a deep impression on

Osho, the famous Indian teacher, and he advised all his pupils to practice the Movements. He was not the only one; many others had already added fragments of Movements to their arsenal of methods, but he was certainly the most influential. His many pupils started to enthusiastically collect information that quickly led to performances for a thousand or so people in India, and courses constantly being given in their center.

At the beginning, they had difficulty collecting authentic material, but their task was eased by members of the Bennett-line of transmission who, at the time, in the openness true to their tradition, taught everything they knew about Movements during work weeks that were open to everyone, and these were attended by many Osho followers. All this snowballed as a result of the fact that the Osho community enjoys a close cohesion and is well represented in the new media. Everyone passed on what they had learned in paid and unpaid courses, so that the Movements are now practiced more in these circles than in the traditional circles of the Gurdjieff Work.

A completely new situation arose in which, for the first time on a large scale, Movements were separated from Gurdjieff's teaching. Likely, Osho followers have less interest in this, as they have, after all, their own teacher and teachings. Is it possible to take a ritual, an esoteric practice, from one spiritual discipline and add it to another completely different one? The answer to this question, given by scientific research into the function, form and history of symbol bearers, is that the more a religious symbol is separated from its ritual function, the more certain it is that it will degenerate into a purely decorative element, just as Eastern symbols in the carpets that decorate the houses of the upper middle class. This does not mean that Osho followers were not truly interested in Movements and even less that this is solely negative, but I will get back to that later.

DUSHKA HOWARTH'S DECISION

The second occurrence is that Gurdjieff's daughter Dushka Howarth died in 2010 and, in her will, placed her entire archive at the disposal of the research department of the New York Public Library, through which any person interested can gain access to it.[2] In fact, the lion's share of this archive was collected by her mother, Jessmin Howarth, and contains countless choreographies. Without a doubt, it is one of the most important archives for Movements. With her decision, which was not a complete surprise to me, because she had hinted as much in the many times we spoke, the secrecy surrounding the outward appearance of Movements was ended for good. How these choreographies will be interpreted in the future is quite another question. The future will tell what the consequences of Dushka Howarth's decision will be, but her decision, which also carries a symbolic message, was certainly a radical one that could have a marked influence on the future of the Movements.

THE QUESTION OF SECRECY

I do not pretend to have an overview of the factors that have led to this current "junction." The motives of an almost impenetrable esoteric circle and its decision-making are too unclear. Even so, I *can* sketch a picture of the theme that is central here and subsequently describe a factor that has been of influence.

2 The shipment of this archive to the New York Public Library has been completed September 2017. Next, the research department of the New York Public Library for the Performing Arts, the Jerome Robbins Dance Division, begins its own archiving process to provide an on-line catalog and non-circulating, public archive access in its secured reading room located at Lincoln Center, NY, NY. For more information *http://catalog.nypl.org* and search for: Author: Howarth, Dushka; Title: Howarth Gurdjieff Archive, 1910-1920

The central theme, the heart of the matter, is how Gurdjieff's pupils and the institute that they established should preserve the integrity and purity of the esoteric part of his teachings entrusted to them. Because the recent developments both have to do with responses to the policies of the Institut Gurdjieff—in the first instance to the film made by that institute and in the second to the absence of trust in that same institute—I can ignore the other lines of transmission. This institute also disposes of the most knowledge because of the activities of the two flag bearers of Gurdjieff's Movements, de Salzmann and Howarth. However, I will limit myself to the first development, the "Osho effect," because the consequences of Dushka's decision are not yet known.

The factor I would like to examine in detail is secrecy. The word is often used in a negative manner. This is unjustified, because it is a historical fact, one shared by all times and religions, that the hidden, esoteric part of a spiritual discipline is not accessible for everyone. In my opinion, the Institut Gurdjieff cannot be blamed for wishing to keep this esoteric knowledge within its walls. I do not see what right a random passer-by might have to that part of its knowledge and experience. I believe that, in general, this institute has fulfilled its task well. The problem does not lie here, but occurred in not being able to resolve the contradiction between publicizing the teachings, through which new pupils could be attracted, and observing strict secrecy. It often demonstrates an unclear, half-hearted attitude in which parts of the teachings are released and others are not.

A good illustration of this confusing situation is the incomplete publication of Gurdjieff's music. But the best example, by far, of this ambiguity, is the instruction of only parts of Movements to its own members. When, in the early 1960s, I arrived at the Dutch branch of this institute, I hoped that a thorough education in Movements would be offered there. The films by Jeanne de Salzmann that I was shown only fortified my hope that I would be able to learn the

Movements shown. This was not the case; the study program only offered me fragments.

Why were only fragments taught and not entire Movements? This was because the classes were given in a single hour—hardly enough time to release someone from a physical habit that has crept in, let alone teach them a more complex Movement. As a result, only part of a Movement can be dealt with. If, in the next class, usually in the following week, yet another Movement is only studied in part, a complete Movement can never be achieved. I do not know to what extent this practice has remained unchanged, but I do know that this was the case for a very long time and that people cannot learn Movements from this manner of instruction.

I suspect that a deeper reason is playing a much larger role here. For a long time an ambivalent policy was maintained: only to release part of their available information and knowledge, out of habit, or as the result of a predetermined policy of secrecy. Whichever of the two variants has caused this, the resulting compromise allowed them to publicize something of the wealth of Gurdjieff's teaching, also to demonstrate the importance of the institute, and at the same time keep the greatest part of Gurdjieff's legacy under wraps.

This institute is not the only channel for publicizing Gurdjieff's teachings. Gurdjieff himself had certainly not shied away from introducing his name to the world, and had published his first book, in which his teachings—although hidden—were described in full. So, why was this route of ambiguity opted for?

TRANSUBSTANTIATION

This question—the why of such ambiguity—is not one I am able to answer, but I *can* shed a new light on it through an indirect approach, especially with regard to the Movements. It concerns the word "transubstantiation," which my trusty dictionary describes as a "change in substance." This is the key to understanding Gurdjieff's practical methods. This word (or concept) is so open to incorrect associations, and is so often interpreted erroneously, that it has more in common with a red-hot key that you can easily burn your fingers on if you try to turn it in the lock. This is why I emphasize that I can only provide my own impression.

Let me give a simple example of what I think is meant by this impossible word "transubstantiation." When someone dies, it is never easy for the relatives to throw away his or her clothes, as in some way they seem to still radiate the life of the deceased. If the person who has died was important, his personal possessions are of great value because of the idea, or the illusion they give, that they still facilitate almost physical contact with the deceased. This is such a general phenomenon that countless examples can be given, varying from the first edition/printing of a famous book, many times more expensive than a copy from the final printing, to the adoration of the relics of saints. In a church in the Dutch town of Hoorn stands a vase containing the heart of one of the country's greatest maritime heroes. It is kept there for future generations to maintain contact with the courage displayed by this hero. Many other examples occur to me. I see before me the wall around the tomb of an Islamic saint in a village in Turkey. The women who push up against it, kiss the stones and weep loudly, exclaiming their despair, and through the wall the strength of the saint will comfort and support them. I will not discuss the Christian religious meaning of "transubstantiation" here.

It is no secret that Gurdjieff believed that everything has a certain substance, even angels' thoughts. But, by its very definition, there is a limitation to the amount of substance. I have good reason to believe that, in the circles of Gurdjieff's immediate pupils, Movements especially were considered as a *substance* that facilitated direct contact with Gurdjieff and his teachings, but through disseminating this among the masses it would lose quality and strength. In simple terms: quality above quantity.

This concept rubs shoulders with the suspect world of superstition and magic, but I too believe it is true. Great parts of Gurdjieff's practical instructions could be considered magical, and some of his inner exercises describe how to establish a link with saints or places where they lived, through which a substance can reach us that feeds us from within. The idea of transubstantiation is not in the slightest foreign to Gurdjieff's teachings.

This idea was reinforced by sociological circumstances. Women live longer than men and are better at Movements than men. This is why, after Gurdjieff's death, a core group was formed, exclusively comprised of women who had known Gurdjieff during the war and shortly afterwards—a period described by them as "intimate"—and who, during these years, had learned Movements that reflected this intimate atmosphere. These were the Movements from the "second" period. In addition to this core group of women being formed, there was the fact that Jeanne de Salzmann preferred to appoint women to the top of the international branches. Gurdjieff's "macho" world had been transformed into a matriarchate, something that not even the greatest visionary could have predicted. The power of this matriarchate and the convincing evidence of their ability was their knowledge of Movements. Everyone was sensitive to this, even the male half of Gurdjieff's pupils. In the uncertain phase that inevitably followed the death of the spiritual teacher, Gurdjieff's Movements were the most tangible form of his legacy and were, rightly, considered as a ritual in which the teaching could be experienced, "transubstantiated." I delved into this theme to clarify how intimate this esoteric part was and is still experienced by his pupils, and I will leave the red-hot key for what it is.

CULTURAL LEGACY?

As though this problem of quality vs. quantity was not difficult enough, another question arises. Has Gurdjieff's legacy not become part of humanity's cultural legacy? If works by Mozart, for example those that he composed for the Freemasons, had remained hidden, would a single sensible person be content with such a situation? Should an institute that professes to represent Gurdjieff's work not verify its responsibilities for sharing cultural values? This question deserves careful consideration.

The Institut Gurdjieff has, in the course of the years, been of great service to thousands of people through introducing them to the practical rudiments of Gurdjieff's teaching, but is the institute sufficiently aware that, in the last decades, the artistic expressions of Gurdjieff's teaching in music and dance have crossed the line between a closed religious climate and the cultural legacy of humanity? Unfortunately, it looks as though, despite its great services in the past, it has adopted a doubtful stance that even borders on disinterest in this matter. It is highly desirable that the Institut Gurdjieff should deliberate on its position.

The interest from Osho's followers in the outward appearance of the Movements demonstrates that the unclear policy of providing fragmented information can have major consequences, and it is unjust to attribute the responsibility for this solely to them (Osho's followers). The paradoxical benefit of this "acceleration" is that, as a result, even though it is from the outside and due to others, the outer appearance of Movements is capturing the attention that it often did not get within the circles of the Institut Gurdjieff. It is also a sign of the changing times, in which people are more open to a physical discipline than to a mental introduction to a spiritual discipline. It also offers the opportunity for an interesting exercise for both parties that have come into contact with each other, and between which there is much distrust. Would it be possible for them to detach the idea of belonging to an esoteric circle from every form of perceived superiority? This would be beneficial for the emotional lives of all those involved, because the idea of belonging to an "elite" is catastrophic for leading a normal emotional life. And finally, about this occurrence: Osho pupils need to realize that practicing Movements without first studying the teachings from which they originate is like following a path with a dead end.

WHAT NEXT?

I have now reached the end of this book, which I have written especially for people unfamiliar with Gurdjieff's teachings and Movements. I admit that the issues considered at length in this final chapter, however, are of little or no use to a new person who is looking to derive wisdom from Gurdjieff's teaching, or to learn the Movements at this time. These readers are perhaps asking themselves: what next? In response to this, most importantly, I recommend that a situation must be found in which Movements can be taught in a responsible manner and, subsequently, the interest in Gurdjieff's teaching be shared among a group of people. These Movements and teachings are unsuitable for practice in an individual vacuum, but finding a good environment is not easy. Common sense is helpful here and people must be allowed the time to familiarize themselves with the environment.

IN CONCLUSION

Throughout this book I have often relied on my own experiences. They are subjective, but have the advantage of being true. The experiences from my childhood, especially, have maintained great significance for me; they are still a touchstone with which I can evaluate others and myself, and provide me with reliable direction. I would like to relate a final memory from my youth that fulfills such a function for me, and so too perhaps will serve others new to this teaching, who are trying to navigate the often-murky world of esotericism.

My early years were spent in a small industrial town, of which the population chiefly comprised a large, usually poverty-stricken working class and a small, rich, elite group. I personally witnessed the devastation of the countryside as a result of the industrial revolution of the nineteenth century and, even though just a child, I instinctively felt great sympathy for the workers and their large families, and an equally instinctive dislike for the clique of over-privileged who lived in grand style thanks to the efforts of others. The poverty I saw was harrowing and I sometimes had the feeling, without having the words to express it, that God, whom everyone was so full of praise of, had abandoned these people to their lot and no longer concerned himself with them.

From time to time, my parents visited the farming families who lived in the countryside around the town—people who had helped our large family with food throughout the war. I will never forget the simplicity of these farmers, their hospitality and the naturalness with which they had reached out to us in our time of need. My memories seem to mingle with the countryside around the farm, and I treasure the impressions they left on my heart as an example of honest and worthy existence. To this day, "ordinary" people are extraordinary for me, in a positive sense, and I distrust people who consider themselves "extraordinary" and who attribute all sorts of illusionary abilities to themselves. Every human development must, similar to the example given to me, be founded on simplicity and an instinctive ability to view matters from another's perspective.

With this reflection, I bring this chapter and book to a close. Relieved, I have just tossed a stack of informative and factual notes that have not been discussed in this book into the wastepaper bin. Not everything has been said, not everything can be said. I consider the task allotted to me as completed.

A sudden silence has occurred within me, quieter than a moonlit landscape under a blanket of snow. It occurs to me that my body encloses an empty form like that of a plaster casting. In the void, there seems to live wickerwork, as though the lines of the arteries and muscles from an old-fashioned medical illustration are illuminated by a weak electric charge. Or, like the image of a city seen from the sky at night, where through darkness, suddenly, the network of roads traces lines as the street lighting is switched on. I think that this is what I have learned through the years from the teachings that I have endeavored to speak in favor of in this book.

Berlin, 2013, Wim van Dullemen

ADDENDA

I.

TITLES AND BACKGROUNDS AS NOTED BY THOMAS DE HARTMANN PRIOR TO THE PERFORMANCES

This list that follows only provides the names of Movements and places of performance, and no further explanation. More material can be found in Gert Jan Blom's "Oriental Suite," Basta Audio Visuals, 2006, The Netherlands.

The extent to which the geographical indications are reliable is debatable. In several cases, there is reason for doubt. For example, the "Sixth Obligatory" is a Mazurka that was probably not danced in Tibet or Kafiristan. Nevertheless, what follows is the only data available to us. "The Big Group" is missing from this list. In other lists, the background for this is not specified.

"Obligatories"
3 taken from the Temple of Medicine at Sar, Tibet
3 from an esoteric school in Kidgera, Kafiristan

"The Initiation of a Priestess"
From a mystery, "The Truth Seekers"

"O-Ya Dervish"
From the Matchna Monks, Keril Oasis, Turkestan

"Camel Step"
Mazari Sherif, Afghanistan

"Trembling Dervish"
From a monastery in Khavar, Kafiristan

"The Great Prayer"
From a monastery in Tangi-Gissar in Kashgar

"Funeral Ceremony"
From the Sukari monastery near Uchan-su in Kashgar

"Turning"
From the "whirling dervishes"

"Manual Labours"
Not specified

"Women's Dances"
Not specified

"Round Dances"
Humushane, Turkey, Oasis of Keril, Transcaucasia

"Pythia"
From the Rudarikar Sanctuary in Chitral

II.

CORRESPONDENCE OF "FRENCH" NUMBERS AND "AMERICAN" NUMBERS ASSIGNED TO MOVEMENTS

The first (left-hand) column represents the "French" numbers of the "39-series." The second (right-hand column) provides the corresponding "American" numbers. The "American" numbers 6, 7, 23, 24, 26, 37 and 38 do not occur in the "French" list, only in the "American" list.

1	14	14	25	27	19
2	3	15	29	28	36
3	21	16	8	29	39
4	27	17	11	30	4
5	2	18	9	31	5
6	28	19	1	32	16
7	30	20	32	33	40
8	20	21	22	34	41
9	31	22	33	35	42
10	10	23	15	36	43
11	18	24	17	37	44
12	13	25	34	38	45
13	12	26	35	39	46

III.

ABOUT THE FILM

GURDJIEFF'S MOVEMENTS
A Body Towards an Aim
A film by Amir Kaufmann

This film is meant as an adjunct to this book.

COMMENTS BY WIM VAN DULLEMEN

Introduction

There seemed to be little sense in writing and presenting my book about Movements (*The Gurdjieff Movements: A Communication of Ancient Wisdom*) if the reader would not get a more complete impression than just words could offer. To offer that possibility became the aim of this film.

When I started writing the first chapters of this book, I met Amir Kaufmann, a filmmaker and multidisciplinary artist, who wished to make (in Berlin, where I reside), a new film dedicated to his own experiences with Gurdjieff's ideas, and possibly incorporating Movements. This background enhanced our communications, and our perceptions merged into a mutual approach. The idea of a joint project was born. From Day One we were in full agreement, and it was decided that both the book and the film should be linked together.

The resulting 60-minute film, *Gurdjieff's Movements: A Body Towards an Aim*, by Amir (camera, director and editor), was made after three years of direct and continuous work. We both felt that the first priority was the need to register Movements in a historically correct format, but another aim and challenge was to register and capture the work atmosphere.

During our many talks in those years of growing friendship, Amir showed great sensitivity to the inner processes evoked by Gurdjieff's Movements and music, and concentrated his work especially upon their effects on human awareness. The fact that Amir is also a photographer allowed him to create various still images that were edited into the film to emphasize certain human shifting-states, probably beyond the scope of what a video clip could capture.

Both Amir and myself felt strongly the dilemma of using a video camera in a sensitive "working" space. A camera has the potential to hinder concentration and quality of presence. I can testify that Amir's quiet behavior and his dedication to the project prevented any negative side effect of the video shooting. Although this was a continuous challenge, his efforts were perceived by all of us as helpful.

Works In Progress

The viewer should be aware that not all the Movements shown in the film are complete and that some are even fragmented. The execution of the Movements can be described with the same words that you see on signs at the side of road works: WORK IN PROGRESS. Nevertheless, we made efforts to present the Movements in the most natural way and the filming, accompanying the rehearsals, were spread over a few months.

Titles

Although the titles cannot really contribute to the "first impression" that the film hopes to offer, they are listed below in the sequence in which they appear in the film, including a brief explanation. The Roman numerals alongside the titles indicate the period from which the Movement dates (for full explanation of these periods see Chapter 17, *The Gurdjieff Movements*, by Wim van Dullemen).

1. **The Little Dance II:** Many completely different Movements share this title. The numbers 3 and 7 have been incorporated ingeniously in 7 positions, alternated with 3 *entremèdes*.

2. Ho Ya I: One of the two warrior or sword dances that were demonstrated in Gurdjieff's performances. The deeper meaning is that the Dervish does not fight an opponent of flesh and blood, but an aspect of himself that he deems undesirable. The words "Ho Ya" mean "Lord God." It is likely that the dance was originally performed with a long dagger. One hand, which makes the "pull and throw" movement, tosses it over the shoulder, and catches it again in the air and then throws it briefly forward to get a better grip on the handle.

3. Title Unknown II: In this Movement, of which the title is unknown to us, a continuous movement is combined with a strict, tempo-marked movement. This is alternated with a complex and dynamic part by two dancers, in which the continuous movement of one of the arms does not change.

4. Tibetan Exercise II: Twenty-four Tibetan words are recited during the Movement. The *entremède* is the word "will" in Morse code.

5. Multiplication 15 II

6. Title Unknown: We do not know if this is an exercise given by one of Gurdjieff's pupils after his death, or a fragment of an authentic Movement.

7. #31, 9 III

8. Om Om Om II: This title is linked to the sound *Om* that is spoken in canon, but not in this recording, in which the head movement is also absent. However, the basic elements are present: the cyclic pattern in the arm, typical of Gurdjieff, with an apparently simple hand movement in two different rhythms.

9. Dervish of 13 January II: This Movement is commonly performed in a class and in canon, but here two dancers mirror each other. The rhythmic breathing occurs in various Dervish Movements, but it is not characteristic for this Movement.

10. Domestic recording: Ya Yu II: Christiane Macketanz practises the basic movements of this complicated Movement and part of one of the *entremèdes*. This Movement is composed of "dash" and "dot," but in this Movement these are in a mathematical pattern and do not represent a word, such as in most Morse Code Movements.

11. Prayer of 26th June II: This is the complete and authentic Movement as given by Gurdjieff. However, this only applies to the dancer on the left, the dancer on the right mirrors this version. The "Whirling Dervish" has been added by us, an experiment in contrast. The accompanying music leaves the well-trodden path of usual Movements music, another experiment. This demanded extreme concentration from the performers.

12. Enneagram 12 II: A study of one of the two roles from this Movement. We continued to work on this Movement and the complete version was performed by us during the 2013 Konya International Mystic Music Festival in Konya, Turkey. A deeper investigation of one of the two roles, as represented here, is certainly justified.

I am indebted to Amir Kaufmann for his work and the patience he has shown while I have been writing this book. More information about his work can be found on his website: *www.amir-artfilm.de*

The copyright of this film belongs to Amir Kaufmann. Copying or public usage/distribution of this film is prohibited without specific written approval of the publisher and copyright holder, and subject to applicable laws.

This film is available for download from the publisher at
http://www.hohmpress.com/video Price: $29.95

INDEX

ABOUT THE AUTHOR

WIM VAN DULLEMEN is a musician who studied with the Dutch composer and piano virtuoso Wolfgang Wijdeveld. He met the Gurdjieff work in 1964, and for twenty years played the Gurdjieff–de Hartmann compositions for Movement classes led by direct pupils of Gurdjieff, particularly Solange Claustres. Interviewed widely on this subject, his numerous articles have been published both in the U.S. and Europe. Since 1995 he has devoted himself entirely to this work. Presently, he leads a group on Gurdjieff's teachings and regularly gives courses and performances in Movements in many countries, most recently in Turkey during the yearly Mystic Music Festival in Konya. He resides in Berlin, Germany with his life-partner and collaborator Christiane Macketanz and their sixteen-year-old son, Sascha.

ABOUT HOHM PRESS

HOHM PRESS is committed to publishing books that provide readers with alternatives to the materialistic values of the current culture, and promote self-awareness, the recognition of interdependence, and compassion. Our subject areas include parenting, transpersonal psychology, religious studies, women's studies, the arts and poetry.

Contact Information: Hohm Press, PO Box 4410, Chino Valley, Arizona, 86323; USA; 800-381-2700, or 928-636-3331; email: hppublisher@cableone.net

Visit our website at www.hohmpress.com

Purchase and download the film, *The Gurdjieff Movements*, at www.hohmpress.com/video